The Word of This Salvation in the Mouths of Christ's Ministers

"In a time when preaching often has more in common with therapy or entertainment, Michael Cooper's book is a welcome call to faithful preaching by retrieving the robust, Christ-exalting, Scripture-saturated theology of preaching found in Benjamin Keach (1640–1704). Keach was one of the most prolific pastors among the early English Particular Baptists, and he is well-worthy of study and imitation. With warmth and scholarship, Cooper demonstrates that true renewal in the pulpit can never come through cultural accommodation, but only through humble retrieval of the scriptural way of preaching, demonstrated by our theo-homiletical heritage, where the Word of God is sufficient, Christ is central, and the Spirit of God provides his strengthening and illuminating power. I heartily recommend this work to every preacher and teacher. It not only diagnoses the crisis but prescribes the biblical cure: preach the word, in season and out, standing on the shoulders of faithful preachers who came before you."

—Tom Hicks, Pastor, First Baptist Church, Clinton, Louisiana

"It is my privilege to commend this volume. Michael Cooper serves pastors by recovering a robust theology of preaching from Benjamin Keach, one that resists reducing the pulpit to mere technique, therapy, or performance. Instead, he restores preaching to its rightful place as the appointed means through which the risen Christ speaks by his word and Spirit. Through careful engagement with Keach, Cooper demonstrates that faithful preaching is far more than a transfer of information—it is God speaking—it is revelatory. This retrieval of Keach is not an exercise in nostalgia, but a model of pastoral ressourcement, providing contemporary preachers with a framework that is historically grounded, confessionally shaped, and thoroughly Christ-centered. Readers who value the glory of God, the authority of Scripture, and the spiritual gravity of expositional preaching in the church will find this work illuminating, invigorating, and restorative."

—David E. Prince, Pastor, Ashland Avenue Baptist Church

"Michael Cooper has provided us with a marvelous introduction to, as well as an interpretation and analysis of, the life, ministry, preaching, and theology of Benjamin Keach (1640–1704), a leader among early English Particular Baptists. In doing so, Cooper does not so much provide a biography of Keach as he offers Keach as a model for preaching in our contemporary context, which brings together word and Spirit, in conjunction with the ordinances and Christian hymnody, to accomplish God's purposes. By connecting Keach's background with an overview of the history of preaching, the distinctive aspects of Baptist preaching, and the influence of the English Reformation, Cooper provides for his readers a thoroughgoing theology of preaching, which is grounded in Scripture and enabled by the Holy Spirit, and which is expositional, experiential, ecclesial, edifying, evangelistic, and evangelical. We join with Michael Cooper in praying that this publication will be used by God to bring about renewal in Baptist preaching and in Baptist churches. It is a genuine joy to recommend this outstanding volume!"
—DAVID S. DOCKERY, President, Southwestern Baptist Theological Seminary

"Michael Cooper Jr. has added a worthy contribution to the study of the early Baptist leader, Benjamin Keach. This new examination of Keach's preaching ministry provides fodder for deeper discussion and encourages even more research. Those who were previously acquainted with Keach will be eager to engage Cooper, and those who are meeting Keach for the first time will surely be blessed by this introduction to the regular ministry of a faithful-but-flawed preacher."
—JONATHAN ARNOLD, Associate Professor of Theological Studies, Cedarville University

The Word of This Salvation in the Mouths of Christ's Ministers

Retrieving a Theology of Preaching as Reflected in the Sermons and Writings of Benjamin Keach (1640–1704)

MICHAEL R. COOPER JR.

Foreword by Matthew F. McKellar

WIPF & STOCK · Eugene, Oregon

THE WORD OF THIS SALVATION IN THE MOUTHS OF CHRIST'S MINISTERS
Retrieving a Theology of Preaching as Reflected in the Sermons and Writings of Benjamin Keach (1640–1704)

Copyright © 2026 Michael R. Cooper Jr. All rights reserved. Except for brief quotations in critical publications or reviews, no part of this book may be reproduced in any manner without prior written permission from the publisher. Write: Permissions, Wipf and Stock Publishers, 199 W. 8th Ave., Suite 3, Eugene, OR 97401.

Wipf & Stock
An Imprint of Wipf and Stock Publishers
199 W. 8th Ave., Suite 3
Eugene, OR 97401

www.wipfandstock.com

PAPERBACK ISBN: 979-8-3852-6787-3
HARDCOVER ISBN: 979-8-3852-6788-0
EBOOK ISBN: 979-8-3852-6789-7

VERSION NUMBER 01/26/26

To Kailie, Sophia, and Lydia.
With all my heart, I love you.

> Ὑπὲρ Χριστοῦ οὖν πρεσβεύομεν ὡς τοῦ θεοῦ παρακαλοῦντος δι' ἡμῶν. δεόμεθα ὑπὲρ Χριστοῦ καταλλάγητε τῷ θεῷ.
>
> THE APOSTLE PAUL, 2 CORINTHIANS 5:20

> Did Christ in Person speak from Heaven to Men on Earth, and make known to them this Salvation? Moreover, he speaks still, he it is that speaks to you now, Day by Day, by us his poor Ministers, who may be you are ready to slight and despise in your Hearts; yet know Christ's faithful Ministers personate him, they are his Ambassadors, they represent the very Person of Christ.... Little do Sinners think what they do when they sleep under the Word, disregard, slight and despise *the Word of this Salvation in the Mouths of Christ's Ministers*, Christ's Ambassadors.
>
> BENJAMIN KEACH
> *A GOLDEN MINE OPENED*

Contents

Foreword by Matthew McKellar — ix

Acknowledgments — xi

Introduction — xiii

CHAPTER 1 Homiletical Retrieval for a Theology of Preaching — 1

CHAPTER 2 Preaching in the Baptist Tradition — 19

CHAPTER 3 The Religious Context of Benjamin Keach — 48

CHAPTER 4 The English Homiletical Setting of the Sixteenth and Seventeenth Centuries — 68

CHAPTER 5 Benjamin Keach's Theology of Preaching — 110

CHAPTER 6 Conclusion — 168

Bibliography — 181

Foreword

I am delighted to recommend heartily the book you hold in your hand. Written by one of Southern Baptist's brightest young scholars, who also serves as a practitioner of preaching in his role as a pastor in a local church context, Michael Cooper's work on Keach's sermons and writings represents a stellar and significant contribution to both classrooms and pulpits in Southern Baptist life as well as the larger context of evangelicalism. Personally, a key reason for my enthusiasm regarding this monograph is the conviction that it addresses a lacuna or, at the very least, a "thin area" in conservative evangelical scholarship with reference to a well-developed, full-throated articulation of a cogent theology of preaching. That is, Cooper ably addresses what attributes and characteristics of God and his revelation should shape and drive what preachers aim to accomplish in the pulpit today.

In the pages that follow, the author takes the reader on a substantive journey that uses Keach's unique contributions, accurately framed in his particular historical context, to link past with present in order to convey not only the appropriate theological foundation for preaching, but also the practical implications and applications of such a foundation in the life and ministry of today's church. In a post-Christian culture marked by shifting societal trends and technological advancements, only a stable foundation can sustain the weight of biblical proclamation. *The Word of This Salvation in the Mouths of Christ's Ministers* meets this challenge through a robust homiletical retrieval within the Baptist tradition. Following the model of historical ressourcement, the study ensures continuity with Baptist heritage while fostering renewal in contemporary preaching.

This book centers on Benjamin Keach, an early English Particular Baptist, whose sermons and writings provide the primary sources for constructing a systematic theology of preaching. By situating Keach within his historical context, his theology of preaching can provide a theo-homiletical framework for contemporary expressions of Baptist preaching. The resulting theology of preaching is comprised of six interconnected elements: epiphanical in its basis, expositional in its object, experiential in its subject, effectual in its means, ecclesial in its context and evangelical in its goal. Each of these elements is derived carefully from Keach's published works and evaluated against a backdrop of timeless homiletical queries. Ultimately, Cooper's purpose is to equip Baptist preachers and teachers with a theologically coherent, historically grounded framework that bridges the gap between past convictions and present practices, enabling faithful and transformative proclamation in today's context.

On a personal note, this book is particularly meaningful to me because of the professional and personal relationship I have enjoyed, and continue to enjoy, with its author. It was my great privilege to serve as his academic supervisor during his doctoral work at Southwestern Baptist Theological Seminary and to observe first-hand the progression of his work on Keach and its preaching implications from proposed dissertation chapters to a completed dissertation and ultimately this book. Indeed, Dr. Cooper is a gifted scholar and treasured friend. He represents a blend of academic acumen and interpersonal ability that is reflected both in this book and in his life.

MATTHEW MCKELLAR
Professor of preaching; George W. Truett Chair of Ministry
Southwestern Baptist Theological Seminary
Fort Worth, Texas
December 2025

Acknowledgments

I find Benjamin Keach to be ordinary. He was an ordinary pastor who sought to preach, teach, and write for the glory of God. Talents and natural giftedness do not matter unless they are grounded in faithfulness. Thus, I cannot help but write this work with a bias. As a student of preaching, I'm fascinated by Keach's preaching. As a pastor, I'm challenged by his homiletical convictions. As a Christian, I'm stirred by his gospel proclamation. Working on this project has reminded me of the enduring tradition of Christian preaching and the eternal gospel of King Jesus. Those of us who preach the gospel stand in this homiletical stream.

This work is a revision of my doctoral dissertation on Benjamin Keach's theology of preaching. Dedicating time and energy to academic work is not a fruitless endeavor. Rather, I am convinced it is virtue forming. It requires discipline. But academic work is always accomplished in community, without which one is destined to fail.

This project is the result of God's kind providence. I thank Dr. Matthew McKellar, my doctoral supervisor. He truly walks with the Lord. His pastoral kindness and scholarly sensitivity made this work a reality. From the first time I mentioned my dissertation topic to this book, he has not ceased to be a consistent source of encouragement. I am thankful for his wisdom and graciousness. I am indebted to the insights from Drs. Chris Osborne and Jonathan Arnold who served as readers on my dissertation committee.

In the words of Keach, "To the congregation with whom I am a member (and the unworthy Overseer) who are in God the Father, and in our Lord Jesus Christ; Grace, mercy, and peace be multiplied."[1] I thank the saints located at Grace Community Church in Mabank, Texas. These faithful followers of Jesus have endured my historical ramblings and

---

1. Keach, *Short confession of faith*.

random tidbits of Baptist preaching trivia. For over a decade, I've had the honor and joy of preaching to Christ's sheep at GCC. Your love toward me and my family is a confirmation of God's profound grace. To the many who read early drafts, helped edit, listened to me work out ideas, and provided encouragement—thank you from the bottom of my heart. To the GCC staff: Cindy, Chris, Brooke, and Matt, only God knows how blessed I feel to serve alongside of you. Thank you for complementing my weaknesses and providing me the space to complete this project.

To my parents, Mike and Dreama, words cannot express my indebtedness to your love. You provided me with the environment to reach my goals and the encouragement to succeed. Dad, thank you for reading every seminar paper I wrote over the past few years and offering feedback. Mom, thank you for challenging me to work hard. I pray I make you proud.

Finally, to my wife, Kailie, and daughters, Sophia Grace and Lydia Joy. Words cannot express my affection for you. The grace that you've shown me during this entire process has been a small reflection of the Lord's forbearance. You've made this journey possible. Kailie, thank you for reading and offering feedback. Your encouragement means more than you know. Even more, thank you for loving me. God's glory and grace shine through you. You are a gift from the Father's heart.

MICHAEL R. COOPER JR.
Mabank, Texas
The First Sunday of Advent 2025

Introduction

ENGLISH CALVINISTIC BAPTIST PREACHER Benjamin Keach declares, "Preaching the Gospel, is the feeding of the Soul."[2] As the pastor of the Horsleydown church on the south side of the Thames, Keach offered himself in service to Christ, the congregation, and the larger network of baptized churches in England.[3] In his *Short Confession of Faith* penned in 1697, Keach writes, "It is the Spirit of God that maketh Prayer, Reading, and especially the Preaching of the Word, effectual to the convincing, converting, building up, and comforting, through Faith, all the Elect of God unto Salvation."[4] Though a signer of the Second London Confession of Faith, Keach notes that the Horsleydown congregation urged him to write a smaller statement synthesizing its content.[5] The fundamental

---

2. Keach, *Golden Mine Opened*, 131–32.

3. Keach used the nomenclature of *baptized churches* to refer to a network of churches that would become known by historians as Particular Baptists. See Keach, "To All the Baptized Churches," 109. Additionally, Keach used the language of Baptist as a way of self-identification. See Keach, *Glory of a true church*, iv. Recent arguments put forth by Bingham challenges the usage of *Particular Baptist* as a mark of identity for early congregationalists who modified their views on baptism. He prefers to call this group *Baptistic congregationalists*. Additionally, he claims, "The very category 'Baptist' was an eighteenth-century development and to impose it upon the mid-seventeenth century is to think anachronistically about the past." See Bingham, *Orthodox Radicals*, 10.

4. Keach, *Short confession of faith*, 19–20. The article reads, "We believe that the outward and more ordinary means, whereby Christ communicates to us the Benefits of Redemption, are his Holy Ordinances, as Prayer, the Word of God, and Preaching, with Baptism, and the Lord's Supper, &c. and yet notwithstanding it is the Spirit of God that maketh Prayer, Reading, &c. and especially the Preaching of the Word, effectual to the convincing, converting, building up, and comforting, through Faith, all the Elect of God unto Salvation. And that it is the Duty of all, that the Word may become effectual to their Salvation, to attend upon it with all Diligence, Preparation, and Prayer, that they may receive it with Faith and Love, and lay it up in their Hearts, and practice it in their Lives."

5. See *Confession of Faith Put Forth*. Keach notes that by 1697 the "larger confession"

articles of the congregation's confession parallel the Second London Confession.⁶ Yet, there are some Keachean nuances. For example, he includes articles on singing hymns, laying on of hands, and the minister's maintenance.⁷

In particular, he includes the article "Of the Means of Grace." This article follows the language of the Westminster Larger Catechism nearly verbatim.⁸ Interestingly, Keach does not state the reasons for including this article, which is absent in the Second London Confession. Yet, the article makes explicit what the Second London Confession implies—namely, "We believe that the outward and more ordinary means, whereby Christ communicates to us the Benefits of Redemption, are his Holy Ordinances . . . the Word of God . . . and Preaching."⁹ Keach makes clear his view of the Reformed means of grace and, chiefly, the salvific results of the preached word. It becomes evident that the proclamation of the word is central to his ministry.

Benjamin Keach was a theologian, hymn writer, and polemicist who stands as a preeminent figure in the life of early British Calvinistic Baptist history.¹⁰ His early theological and ministerial formation provided him a unique opportunity to minister in the Particular Baptist movement of seventeenth-century England. Keach became "instrumental in guiding

---

was out of print and many in his congregation could not purchase remaining copies due to the price. Keach, *Short confession of faith*, author's introduction.

6. Also see Lumpkin, *Baptist Confessions of Faith*, 217. Lumpkin writes, "The Particular Baptists of London and vicinity determined, therefore, to show their agreement with Presbyterians and Congregationalists by making the Westminster Confession the basis of a new confession of their own. A circular letter was sent to the Particular Baptist churches in England and Wales asking that representatives be sent to a general meeting in 1677." Following the Act of Toleration in 1689, seven London pastors, including Benjamin Keach, called for a general meeting of Baptists, thereby reissuing the Confession. Lumpkin also notes, "Benjamin Keach of the Horsleydown Church, London, who had been associated with Collins in reissuing the Confession in 1688, worked over and condensed the Confession in 1697." See Lumpkin, *Baptist Confessions of Faith*, 221.

7. Keach, *Short confession of faith*, 23–24; 27; 29–30.

8. See questions 154–55 in Westminster Assembly, "Larger Catechism," 333–35. This article also follows the Baptist Catechism, commonly called Keach's Catechism. See questions 93–95 in Keach, *Baptist Catechism*, 26–27. For the development of the so-called Keach Catechism see Arnold, *Reformed Theology*, 53–54. Also, for a textual comparison of the documents see Renihan, *True Confessions*, 196–231.

9. Keach, *Short confession of faith*, 19–20.

10. For a short introduction on the theology and controversies in Keach's ministry see Nettles, *Beginnings in Britain*, 163–95.

and encouraging the next generation of Particular Baptist leaders."[11] His congregation "quickly grew to one of the largest and most influential London Baptist Churches."[12] Reflecting upon the impact of his predecessor's ministry, Charles Haddon Spurgeon writes, "Benjamin Keach was one of the most useful preachers of his time. . . . His teaching was sweetly spiritual, intensely Scriptural, and full of Christ. Whoever else kept back the fundamental truths of our holy gospel, Benjamin Keach did not so."[13] Spurgeon concludes that the spiritual strength of the congregation could be traced back to his "illustrious predecessor, Benjamin Keach."[14]

Additionally, accounts of Keach's life further confirm his passion for preaching. Thomas Crosby in *The History of the English Baptists* writes of his father-in-law, "Preaching the Gospel was the very pleasure of his soul, and his heart was so engaged in the work of the ministry, that from the time of his first appearing in public to the end of his days, his life was one continued scene of labour and toil."[15] Another Baptist historian, William Whitley, writes of Keach's preaching that "he devoted himself almost entirely to Biblical exposition."[16] As a pastor he published over forty different works, including 224 sermons.[17] Austin Walker states, "The sermons of Benjamin Keach constitute the greater part of his writings."[18] Due to the amount of his published material, Keach most certainly was viewed as a Baptist authority on various issues.[19] Yet, "above all else he was a preacher of the gospel."[20]

As one whose pleasure was preaching the gospel, what did Benjamin Keach think about the task of preaching? Do his writings and published sermons detail a theology of preaching? Furthermore, what can

---

11. Ward, *Pure Worship*, 184.
12. Ward, *Pure Worship*, 184.
13. Spurgeon, *Autobiography*, 306.
14. Spurgeon, *Autobiography*, 397.
15. Crosby, *History of the English Baptists*, 304.
16. Whitley, *History of British Baptists*, 177.
17. Nettles, *By His Grace*, 10. For a discussion regarding Keach's sermons see Holmes, "Role of Metaphor," 41–78.
18. Walker, "Tailor Turned Preacher," 31. The print culture of late seventeenth-century nonconformity was vital for promoting their ideas, encouraging literacy, and establishing orthodoxy. Keeble argues that nonconformist ministers created a unique literary culture, and publishing was the means of its survival. See Keeble, *Literary Culture*.
19. Arnold, *Reformed Theology*, 41.
20. Walker, *Excellent Benjamin Keach*, 9.

preachers today learn from Keach's theology of preaching? The purpose of this book is to encourage Baptist preachers and homiletical teachers to consider a retrieved theology of preaching from within their tradition. By highlighting the theo-homiletical convictions of Benjamin Keach, the hope is, though he is dead, he will still speak to us. But the intention is not merely to record what Keach thought about preaching within his context. Rather, the aim is to apply the retrieved framework presented to our own homiletical practice. Keach's homiletical theology—which is epiphanical (basis), expositional (object), experiential (subject), effectual (means), ecclesial (context), and evangelical (goal)—offers contemporary Baptist preachers a foundation and framework for proclamation. Therefore, this book attempts to operate within the spirit of historical ressourcement by retrieving a theo-homiletical framework for contemporary expressions of preaching. Theological retrieval for the sake of spiritual renewal is not a new project.[21] However, as it relates to homiletics, not much is written in this area.[22]

Chapter 1 will introduce the topic of homiletical retrieval and a theology of preaching. Within homiletical scholarship, especially in the twentieth and twenty-first centuries, theologies of preaching have emerged from various denominational traditions. While many contemporary theologies of preaching seek to balance various modern/postmodern concerns, the questions asked by homiletical scholars are timeless. By exploring contemporary theology of preaching scholarship, we can identify particular questions and use them as a means of evaluation. In this way we can engage in the work of homiletical retrieval.

Chapter 2 will set Keach within the larger Baptist preaching tradition. Since the book is primarily concerned about Baptist homiletics, it is necessary to show the warrant for the claim being made. This chapter shows that Baptists throughout history have thought deeply about a theology of preaching. They have asked questions, provided answers, and have wrestled with theo-homiletical issues.

Chapter 3 will begin with a history of the English Reformation and progress to the dissenting traditions in the seventeenth century. At this point, Keach's pastoral and preaching ministry will be considered. Chapter 4 will examine the English homiletical setting of the sixteenth

---

21. For specific works see Allen and Swain, *Christian Dogmatics*, and Ortlund, *Theological Retrieval for Evangelicals*.

22. A helpful example of historical ressourcement as it relates to preaching is Hofer's recent work. See Hofer, *Power of Patristic Preaching*.

and seventeenth centuries. Special attention will be given to the English Reformed preaching tradition.

Chapter 5 will apply the six theo-homiletical questions to the sermons and writings by Keach. Additionally, this chapter will summarize the content into a systematized theology of preaching. What will be demonstrated is that Keach's theology of preaching was epiphanical, expositional, experiential, effectual, ecclesial, and evangelical. Chapter 6 will explore how the retrieved theo-homiletical framework can serve as a basis for contemporary Baptist preaching.

CHAPTER 1

Homiletical Retrieval for a Theology of Preaching

THE LATE BAPTIST HOMILETICAL historian E. C. Dargan writes, "Preaching is distinctively a Christian institution, and yet is founded on certain fundamental things in human character and history. As one of the most widely employed and useful forms of public speech, it has held for all the Christian ages an assured place among the institutions of human society."[1] While preaching is certainly a central feature in Christianity, at times within the history of the church the primacy of proclamation has ebbed and flowed.[2] Contemporary preaching in the West is experiencing such a moment. The pulpit has lost a bit of its power and grandeur.

This attitude is reflected in many contemporary evangelical churches, where the pulpit has been relegated to a political soapbox, a therapeutic couch, or even a bad infomercial. Preachers have used the word *crisis* to describe the state of preaching. As Akin writes in the introduction to *Engaging Exposition*,

> A crisis is in our pulpits, and this situation is critical. Seduced by the sirens of modernity, preachers of the gospel have jettisoned a word-based ministry that is expository in nature. Skiing across the surface needs of a fallen, sinful humanity, we have turned the pulpit into a pop psychology sideshow and

---

1. Dargan, *History of Preaching*, 1:552.
2. For a contemporary overview of the history of preaching see Edwards, *History of Preaching* and Old, *Age of the Reformation*.

a feel-good pit stop. We have neglected preaching the whole counsel of God's Word.[3]

Twenty-first-century preaching must wrestle with shifting trends within society, the advancement of technology, and the decline into a post-Christian culture. However, the church must be reminded that "the great appointed means of spreading the good tidings of salvation through Christ is preaching—words spoken whether to the individual, or to the assembly. And this, nothing can supersede."[4]

HOMILETICAL RETRIEVAL

This project is not primarily concerned about the postmodern context of homiletics, which is a worthy endeavor itself. Rather, the book is focused on homiletical retrieval and how it shapes contemporary preaching. The context of this work is written within the Protestant stream of Christianity, in particular, the Southern Baptist expression. As Baptists we consider ourselves "people of the book" with a fascination with preaching.[5] It is evident that preaching is at the forefront of Baptist ecclesiological praxis when one surveys the homiletical works written by Baptists in the twentieth and twenty-first centuries.[6] Rightfully so since preaching is the means by which faith is formed. As Baptists continue to reflect on their place within the broader Christian tradition, homiletical retrieval should be taken into consideration.[7] But the work of retrieval for the sake of renewal requires patience. Timothy George writes,

---

3. Akin et al., *Engaging Exposition*, 1.

4. Broadus, *Treatise*, 2.

5. Chute, Finn, and Haykin write, "Baptists are a 'people of the book,' and even though they read that book differently from time to time, they understand that nothing else carries the same authority over their lives as the Bible." See Chute et al., *Baptist Story*, 6. Also, Hobbs, "People of the Book," 12–16.

6. Only a few are mentioned: Ray, *Expository Preaching*; Brown et al., *Steps to the Sermon*; Vines, *Practical Guide to Sermon Preparation*; Vines, *Guide to Effective Sermon Delivery*; McDill, *12 Essential Skills*; Vines and Shaddix, *Power in the Pulpit*; York and Decker, *Preaching With Bold Assurance*; Mohler, *He Is Not Silent*; Akin et al., *Text-Driven Preaching*; Akin et al., *Engaging Exposition*; Dever and Gilbert, *Preach*; Smith, *Recapturing the Voice of God*; Merida, *Christ-Centered Expositor*; Gallaty and Smith, *Preaching for the Rest of Us*.

7. For a helpful work on Baptists and the Christian tradition see Emerson et al., *Baptists and the Christian Tradition*.

What is retrieval? It is not just refurbishment. It is not just going back and finding something or someone famous four or five hundred years ago and dusting them off and letting them shine again in all of their glory. There is nothing wrong with that, but more is involved in retrieval. Retrieval is more of a rescue operation. It recognizes that there's a great deal of our Christian past that has become obscure, that we just don't know about anymore. Retrieval looks at these figures as our fellow sojourners in the life of faith. We are one with them in Jesus Christ. They are guiding lights for the people of God throughout the ages. That sometimes means we have to ask new and different questions of them, different from what they were asking in their own day. We have the right, and even the responsibility, to do just that.[8]

Two thousand years of the Christian tradition offers preachers a wealth of resources to develop as effective communicators of the word. However, there is a tendency to speak before we listen. Listening to those who have gone before us is a reminder of the church's deep homiletical tradition. We inherit methods, theology, and perspectives that have been handed down to us. Equally, it is a reminder of how much we need our past to speak into the present. Retrieval is a rescue operation for our present moment. As Gavin Ortlund writes, "Sometimes the best way to go forward is, paradoxically, to go backward."[9]

As it relates to the Baptist context, others have sought to retrieve a historic Baptist vision of ecclesiological life and the Christian faith.[10] My objective is to engage in a similar process within the discipline of homiletics. Thus, the goal of this book is to encourage Baptist preachers and homiletical teachers to consider a retrieved theology of preaching from within our own tradition. This exercise in homiletical theology is predicated on "the model of the *sanctorum communio*—the belief that we are neither isolated Christians nor objective scientists but rather within a church and stream of tradition."[11] It is noted that Baptist history and the subsequent theological developments are not monolithic. Nevertheless, there are indeed theo-homiletical truths that transcend nuances within the tradition(s).[12] This work presents a Baptist theology of preaching

---

8. George, "Retrieval for the Sake of Renewal," 73.

9. Ortlund, *Theological Retrieval for Evangelicals*, 45.

10. Haykin's resources are an excellent example of this type of work. See Haykin, *Kiffen, Knollys, and Keach*; and *Amidst Us Our Beloved*.

11. Canlis, *Calvin's Ladder*, 23.

12. *Theo-homiletical* is used interchangeably with *theology of preaching* and

drawn from one of the earliest English Baptists, Benjamin Keach. The following framework does not attempt to reorient Baptist homiletics completely. That is unrealistic nor is it warranted. Rather, the present proposal is intended to aid Baptist preachers by providing homiletical continuity with their own ecclesial tradition, which subsequently shapes contemporary preaching praxis.

So, why Benjamin Keach? What makes him a significant historical figure to evaluate for a Baptist theology of preaching? First, Keach is the most published among the earliest generation of British Calvinistic Baptists.[13] He published works including a children's catechism/grammar primer, material on baptism, covenant theology, a hymnal, and an allegorical novel. These works are important. Yet, the bulk of Keach's published material consists of sermons. Suffice to say, his published sermons allow scholars ample opportunity to dive into the depths of his thought in order to explore various aspects of his theological formulation. Throughout his sermons, he makes clear references to the work of preaching. From a pastoral perspective, Keach is helping his hearers understand the work of proclamation.

Second, he was interested in the role and function of the church. He is the first Baptist to write an ecclesiological primer in his publication *The Glory of a True Church*.[14] He also has a vested interest in worship as reflected in the hymn-singing controversy.[15] Likewise, Keach is the principle author of the seventeenth-century work titled *The Gospel Minister's Maintenance Vindicated*.[16] While the document specifically argues that a local church has the responsibility to financially support their pastor, Keach considers the duty of a preacher in the final section, "The Great and Weighty Work of a True Gospel

---

homiletical theology. It expresses the unique theological presuppositions that provide the basis for preaching.

13. MacDonald writes, "He [Keach] was clearly the single most important apologist for Calvinistic Baptist views in the period 1689–1702. He not only published on congregational hymn singing, but on ministerial maintenance, laying on of hands on baptized believers, first-day worship, enthusiasm, eschatology, the church of Rome, believer's baptism and justification. He produced a confession of faith, a church order, a catechism, a political poem dedicated to William and Mary, a hymnbook, and many sermons." See MacDonald, *London Calvinistic Baptists*, 84.

14. Keach, *Glory of a true church*.

15. Keach, *Breach repaired in God's worship*. Due to the scope of this book, the issue of Keach's role in the hymn-singing controversy is not discussed in detail. However, see Stanton, *Liturgy and Identity*.

16. Keach, *Gospel minister's maintenance vindicated*, 29. Also see Keach, "To All the Baptized Churches."

Minister Opened." It is in this section where the author expounds on the preacher's role in preaching. Therefore, it stands to reason that an individual who is writing and thinking about the nature of the church, the role of worship, and the function of ministers would have much to say about the central role of preaching. Jonathan Arnold notes, "As with all of his [Keach] publications, his over-arching goals were theological in nature."[17] Thus, one should not regard Keach as a "simple-minded, uneducated" practical theologian.[18] Rather, taken as a whole, Keach should be regarded as an *ecclesial-theologian* who is operating within his own distinct expression of Reformed orthodoxy. As such, his theological and practical contributions should be interpreted through the lens of his pastoral function.

Third, Keach had a transatlantic influence among Baptist communities. He was most certainly viewed as a Baptist authority on various issues.[19] Keach's son Elias served as a pastor in Philadelphia from 1687 to 1692 and carried his father's influence with him.[20] The Philadelphia Baptist Association printed Keach's book on the parables.[21] Of course, the Baptist Catechism is often associated with Benjamin Keach and was widely published among the early American Baptists.[22]

RELEVANT LITERATURE

Arnold notes that past scholarship was inclined to pit Keach's practical theology against his other theological contributions.[23] However, recent scholarship has shown that Keach possessed significant theological insight and should be placed in conversation with other leading theologians of his day.[24] Indeed, the practical and theological concerns of Keach should not conflict with each other. To my knowledge, there are only three dissertations that focus explicitly on an element of Keach's preaching.[25]

---

17. Arnold, *Reformed Theology*, 55.

18. Arnold claims that the early work of Spears and Vaughn painted Keach in this light. See Arnold, *Reformed Theology*, 221.

19. Arnold, *Reformed Theology*, 41.

20. Garrett, *Baptist Theology*, 115–16.

21. Gillette, *Minutes of the Philadelphia Baptist Association*, 119.

22. For the development of the so-called Keach Catechism see Arnold, *Reformed Theology*, 53–54.

23. See Arnold, *Reformed Theology*, 7–10, 221.

24. See Riker, *Catholic Reformed Theologian*.

25. This includes my dissertation; this book is a revision of that project. See Cooper,

James Christopher Holmes's contribution demonstrates the role of metaphor in his preaching. He argues, "Keach regularly incorporated metaphorical imagery into his sermons to connect the content of his messages with the intellect and emotions of his audience."[26] He concludes,

> In the task of preaching, Keach was convinced that using metaphorical language . . . was an usually powerful way of communicating with virtually every individual in his audience. Keach believed that the abundance of metaphors in the Bible was God's clear sanction for their use in the preaching act, an activity that Keach fervently believed was God's specially ordained means of broadcasting the truths of His Word.[27]

Holmes does mention specific aspects of Keach's theology of preaching. For example, Keach's preaching focused on the centrality of the Bible and was expositional. Holmes's work shows Keach's originality in preaching and his desire to communicate effectively to his congregation. Moreover, Holmes's dissertation opens an avenue into the nuances of early English Baptist preaching.

Shane Jonathan Deane explores the Christocentric nature of Keach's preaching.[28] He argues that Keach preached Christ in two specific ways. First, he followed the "*Tropologia* method of preaching," and second, he employed the "Sin-Salvation method of preaching."[29] Furthermore, Deane compares Keach's method with contemporary homiletical methods of preaching Christ (Christotelic, Christiconic, Christo-promise, Christ centered).[30] Deane argues that Keach's method aligns with the Christ-centered method.

His research further illuminates an aspect of Keach's preaching and its subsequent relevance for modern-day homiletics. Even more, it demonstrates that Keach's theological hermeneutic shaped his homiletic. Deane establishes Keach within the Puritan preaching tradition while showing the nuances of his hermeneutical method. Both Deane and Holmes focus on various aspects of Keach's homiletical methodology.

"Word of this Salvation."
26. Holmes, "Role of Metaphor," 40.
27. Holmes, "Role of Metaphor," 169.
28. Deane, "Golden Mine Opened."
29. Deane, "Golden Mine Opened," 5–8.
30. Deane, "Golden Mine Opened," 237–63.

This present work approaches Keach's preaching from a different angle, which in the end will complement their contributions.

Important "practical theology" dissertations, such as Spears and Vaughn, provide some information on Keach's preaching.[31] Spears tends to focus on Keach's method of preaching rather than the theology that supports it. Vaughn, on the other hand, does make an intriguing observation regarding the spirituality/sacramentality of Keach's preaching.[32] He claims that Keach viewed preaching as a vehicle of divine truth, thus communicating grace to the hearers.[33] While I do not dispute this (a similar argument will be made), the limited evidence that Vaughn provides does not substantiate his claim adequately. There are a few academic articles that mention Keach's preaching. Raymond Brown's article on Baptist preaching makes passing references to Keach.[34] Midwestern Baptist Theological Seminary preaching professor Jared Bumpers places Keach in dialogue with John Broadus.[35] McKibbens includes a small section concerning Keach in his book *The Forgotten Heritage*.[36]

The only biography on Keach's life was published in 2004 and republished in 2015.[37] While Walker does an exceptional job at grounding Keach within his historical context, he spends little time on the subject of preaching. However, Walker's chapter in *Pulpit and People* does provide a broad perspective of Keach's preaching, which proves to be helpful in terms of a theology of preaching.[38] Significantly related to a theology of preaching is his discussion on Keach's view of a gospel minister.[39] Though the section is short, he comments on *The Gospel Ministers's Maintenance* as a key source for understanding Keach's homiletical theology.

---

31. Spears, "Baptist Movement in England," 143–74. Vaughn, "Public Worship Practical Theology," 85–123.
32. Vaughn, "Public Worship Practical Theology," 123.
33. Vaughn, "Public Worship Practical Theology," 118–21.
34. Brown, "Baptist Preaching."
35. Bumpers, "Worse than Idle."
36. McKibbens, *Forgotten Heritage*, 16–19.
37. Walker, *Excellent Benjamin Keach*.
38. Walker, "Tailor Turned Preacher."
39. Walker, "Tailor Turned Preacher," 29–31.

METHODOLOGY

Since Keach did not write a preaching manual, evaluating and categorizing homiletical statements from his sermons and writings is the next viable option. By doing this we can piece together his homiletical theology. However, this presents various challenges, as Stout notes:

> Published sermons present limitations because they are not necessarily representative of regular preaching, nor can we be certain they are the best index to what the clergy offered the public on a weekly basis.... As such they provide an inexact and even misleading guide to what was being said publicly in most churches on Sundays.... The most accurate guide we therefore have to what people actually heard are the handwritten sermon notes that ministers carried with them into the pulpit.[40]

Even with the challenges, Keach's sermonic material is extensive, representing what seems to be his normal homiletical method.[41] As Holmes argues, "With Keach, no manuscripts, transcriptions, or sermon notes of any kind are known to exist. Thus, while conclusions drawn must be limited, Keach's published sermons are still capable of providing substantial information about Keach and his preaching."[42] Keach's other writings, such as *Tropologia*, provides relevant information related to preaching.[43]

Thus, in evaluating Keach's statements on preaching, his published sermons and writings will be treated similarly, both as authentic representations of his reflections on preaching. Even if Keach includes additional statements in his published sermons that were not originally within the preached sermon (which readers cannot know), this does not

---

40. Stout, *New England Soul*, 4.

41. Hunt argues that the sixteenth-century Puritans placed a greater emphasis on the spoken word rather than the printed word. Yet, by the seventeenth century, "the word read by the eye and the word heard by the ear, would all be assimilated into a single category of verbal expression." Hunt, *Art of Hearing*, 59; see 30–42 for the fuller discussion. Keach, however, claims "I understand not that reading out of a book, is any more praying, *than the reading a sermon out of a book is preaching*." See Keach, *Exposition of the Parables*, 436. Keach did not necessarily equate the printed sermon to the spoken sermon. He did maintain that reading the word was an ordinance given by Christ. See Keach, *Short confession of faith*, 19–20. Nevertheless, he utilized the publishing world to his advantage.

42. Holmes, "Role of Metaphor," 42.

43. Keach, *Tropologia*. *Tropologia* was originally a two-volume work. Volume 1 is called *Tropologia* (Book 1) and volume 2 is called *Troposchēmalogia* (Book 2–4). The 1856 edition is used throughout this work unless noted otherwise.

change how one interprets his direct and indirect statements pertaining to a theology of preaching.[44]

In analyzing Keach's sermons and writings for a theology of preaching the following methodology will be applied. Statements directly and indirectly related to preaching will be categorized using the six theo-homiletical convictions of preaching, which will be discussed further in this chapter. Contextual sensitivity is important when evaluating the statements to establish authentic comments germane to preaching.

A THEOLOGY OF PREACHING

A word is warranted concerning the topic of a theology of preaching. What is it? How is a theology of preaching discerned? Aaron Edwards observes, "The vast majority of contemporary homiletical approaches are overwhelmingly freighted towards the technical, practical element of preaching. . . . Indeed, preaching is usually seen as a practice of applied theology rather than something which warrants its own theological reflection."[45] This is evident when one considers the most popular homiletical textbooks in the twentieth and twenty-first centuries. A theology of preaching is intent on understanding the conceptual question, "How does one understand preaching?"[46] A theology of preaching will subsequently shape sermonic method and delivery. Therefore, it is imperative to reflect on the theological basis for proclamation. James Kay writes, "The 20th century arguably witnessed the most intense period of theological concentration on Christian proclamation since the Reformation."[47] Homiletics as a discipline was influenced by various scholars, in particular Karl Barth and Rudolf Bultmann, at the beginning of the twentieth century.[48] As a result, their conclusions impacted American hermeneutics and homiletics during the 1950s–1970s.[49] During this period, various ways of thinking about preaching (i.e., theologies of preaching) emerged in homiletical discussions.[50] Fred Craddock argues that a theology of preaching is important,

---

44. Keach mentions he added additional material in printed sermons that were not in the spoken sermon. See the introduction of Keach, *Golden Mine Opened*.
45. Edwards, *Theology of Preaching and Dialectic*, 5.
46. Edwards, *Theology of Preaching and Dialectic*, 5.
47. Kay, "Theology of Proclamation," 493.
48. Kay, "Theology of Proclamation."
49. See Campbell, *Preaching Jesus*.
50. This is particularly true in the case of those who tend to follow the "new

because effective preaching sustained over a long period of time must have some sense of its own nature, its own significance, its own role in the redeeming and caring work of God in the world. What is preaching and what is its place in the larger purposes of God? These are theological questions which must be addressed by the one who preaches. . . . A theology of preaching sustains and nourishes the pulpit with a constancy that survives the ebb and flow of the feelings of the one standing in it as well as the smiles and frowns of those who sit before it.[51]

A theology of preaching can be seen as a "frame of reference."[52] Kay notes that three frames of reference "currently inform homiletics . . . rhetoric, poetics, and theology."[53] Commenting on the theological element of preaching, Mark Thompson aptly notes, "we need to see preaching as a richly theological activity, not just in terms of its content (ensuring that we are talking about God rather than just ourselves) but also as an activity (ultimately this is something God is doing)."[54] Additionally, William Willimon echoes this when he states, "Preaching is a theological act, our attempt to do business with a God who speaks. It is also a theological act in that a sermon is God's attempt to do business with us through words."[55] Preaching is more than just a mere practical discipline. Indeed, homiletics should be concerned about sermonic method and delivery (poetics and rhetoric). Yet, it also entails a theological frame of reference which should govern the whole homiletical process.

Scholars have sought to provide a broad overview of various theologies of preaching. Here are a few examples. David Greenhaw states that a "theology of preaching is concerned with the role and place of preaching in the life of the Christian church. . . . Theology of preaching struggles with the question of what the church is doing when it preaches; that is, a theology of preaching is concerned with the expectations of preaching."[56] He lists various theologies of preaching. He begins with Schleiermacher, who "understood preaching to play an important role in shaping the

---

homiletic." See Campbell, *Preaching Jesus*, 147–65.

51. Craddock, *Preaching*, 48.
52. Kay, *Preaching and Theology*, 1.
53. Kay, *Preaching and Theology*, 3. Rhetoric is concerned with sermon delivery. Poetics pertains to the nature of the text and exegesis. Theology relates to what is taking place in the preaching moment.
54. Thompson, "Declarative God," 18.
55. Willimon, *Proclamation and Theology*, 2.
56. Greenhaw, "Theology of Preaching," 477.

hearer's experience of God. . . . Preaching awakens the experience of the divine."[57] He contrasts this with Barth who "stressed the objective character of preaching. What is to be expected of preaching is nothing short of God speaking."[58] He concludes, "For Barth, preaching is not stating the meaning of the Bible but is itself revealing the word of God, because in the very human words of preaching, God is speaking."[59] In noting the preaching development of Moltmann, he highlights the eschatological nature of preaching.[60] This, in turn, shaped the development of liberation preaching, as seen in Gutierrez, McFague, and Mitchell.[61]

Likewise, John McClure notes that a theology of preaching is "the preacher's understanding of the kind of theological event or transaction with God taking place during preaching. Theologies of preaching ask questions such as: What is God doing during the sermon? What is the nature of the Word of God in preaching?"[62] McClure identifies four theologies of preaching. First is an existential theology of preaching. This primary concern relates to a divine solution to a human problem as demonstrated in Paul Tillich.[63] Second is the transcendent theology, in which "the Word of God has absolute priority," which is reflected in Karl Barth.[64] Third is the ethical-political theology of preaching, which provides the foundation for liberation preaching.[65] Finally is the organic-aesthetic theology of preaching. The theology is less "word-centered" and relies upon subjective experiences.[66]

Last, Donald McKim states that a theology of preaching is "the understanding that there is a theological basis for the proclamation that occurs in preaching and that preaching is a means God uses to convey a knowledge of God and to communicate with people. Included are understandings of God's Word, the Holy Spirit, the power of language, etc."[67] A theology of preaching is concerned about the theological basis

---

57. Greenhaw, "Theology of Preaching," 479.
58. Greenhaw, "Theology of Preaching," 479.
59. Greenhaw, "Theology of Preaching," 479.
60. Greenhaw, "Theology of Preaching," 480.
61. Greenhaw, "Theology of Preaching," 480–81.
62. McClure, *Preaching Words*, 137.
63. McClure, *Preaching Words*, 138.
64. McClure, *Preaching Words*, 138.
65. McClure, *Preaching Words*, 139.
66. McClure, *Preaching Words*, 139.
67. McKim, *Westminster Dictionary of Theological Terms*, 245.

for proclamation itself. This basis shapes the other homiletical frames of reference and the whole of the preaching task.

Based on these insights, various implications can be drawn. First, a theology of preaching is concerned with the activity of the proclamation event. Second, this event is a theological transaction that occurs between the divine, human, and the biblical text. Third, a theology of preaching is equally interested in the goal of proclamation. Fourth, a theology of preaching seeks to identify how preaching is effective in the lives of those who hear. Fifth, a theology of preaching asks questions regarding the one speaking and the context in which speaking occurs. Last, and most significantly, a theology of preaching simply asks, Why preach in the first place?

UNIQUE CONTRIBUTIONS TO A THEOLOGY OF PREACHING

The following section looks at unique theologies of preaching, which further define how one can ascertain a theology of preaching. As claimed, twentieth- and twenty-first-century homiletical scholarship has produced various theologies of preaching.[68] It is not the goal to critique these contributions positively or negatively in the following section. Rather, it is to show the development of the subject within scholarship and establish how the field evaluates a theology of preaching. In highlighting these contributions, a rubric for evaluating a theology of preaching becomes clear.

A Barthian Theology of Preaching

It can be argued that Karl Barth's theological project is interpreted through the lens of proclamation.[69] Barth writes, "Proclamation is human speech in and by which God Himself speaks like a king through the mouth of his herald, and which is meant to be heard and accepted as speech in and by which God Himself speaks."[70] Barth does not see proclamation as mere "practical theology." Rather, proclamation is central

---

68. These works cannot be discussed fully in this section, yet they should be mentioned as important contributions: Chan, *Preaching as the Word of God*; Lischer, *Theology of Preaching*; Bartow, *God's Human Speech*; Buttrick, *Captive Voice*; Forde, *Theology Is for Proclamation*; Coggan, *Preaching*; Wingren, *Living Word*.

69. See Willimon, *Conversations with Barth on Preaching*.

70. Barth, *Church Dogmatics*, 52.

to the entire theological task. For Barth, preaching is paramount to revelation.[71] It is done within the context of the church.[72] It ought to be done in conformity to the church's confession under the divine command.[73] It is done by those called into the ministry.[74] Preaching is both divine and human heralding.[75] Preaching is based on Scripture.[76] Preaching involves human originality.[77] Proclamation is directed at specific people at a specific time.[78] Preaching is empowered by the Spirit.[79] In the end, Barth describes this as the nine constitutive elements of preaching.

A Catholic Theology of Preaching

Domenico Grasso wrote *Proclaiming God's Message* in 1965.[80] He draws attention to the "crisis of preaching" that has resulted from a lack of a homiletical theology.[81] Grasso attempts to identify a theology of preaching by looking at the different elements involved in the preaching process. Thus, he is concerned about the object/content of preaching,[82] the principal subject,[83] the relationship between the human and divine word,[84] the preaching event,[85] the hearers' response,[86] the dimensions of preaching,[87] and the efficacy of the word.[88] While written for a Roman Catholic audience, Grasso's work asks the appropriate questions for discerning a theology of preaching. Moreover, this work represents a retrieval project

71. Barth, *Homiletics*, 47.
72. Barth, *Homiletics*, 56.
73. Barth, *Homiletics*, 66.
74. Barth, *Homiletics*, 67.
75. Barth, *Homiletics*, 72.
76. Barth, *Homiletics*, 79.
77. Barth, *Homiletics*, 81.
78. Barth, *Homiletics*, 84.
79. Barth, *Homiletics*, 86.
80. Grasso, *Proclaiming God's Message*.
81. Grasso, *Proclaiming God's Message*, xxx.
82. Grasso, *Proclaiming God's Message*, 1.
83. Grasso, *Proclaiming God's Message*, 23.
84. Grasso, *Proclaiming God's Message*, 47.
85. Grasso, *Proclaiming God's Message*, 69.
86. Grasso, *Proclaiming God's Message*, 86.
87. Grasso, *Proclaiming God's Message*, 111.
88. Grasso, *Proclaiming God's Message*, 125.

as Grasso roots preaching within the context of the Catholic tradition. Frequently he appeals to patristic and Medieval theologians. As such, the categories discussed by the author help scholars think through the various theological implications of the preaching event.

A Historically Informed Evangelical Theology of Preaching

Mike Pasquarello's work *Christian Preaching* attempts to provide a broadly evangelical approach to preaching. He claims that the book is written "within a theological tradition that acknowledges that throughout most of Christian history the practice of preaching was believed to take place in, with, and through the initiative and activity of the Triune God."[89] Therefore, preaching is "the gift of the Spirit," a "conversation initiated by God in which the church is addressed by the Father through the Son."[90] As a result, Christ continues to speak through preaching.[91] This event takes place within the church.[92] It possesses unique pastoral significance.[93] Additionally, preaching is grounded in Scripture.[94] The focus of preaching is the cross, the word of salvation.[95] It has for its end goal the worship and praise of God.[96] Pasquarello's work attempts to draw together the historic Christian orthodox view of proclamation with an evangelical audience in mind. Preaching, therefore, is the speaking of God and the sermon is doxological speech.[97]

A Mainline Protestant Theology of Preaching

William Willimon demonstrates the need to reflect theologically about the task of preaching in his work *Proclamation and Theology*. He makes the claim that "preaching is God speaking."[98] He asserts that this

---

89. Pasquarello, *Christian Preaching*, 13.
90. Pasquarello, *Christian Preaching*, 31.
91. Pasquarello, *Christian Preaching*, 80.
92. Pasquarello, *Christian Preaching*, 87.
93. Pasquarello, *Christian Preaching*, 129.
94. Pasquarello, *Christian Preaching*, 147.
95. Pasquarello, *Christian Preaching*, 149.
96. Pasquarello, *Christian Preaching*, 204.
97. Pasquarello, *Christian Preaching*, 213.
98. Willimon, *Proclamation and Theology*, 8.

governing theological axiom is revealed in Luther's theology, the Second Helvetic Confession, Calvin, and Barth.[99] Willimon grounds preaching in the reality that God speaks.[100] The word that God speaks is prophetic, a word "that comes to us from outside our personal experiences or interior ruminations."[101] Likewise, God continues to speak in the biblical word. Willimon claims, "Scripture itself is homiletical in intent."[102] As a result, "a sermon begins in encounter with the biblical text."[103] Foundational to this assertation is that the sermon is a human attempt to "get the sermon off the printed page and into an oral form."[104] He draws the conclusion then, "We really believe that when we are encountered by Scripture, we are not simply encountering a set of interesting ideas about God, we are encountering the risen Christ."[105] The risen Christ, who is the incarnate God, makes the divine-human communion possible.[106] Thus, Willimon roots preaching in the incarnation.[107]

In a sense, Christ is God's sermon personified since Christ is the self-communication of God to humanity. Preaching is the Father speaking in the Son through the Spirit.[108] This is made a reality through human lips. Thus, all preaching is cruciform.[109] And all preaching is made possible by the resurrection of Christ.[110] This leads Willimon to conclude that preaching is political. He writes, "All faithful Christian preaching is in this sense 'political' because it always involves a dispute over just who is in charge of our world and therefore our lives."[111] While Willimon certainly develops and sets forth an important contribution, some of his theological conclusions tend to be outside of the norm of

---

99. Willimon, *Proclamation and Theology*, 7–16.
100. Willimon, *Proclamation and Theology*, 10.
101. Willimon, *Proclamation and Theology*, 19.
102. Willimon, *Proclamation and Theology*, 39.
103. Willimon, *Proclamation and Theology*, 41.
104. Willimon, *Proclamation and Theology*, 42.
105. Willimon, *Proclamation and Theology*, 46.
106. Willimon, *Proclamation and Theology*, 52.
107. Willimon, *Proclamation and Theology*, 54.
108. Willimon, *Proclamation and Theology*, 62.
109. Willimon, *Proclamation and Theology*, 68.
110. Willimon, *Proclamation and Theology*, 81.
111. Willimon, *Proclamation and Theology*, 92.

conservative theological approaches. For example, he jettisons the inerrancy conversation.[112]

A Reformed Theology of Preaching

Peter Adam's work *Speaking God's Words* represents a Reformed approach to preaching. He claims, "My aim in this book is to provide a robust practical theology of preaching. . . . I want to provide a theology of preaching, because only theological arguments are convincing in the long term."[113] He grounds preaching in three foundations: (1) God has spoken; (2) it is written; (3) preach the word.[114] He argues, "Preaching is best understood as one part of the ministry of the Word, and it derives its theological character from the biblical basis for all aspects of the ministry of the Word."[115] He states that preaching is "the explanation and application of the Word in the assembled congregation of Christ."[116] He furthers his argument by claiming that "preaching is essentially a corporate activity, and its most useful aim is corporate edification."[117] The crux of Adam's argument is: "God's words are part of his self-revelation. God's words are not remote from him: he is present in his words. Our preaching of God's words is not an invitation to consider something remote from God, but an invitation to meet the living God in his words."[118] In considering the statement, "Preaching the Word of God is the Word of God," he provides a simplistic understanding of its implications. He argues, "To claim that Christ may be heard through preaching or that God makes his appeal through preaching is not to claim that the preaching itself is the Word of God."[119] Additionally, "If our preaching is true to Scripture, it will be the means by which God brings the Word of God to those who hear us."[120] Adam's work helps provide a solid foundation for expository preaching.

---

112. Willimon, *Proclamation and Theology*, 39.
113. Adam, *Speaking God's Words*, 9.
114. Adam, *Speaking God's Words*, 15–56.
115. Adam, *Speaking God's Words*, 15.
116. Adam, *Speaking God's Words*, 61.
117. Adam, *Speaking God's Words*, 70.
118. Adam, *Speaking God's Words*, 55–56.
119. Adam, *Speaking God's Words*, 118.
120. Adam, *Speaking God's Words*, 120.

A RUBRIC FOR EVALUATING A THEOLOGY OF PREACHING

Aaron Edwards writes, "Preaching, particularly in the Protestant tradition, has always carried immense significance not simply as an act of Scriptural exposition, but as a unique, revelatory activity."[121] Summarizing contemporary scholarly work, theologies of preaching seek to explain this revelatory activity of proclamation. Generally, theologies of preaching ask specific historical and theological questions about the nature of Scripture, the role of the Spirit, and the context of preaching. An overview of the unique contributions in the field demonstrates similarities regarding how scholars understand what is happening in the event of proclamation. Therefore, to synthesize the vast amount of material into a workable rubric for evaluating a theology for preaching, the following definition and six questions will be applied: *A theology of preaching attempts to understand the theo-homiletical convictions (the why) and the activity of proclamation (the what) by asking: (1) What is the basis for preaching? (Basis); (2) What is being preached? (Object); (3) Who is doing the preaching? (Subject); (4) How is preaching made effective? (Means); (5) Where is preaching taking place? (Context); (6) What is the purpose of preaching? (Goal).*

These questions govern the scope of this project. It is acknowledged that this rubric can be nuanced in various ways. However, the broadness of this definition and the subsequent questions help establish a paradigm for understanding theo-homiletical presuppositions. As it specifically relates to Benjamin Keach, the historical subject under consideration, the general nature of the questions allows for deeper discoveries in Keach's preaching. These questions attempt to explore different elements of the preaching activity. *The basis* for preaching is focused on the nature of God as communicator and the Bible. *The object* of preaching explores how one articulates the gospel. *The subject* investigates the role of the human preacher and the divine preacher. The third question, *the means*, aims at understanding the role of the Spirit and rhetoric in preaching. *The context* details the ecclesiological setting of preaching with other liturgical elements. Last, the final question, *the goal*, examines the intended purpose of proclamation for Christians and non-Christians.

Therefore, what will be demonstrated is that Keach's homiletical theology, which is epiphanical (basis), expositional (object), experiential (subject), effectual (means), ecclesial (context), and evangelical (goal),

---

121. Edwards, *Theology of Preaching and Dialectic*, 134.

offers contemporary Baptist preachers a foundation and framework for proclamation. A qualification is acknowledged at this point. These convictions are often assumed in modern preaching. The claim of this book is not that these features are entirely unique to Keach or even the larger Baptist homiletical tradition. Indeed, many of the theo-homiletical convictions are shared by others in various denominational traditions that emerged out of the Protestant Reformation. Rather, the claim is that Baptists have a figure located at the beginning stages of our own history who thought deeply about the task of preaching. His thoughts on preaching can shape our homiletical convictions. This is retrieval done within the *sanctorum communio*. As McKibbens notes, "Baptists in England during the seventeenth century had an extraordinary number of evangelistic and learned leaders. Benjamin Keach was among the most well-known, and his influence is still with us."[122] While Baptists will disagree with some Keachean nuances, the six theo-homiletical convictions provide an avenue to understand the task of preaching more robustly.

---

122. McKibbens, *Forgotten Heritage*, 18.

CHAPTER 2

Preaching in the Baptist Tradition

THIS CHAPTER IS DEDICATED to the question *why*. Why make the effort to retrieve a Baptist theology of preaching? Is it warranted? Perhaps this entire project runs the risk of being anachronistic. Are we imposing modern questions on historical figures? My goal in this chapter is twofold. First, it is to show that Baptists throughout history have wrestled with theo-homiletical questions. Second, this chapter shows homiletical continuity to our present day. In other words, a *Baptist sanctorum communio*. This chapter could be unnecessarily long as it explores the roughly four hundred years of the Baptist homiletical tradition. Therefore, I have chosen to limit myself to well-known Baptist preachers and Baptist confessions.

HISTORICAL CONTEXT

What is a *Baptist* in the first place? Leon McBeth writes, "The Baptist denomination, as it is known today, emerged by way of the English Separatist movement. The best historical evidence confirms that origin."[1] Additionally, "Baptists are children of the Puritans, a movement with roots stretching back to the European Reformation in the sixteenth century."[2] The Reformation impulses of the Puritan attitudes and aims ignited various dissenting traditions. In particular, these attitudes and priorities

---

1. McBeth, *Baptist Heritage*, 31.
2. Chute et al., *Baptist Story*, 14.

shaped the English Separatist movement in the later part of the sixteenth century.[3] Bebbington summarizes the origins:

> Like the Independents, Baptists were the heirs of the Reformation, Puritanism, and separatism. They adopted the same principles of punctilious loyalty to the word of God, of passionate desire to worship the Almighty correctly, and of willingness to restructure the church in accordance with God's precepts. Their biblical, liturgical, and ecclesiastical priorities drove them through Puritan loyalties into separatism and, eventually, to the further step of repudiating infant baptism. Baptists were the people who took Reformation principles to their ultimate conclusion.[4]

Regarding the specific origins of the two groups of Baptists—General and Particular—it is accepted that "these two groups did not 'divide;' instead, they had quite different origins, at different times and places, and with different leaders."[5] For this work, the origins of the Particular Baptist movement will be the focus.

Regarding Baptist origins, historians accept that Robert Browne's publication *A Treatise of Reformation without Tarying for Anie* served as a launching pad.[6] Browne argued that the magistrate possessed no authority over the affairs of a congregation. He writes, "Yea the Church hath more authoritie concerning Church gouernement then Magistrates."[7] The congregation possessed authority over its own decisions.[8] Significantly, his work is the first known attempt at producing "a consistent doctrine of the Church" outside of the established church.[9] These Separatist impulses shaped ministers, such as John Smyth, who adopted these doctrines and established Separatist churches.[10] Smyth went on to embrace believer's baptism and renounce his Calvinistic doctrine while in Holland. Bebbington states, "In 1609 Smyth baptized himself and created the earliest

---

3. White, *English Separatist Tradition*, 19.
4. Bebbington, *Baptists Through the Centuries*, 23.
5. McBeth, *Baptist Heritage*, 39.
6. Haykin, "Separatists and Baptists," 115.
7. Browne, *Treatise of Reformation*, 28.
8. White, *English Separatist Tradition*, 63.
9. White, *English Separatist Tradition*, 66.
10. Haykin, "Separatists and Baptists," 119. Smyth would flee to Amsterdam and start a Separatist church. He seemed to be controversial in various ways. He would find himself in disagreements with Francis Johnson and John Robinson. Robinson's congregation would leave the Netherlands and land at Plymouth Massachusetts in 1620.

Baptist church."[11] Eventually, he applied for membership in a Mennonite congregation. Thomas Helwys split from Smyth, traveled back to England, and settled what would become known by historians as the first General Baptist congregation.[12]

PARTICULAR BAPTIST ORIGINS

Ian Birch notes that Particular Baptists considered themselves to be "true Puritans . . . by virtue of their separation" and became "an identifiable collective organization in the mid-seventeenth century."[13] In his work *Orthodox Radicals*, Matthew Bingham proposes the term *Baptistic congregationalists* as a way of describing those who affirmed credobaptism and congregational polity.[14] His intent is not primarily redefinition. Rather, he regards his work as an attempt to understand this group in relationship to their theological/ecclesiological network.[15] He argues, "The very category 'Baptist' was an eighteenth-century development and to impose it upon the mid-seventeenth century is to think anachronistically about the past."[16] Furthermore, he writes, "The so-called Particular Baptists of mid-seventeenth century England were no such thing. They were practitioners of the congregational way who modified their views on baptism without thereby wholly deconstructing the wider theological framework and relational networks that had previously defined them."[17] The label of Particular Baptists should be avoided "chiefly because it is insufficiently sensitive to the self-identity of those which it purports to describe."[18]

Bingham's work demonstrates the interrelationship of these Baptistic congregationalists within the larger Puritan attitude. Those who aligned themselves with this group of churches were both "theologically and relationally intertwined with the congregationally-minded puritan diaspora."[19] These "Calvinistic baptistic congregationalists" maintained

11. Bebbington, *Baptists Through the Centuries*, 31–32.
12. Haykin, "Separatists and Baptists," 120–22.
13. Birch, *To Follow the Lambe*, 30, 1.
14. Bingham, *Orthodox Radicals*, 40.
15. Bingham notes that he is inclined to identify so-called General Baptists as Baptistic Separatists. See Bingham, *Orthodox Radicals*, 153.
16. Bingham, *Orthodox Radicals*, 10.
17. Bingham, *Orthodox Radicals*, 61.
18. Bingham, *Orthodox Radicals*, 44.
19. Bingham, *Orthodox Radicals*, 45. Bremer states, "In many respects Baptists

their relationships with the broader Reformed community. Nevertheless, by the late seventeenth century, the title *Baptist* was being applied by those involved in the movement.[20] As Renihan argues,

> While the Particular Baptists and their churches were closely allied with the congregational Independents and Separatists in the 1640s, it was the idiosyncrasies of their doctrine of the church which eventually pulled the groups apart. Close ties could not be maintained between parties with fundamentally different notions regarding the complexion of the Christian assembly. This is not to say that their views were mutually exclusive, it is simply to say that ecclesiology was the driving force behind the Baptist movement, and provided it was a self-conscious identity distinct from that of the Independents.[21]

Unique characteristics regarding ecclesiology, baptism, and covenant theology marked this group of baptized churches.[22] Therefore, the usage of the term *Particular Baptists* is not thinking "anachronistically about the past" as much as it is attempting to provide a category for a group that was already expressing unique theological elements in their day.

Particular Baptists can be traced back to "a congregation of independent Puritans found by Henry Jacob in Southwark London, in 1616."[23] Jacob left England in 1622 for Virginia due to opposition. Following his departure, John Lathrop was called as the pastor of this congregation. In 1633, under Lathrop's leadership, Samuel Eaton separated to form a new congregation.[24] The reason for separation seemed to be over the issue of baptism, as Burrage states: "Mr. Eaton with Some others receiving a further baptism."[25] Bingham states, "This split indicated not

---

were puritans who simply disagreed on the subject of infant baptism.... English Congregationalists were generally content to view Particular Baptists as fellow puritans, members of the broader godly community." See Bremer, *Lay Empowerment*, 127–30.

20. Keach used the language of Baptist as a way of self-identification that distinguished the association of churches he belonged to from the congregational churches. He says, "Many *Reverend Divines* of the *Congregational way*, have written most excellently (it is true) upon the Subject ... and our *Brethren* the *Baptists* have not written (as I can gather) on this Subject by itself." See Keach, *Glory of a true church*, iv. Moreover, Keach saw continuity with the seven London Baptist churches of 1644. See Keach, "To All the Baptized Churches," 109.

21. Renihan, *Edification and Beauty*, 37.
22. See Coxe, *Discourse of the covenants*.
23. Birch, *To Follow the Lambe*, 2.
24. White, *English Baptists*, 59.
25. Burrage, *Illustrative Documents*, 299.

just a changing perception of the national church, but also, for the first time among the Jacob-Lathrop-Jessey circle, a changing perception of the national church's baptism."[26]

Following Lathrop, in 1637, Henry Jessey became the pastor of the independent church. Yet, by 1638, a new congregation was formed and pastored by John Spilsbury who was convinced that baptism was for professing believers and not infants.[27] Thus, "John Spilsbury's church, emerging from Puritan Separatism, offers a historically and theologically identifiable lineage for the Particular Baptists."[28] In 1640, the Jacob-Lathrop-Jessey church had grown, which resulted in the church becoming "two by mutuall consent."[29] Half of the church was led by Praise-God Barebones while the other remained under the pastoral care of Jessey.

The following year in 1641, fifty-two members of Jessey's church "were rebaptized by Richard Blunt and Samuel Blacklock."[30] This was prompted by Blunt "being convinced of baptism . . . ought to be by diping ye Body into ye Water, resembling burial and riseing again."[31] In this period, William Kiffin became convinced of believer's baptism and joined Eaton's church. He preached to the congregation during Eaton's imprisonment and was later called as pastor.[32] The issue of baptism prompted others to separate and form new churches. By 1644, "those that were so minded had communion together were become Seven Churches in London."[33]

The two groups of baptized believers, the General and Particular, originated in different ways. These streams reflect diverging ecclesiological developments shaping late sixteenth- and early seventeenth-century England. Though Baptist origins are not the primary focus, it is important to establish the historical context.

---

26. Bingham, *Orthodox Radicals*, 16.

27. Burrage, *Illustrative Documents*, 302. This evidence is found in the "Kiffin Manuscript."

28. Renihan, *From Shadow to Substance*, 13.

29. Haykin, "Separatists and Baptists," 125. Burrage, *Illustrative Documents*, 302.

30. Bingham, *Orthodox Radicals*, 17. Burrage, *Illustrative Documents*, 304.

31. Burrage, *Illustrative Documents*, 302.

32. Haykin, "Separatists and Baptists," 125.

33. Burrage, *Illustrative Documents*, 304.

SEVENTEENTH-CENTURY BAPTIST PREACHING

This section and those that follow are by no means exhaustive. The goal is to provide a broad representation of Baptistic thought on preaching. This seventeenth-century survey does not include selections from Keach, as those comments will be contained in chapter 5.

Thomas Helwys

The earliest English Baptist confession of faith in the seventeenth century was written in 1611 by Thomas Helwys.[34] The confession sets forth articles of faith that articulate Arminian doctrine. Helwys mentions preaching in a few articles. For example, the word and Spirit separates the church of Christ from the world.[35] Likewise, preaching the gospel precedes the ordinance of baptism and church membership.[36] Though the statement of faith does not go into details on preaching, it nevertheless assumes proclamation to be a key role in the church.

The First London Confession

The First London Confession (1644) makes specific statements as it relates to preaching. Article 24 states "that faith is ordinarily begotten by the preaching of the gospel, or word of Christ, without respect to any power or capacity in the creature, but it is wholly passive, being dead in sins and trespasses, does believe, and is converted by no less power, than that which raised Christ from the dead."[37] Additionally, the Confession also states,

> That the tender [preaching] of the gospel to the conversion of sinners, is absolutely free, no way requiring, as absolutely necessary, any qualifications, preparations, terrors of the law, or preceding ministry of the law, but only and alone the naked soul, as a sinner and ungodly to receive Christ as crucified, dead, and buried, and risen again, being made a prince and a Savior for such sinners.[38]

---

34. Early, *Life and Writings of Thomas Helwys*, 29. Helwys, *Declaration of Faith*.
35. Helwys, *Declaration of Faith*, 11.
36. Helwys, *Declaration of Faith*, 12.
37. *Confession of Faith of those Churches*, 10.
38. *Confession of Faith of those Churches*, 10.

This statement is revealing for the early Baptists in 1644. The doctrine of preparation was an aspect of Reformed preaching.[39] However, it seems to be the case that the early Particular Baptists nuanced preparationism.[40] It was not necessary for a sinner to be prepared to receive the gospel. Rather, the preaching of the gospel was "absolutely free."

Benjamin Coxe

Additionally, Particular Baptist minister Benjamin Coxe penned an appendix to the 1644 London Confession. In article 5, Coxe affirms particular redemption for the elect. However, he states in article 6,

> Though some of our opponents do affirm that by this doctrine [particular redemption] we leave no gospel to be preached to sinners for their conversion; yet through the goodness of God we know and preach to sinners this precious gospel: "God so loved the world, (that is, has been so loving to mankind) that He gave His only begotten Son, that whosoever believeth in Him should not perish, but have everlasting life" (John 3:16); and this faithful saying, worthy of all acceptation, "That Jesus Christ came into the world to save sinners" (1 Tim. 1:15), viz., all those sinners (how vile and grievous) not only which already do, but also which hereafter shall believe on Him to life everlasting (1 Tim. 1:16), and that "to Christ all the prophets give witness, that through His name, whosoever believeth in Him shall receive remission of sins" (Acts 10:43). And this is called "The word of the Gospel" (Acts 15:7). This is the gospel which Christ and His apostles preached, which we have received, and by which we have been converted, unto Christ. And we desire to mind what Paul says in Gal. 1:9: "If any man preach any other gospel unto you than that ye have received, let him be accursed."[41]

This provides evidence of a free-offer gospel among the earliest Particular Baptist ministers. They saw no theological contradiction between particular redemption and the proclamation of the gospel. Furthermore, Coxe writes, "The preaching of the Gospel, [is] both for the conversion of

---

39. Beeke and Smalley, *Prepared by Grace, for Grace*. They write, "Puritan preparation is the doctrine that God prepares sinners for faith by overcoming obstacles in their minds and consciences to the claims of the gospel," 17–18.
40. Wenkel, "Only and Alone the Naked Soul."
41. Coxe, *Appendix*, 10.

sinners, and the edifying of those that are converted."[42] The dual nature of proclamation is reflected throughout the preaching of early English Particular Baptists. While nonconformist preaching aimed at these dual goals, Particular Baptists made conversion an explicit objective in their proclamation. Ward claims, "But whereas the [Westminster] Directory gave edification and not salvation as an application of the sermon, the Baptists sought both. . . . Particular Baptists consistently made the presentation of salvation one of the 'uses' in their sermons."[43]

John Spilsbury

John Spilsbury published a work titled *God's Ordinance* in 1646. It is a collection of two sermons, one dedicated to the ordinances and the other focused on particular redemption. While the first sermon is not specifically on preaching, Spilsbury mentions the role of proclamation. In the context of the sermon, he is refuting those who question the authority of preaching. He states,

> We have the same Spirit, who enables men to preach Christ crucified, which though to some a stumbling blocke, and to others foolishnesse, yet to many appears to be the power of God, by which they are brought to believe in Jesus Christ for eternall life and glory. And thus we have the same Gospel, the same faith, the same Christ, and so the same way to salvation as they formerly had; and these meanes doth God appoint, and approve, and blesse, for the effecting of this great worke of salvation to us now.[44]

He continues,

> No man can truly preach the Gospel, but he that hath the same Spirit of God that the Apostles had, And so I come to answer their demand briefly thus: 1. As preaching is to deliver a Message received of the Lord, thus it is now afoote; 2. As preaching is a publishing of the Gospel of Christ occasionally, to bring men to the truth, as so it is now afoote; 3. As the Disciples were to preach the Gospel of Christ freely to all persons without exception, thus it is now afoote. Lastly, as men are to trade with

---

42. Coxe, *Appendix*, 10.
43. Ward, *Pure Worship*, 166–67.
44. Spilsbury, *Gods Ordinance*, 19.

that abilitie given them of Christ, for their Lords advantage, as so preaching the Gospel is now afoote.[45]

Spilsbury claims that contemporary preachers possess the same Holy Spirit of the apostles and must preach in accordance with his power. Likewise, preaching has the same power as it did during the first century. Those gifted are called upon to preach the gospel "without exception." These statements indicate important Reformed homiletical presuppositions. He states,

> They are those Scriptures that are necessary to bring God and man together unto a onenesse in Christ. And this is the Gospel, which is called the *Word of Reconciliation*, the *Gospel of the Kingdome*; which holds forth Christ to be King, Priest, and Prophet, and the onely way unto the Father; and brings persons to be of the houshold of God.[46]

For Spilsbury, the goal of preaching is to bring "God and man together unto a onenesse in Christ." This parallels the Reformed goal of preaching. Additionally, the Scriptures and the gospel are inseparable. It is in the Bible that the word of the gospel is made known. Specifically, this gospel concerns the person and work of Christ.

Hanserd Knollys

Hanserd Knollys published an exposition on the Song of Solomon in 1656. This work is unique since it demonstrates an allegorical, historical, prophetical, and spiritual approach to understanding the book.[47] Knollys sees the proclamation of the gospel in the phrase *with the kisses of his mouth*. He states,

> One Pledge of Christs love, one Manifestation of his Grace, one Injoyment of himself could not satisfie the Spouse, She doth affectionately desire and pray for Kisses, that is to say, abundance of Grace and peace, joy and comfort, blessings and favours from Christ, which God blesseth his poor Saints with all in Christ Jesus. . . . *Of his mouth*, that is, the words of Christs mouth . . . in Christ, his mouth is most sweet. . . . The gracious words of Christ spoken in the Ministery of the Gospel to the ear, and

---

45. Spilsbury, *Gods Ordinance*, 20–21.
46. Spilsbury, *Gods Ordinance*, 22.
47. Knollys, *Exposition of the First Chapter*, introduction.

applyed by the Spirit of God to the heart of his Spouse and people, do communicate abundant grace, peace, and spiritual blessings unto their Souls.[48]

The "kisses of his mouth" are the words of Christ as mediated in the ministry of the gospel. This is a common reference to preaching. These "kisses" are applied by the Spirit to those who believe the word. Thus, "Christ doth thus feed his flocks (to wit, his Churches and Saints) by his faithful Ministers, and Elders of the Churches of God, whom the holy Spirit maketh overseers over the Flock."[49] Knollys demonstrates a Reformed spirituality/sacramentality of preaching.

In *Christ Exalted*, Knollys argues, "God does offer Christ to lost sinners without price. . . . He invites them, that have no money to come and buy wine and milk without price. And anyone, that will, are invited to take Christ freely. And whosoever will, let him take the water of life."[50] He connects this offer of Christ to the proclamation of the word.

Thomas Grantham

Another publication addressing the role of the preacher and preaching was written in 1678 by a General Baptist, Thomas Grantham, titled *Christianismus Primitivus*.[51] Chute, Finn, and Haykin write, "*Christianismus Primitivus* not only contains a thorough elaboration of Grantham's doctrine of salvation but also provides in-depth discussions of other issues important to Baptists in this era."[52] In it, Grantham mentions the role and responsibility of elders, who are called to "feed the flock, as faithful stewards of the mysteries of God . . . they must be to bring forth the sincere, or incorrupt Milk of the Word."[53] While Grantham does not explicitly elaborate on how the minister is to perform the task, he notes that this is the primitive practice of the church.

---

48. Knollys, *Exposition of the First Chapter*, 6.
49. Knollys, *Exposition of the First Chapter*, 29.
50. Knollys, *Christ Exalted*, 12.
51. Grantham, *Christianismus Primitivus*. Also see Plumlee, "Baptist Primitivist."
52. Chute et al., *Baptist Story*, 50.
53. Grantham, *Christianismus Primitivus*, 2.9.123.

The Orthodox Creed

The Orthodox Creed, a General Baptist confession, explicitly declares, "Justifying faith is a grace, or habit, wrought in the soul, by the Holy Ghost, through preaching the Word of God."[54] Additionally, the confession articulates the relationship of the word and the Supper.[55] The right preaching of the Bible is a mark of a truly constituted church.[56] In the article on the family, the document states that it is the familial duty to spend the Sabbath attending public worship, "especially the reading of the Scriptures, and hearing the Word preached."[57]

Nehemiah Coxe

Nehemiah Coxe preached an ordination sermon addressing the various responsibilities of pastors. Though he briefly mentions preaching, he focuses primarily on the identity of the preacher. He says, "As he [the preacher] is to be the Mouth of God to the People," the minister has the responsibility to "speak to them in his Name."[58] In the sermon, he gives three recommendations to those charged with preaching the gospel. He states,

> Let your Care be, to deal with the Souls and Consciences of Men, as knowing that it is the Salvation of Souls which you are to labor after, a Care of Souls that is committed to you, and an account of them that you must make to God. . . . 2. That this may be accomplished; Be sure that you speak *as the Oracles of God*; and deliver that Doctrine to the People which is drawn from the pure Fountain of God's Word. . . . 3. Remember that the Duty of your Place is, *Not to preach your selves but Christ Jesus the Lord*; His Glory must be the Mark aimed at by all your Labors, and his Grace the principal Subject of all your Discourses.[59]

Likewise, pastors are "Ministers of the New Testament, and God's Ambassadors unto Men, who are to dispense the Mysteries of God to his Church."[60] He concludes this section of the sermon with the exhortation,

---

54. *Orthodox Creed*, 31.
55. *Orthodox Creed*, 45.
56. *Orthodox Creed*, 41.
57. *Orthodox Creed*, 68.
58. Coxe, *Sermon Preached*, 23.
59. Coxe, *Sermon Preached*, 24–26.
60. Coxe, *Sermon Preached*, 24.

"Therefore I will not only say, Let there be . . . something of Christ in every Sermon, but let Christ be the beginning, middle, and end of your Discourses."[61] These statements parallel the English Reformed preaching tradition, particularly the primacy of preaching. Also, Coxe uses the term *Ambassador* to describe the preaching function of the minister. Chapter 4 will show that the ambassador metaphor is an important Reformed identifier for the preacher. Last, Coxe identifies the interrelationship between the words of the minister and the word of God. The minister is the "mouth of God" unto the people of God. This language testifies to the larger Reformed view of proclamation.[62]

The Second London Confession

The Second London Confession also mentions preaching in a similar fashion as the First Confession. As chapter 20 states,

> Although the gospel be the only outward means of revealing Christ and saving grace, and is, as such, abundantly sufficient thereunto; yet that men who are dead in trespasses may be born again, quickened, or regenerated, there is moreover necessary an effectual insuperable work of the Holy Spirit upon the whole soul, for the producing in them a new spiritual life; without which no other means will effect their conversion unto God.[63]

This article expresses the twofold work of preaching, akin to Calvin's *minister externus* and *minister internus*.[64] Preaching serves a vital role in the context of Sunday worship.[65] Furthermore, the gospel is to go to all nations.[66] Preaching repentance is an absolute necessity.[67] Additionally, it is the role of the pastor to preaching the gospel; however, this task is not limited solely to those ordained.[68] Baptist preaching in the seventeenth

---

61. Coxe, *Sermon Preached*, 26.

62. Calvin writes, "For, among the many excellent gifts with which God has adorned the human race, it is a singular privilege that he deigns to consecrate to himself the mouths and tongues of men in order that his voice may resound in them." See Calvin, *Institutes*, 4.1.5.

63. *Confession of Faith Put Forth*, 69.

64. Calvin, "Summary of Doctrine," 173.

65. *Confession of Faith Put Forth*, 75.

66. *Confession of Faith Put Forth*, 68–69.

67. *Confession of Faith Put Forth*, 51.

68. *Confession of Faith Put Forth*, 90–91.

century is an outflow of the Reformation vision of preaching. It is word driven and Spirit empowered. For both the General and Particular expressions of the Baptist tradition, the preaching of the gospel was the means by which faith was wrought by the Spirit.

An intriguing aspect among Particular Baptists is their clarity regarding the free offer of the gospel. From 1644 to the end of the seventeenth century, there is an effort to balance particular redemption and the offer of salvation to hearers. This theo-homiletical conviction will be further exaggerated in eighteenth-century Particular Baptist preaching. While this section has intentionally neglected to mention Keach, chapter 5 will detail how he played a role in providing clarity on this specific issue.

EIGHTEENTH-CENTURY BAPTIST PREACHING

Hercules Collins

By the beginning of the eighteenth century, Baptist preacher Hercules Collins published *The Temple Repair'd*, which aimed to give "proper directions as to study and preaching."[69] It is a practical primer to younger ministers and shares similarities with Perkins's *The Art of Prophesying*. He asserts, "Now I shall sum up all into one Doctrine: That it is the Duty of every Gospel-Minister so to study as they may approve themselves to God; and so divide the Word of Truth, that they may not be ashamed, but rather have the Honor that belongs to that calling."[70] The work does not explicitly develop a theology of preaching. It does, nevertheless, assume theo-homiletical convictions. For example, the work of the Spirit is necessary to make the word effectual in proclamation.[71] The presence of God is made known through preaching.[72] The minister is called to administer the ordinances, the primary being that of preaching.[73]

---

69. See the title page of Collins, *Temple Repair'd*.
70. Collins, *Temple Repair'd*, 8.
71. Collins, *Temple Repair'd*, 9.
72. Collins, *Temple Repair'd*, 15.
73. Collins, *Temple Repair'd*, 23.

John Gill

Prominent Baptist preacher John Gill penned his *Doctoral and Practical Divinity* in 1769. He devotes several pages to discussing the role of preaching.[74] Gill claims that biblically qualified and congregationally affirmed ministers are directed "to preach the gospel; it is the glorious gospel of the blessed God, which is committed to their trust; and there is a woe upon them if they preach not the gospel." He argues, "Christ and him crucified is the subject-matter, the sum and substance of the gospel ministry." This Christ-centered proclamation includes "peace by the blood of his cross," "reconciliation of God's elect in one body," and "the atonement and expiation of their sins."[75] Gill asserts that "the chief and principle work" of a pastor is "to feed the church of God committed to their care."[76]

Concerning preachers, Gill writes, "Ministers of the gospel are not only fellow-laborers with one another, but with the Lord himself, in his church; the manuring, cultivation, planting, and watering his vineyard, and the building up of his people in a church-state." Thus, "the presence of the Lord [is] with them, and the operation of his hands [is] seen in their ministry."[77] The laborious activity of proclamation is both human and divine. He boldly claims, "In the ministry of the word . . . they [pastors] are the mouth of God to the people, and speak in his name, and are ambassadors in Christ's stead."[78] This is nearly identical to statements made by Coxe and other Puritan ministers in the seventeenth century.

Gill believes that it is the Spirit of God that makes preaching efficacious. The Spirit is the primary cause of regeneration.[79] He says, "It is the Spirit of wisdom and revelation who leads men into the knowledge of Christ."[80] Additionally, "By hearing the word, the Spirit of God, his gifts and graces, are conveyed into the hearts of men."[81] As it relates to human agency Gill argues, "They [ministers] must be studious in the Scriptures, and have a competent knowledge of things contained in them" but should

---

74. Gill, *Doctrinal and Practical Divinity*, 660–71.
75. Gill, *Doctrinal and Practical Divinity*, 668.
76. Gill, *Doctrinal and Practical Divinity*, 582.
77. Gill, *Doctrinal and Practical Divinity*, 665.
78. Gill, *Doctrinal and Practical Divinity*, 589.
79. Gill, *Cause of God and Truth*, 36.
80. Gill, *Doctrinal and Practical Divinity*, 586.
81. Gill, *Doctrinal and Practical Divinity*, 681.

not rely on their own giftedness.[82] Gill calls preaching "the principal means of maintaining and preserving life."[83]

While some scholars seek to minimize Gill's hyper-Calvinist tendencies,[84] there is evidence that his theological system gravitated toward this extreme position.[85] He seems to believe that the Spirit of God can regenerate unbelievers with or without the proclamation of the word.[86] He claims that the effectual call to save "sometimes . . . is brought about by some remarkable providence, and without the word; but generally, it is by it."[87] This nuance stands in contrast to the Baptists of the seventeenth century who made it an explicit theo-homiletical conviction that the Spirit works in tandem with the word to regenerate unbelievers. Additionally, Gill makes the distinction between offering the gospel and declaring the gospel to all. "It is true, the ministers of the gospel, though they ought not to offer and tender salvation to any, for which they have no commission, yet they may preach the gospel of salvation to all men."[88] Commenting on Isa 55:1, Gill states, "These words are no call, invitation, or offer of grace to dead sinners."[89] Gill's main objection concerns the notion that ministers can offer Christ to sinners.[90] However, this stands in contrast to seventeenth-century Baptists such as Knollys who clearly articulated that it is the role of the minister to offer Christ to sinners through the preaching of the gospel.

---

82. Gill, *Doctrinal and Practical Divinity*, 666.

83. Gill, *Doctrinal and Practical Divinity*, 652.

84. Nettles, *By His Grace*, 54. Nettles writes, "One can accuse Gill of 'non-invitation, non-application' only by clinging to an unbiblically narrow concept of 'invitation,' as if it were a call to physical activity at the end of a preaching service." However, "the unbiblically narrow concept" of a physical activity is not the issue.

85. Toon writes of hyper-Calvinism: "It was a system of theology, or a system of the doctrines of God, man and grace, which was framed to exalt the honour and glory of God and did so at the expense of minimizing the moral and spiritual responsibility of sinners to God. . . . So Hyper-Calvinism led its adherents to hold that evangelism was not necessary and to place much emphasis on introspection in order to discover whether or not one was elect." Toon, *Emergence of Hyper-Calvinism*, 144–45.

86. Gill, *Cause of God and Truth*, 27.

87. Gill, *Doctrinal and Practical Divinity*, 129.

88. Gill, *Cause of God and Truth*, 303.

89. Gill, *Cause of God and Truth*, 36.

90. Nettles writes, "Gill has no objections to encouraging sinners to come to Christ, but considers the phrase 'offer Christ and Grace' as strictly without theological foundation. Grace strictly refers to the sovereign bestowment of unmerited salvific blessings and cannot, therefore, be offered, not even to the elect." Nettles, *By His Grace*, 48.

Baptist Preaching in the Evangelical Revival

Into the mid-eighteenth century, various influences shaped preaching. First, the plain style of preaching slowly began to give way to a more textual approach proposed by Jean Claude.[91] British Baptist preacher Robert Robinson translated Claude's work into English in 1779.[92] Though Robinson's translation of Claude's work contains explanatory comments, which at times overwhelm the primary text, this work proved to be a significant contribution to Baptist preaching.[93] As Old notes, Robinson's translation of Claude's work "apparently became a favorite homiletical guide among Baptists."[94]

Second, the Evangelical Revival possessed a transatlantic influence on Baptists.[95] To be more specific, the Edwardsean tradition shaped English and American Baptists. Those who embraced the tradition maintained a Calvinistic framework with an evangelistic/revivalistic impulse.[96] Edwardsean theology, particularly the emphasis on the natural ability and moral inability distinction, reoriented confessional categories. This adoption and further adaptation gave rise to increased evangelistic efforts.[97] By the 1760s, the English Particular Baptists began to experience the effects of the revivalism in their theology and practice.[98] For example, some Baptists were being influenced by Philip Doddridge's writings, which promoted evangelical teaching.[99] The Northamptonshire Baptist Association was formed in 1764.[100] In 1770 the Baptist college in Bristol was reorganized under Caleb Evans, who was significantly impacted by Jonathan Edwards.[101]

---

91. See Autrey, "Factors Influencing."
92. Claude, *Essay on the Composition*. Also see Haykin, "Those Who Plead for Thee."
93. Wright, "Preacher and His Sermon."
94. Old, *Modern Age*, 730.
95. As it relates particularly to revivalism see these two chapters: Haykin, "Lord Is Doing Great Things," and Nettles, "Baptist Revivals." Scholars have explored the Edwardsean influence in Andrew Fuller: Chun, *Legacy of Jonathan Edwards*; Rindels, *Andrew Fuller's Theology of Revival*. See Todd, *Baptist at the Crossroads*, on the Edwardsean influence in the life of American Baptist Richard Furman.
96. Todd, *Southern Edwardseans*, 49.
97. Kidd, *God of Liberty*, 48.
98. Noll, *America's God*, 163.
99. Noll, *Rise of Evangelicalism*, 163.
100. Noll, *Rise of Evangelicalism*, 163.
101. Noll, *Rise of Evangelicalism*, 163.

Baptist preaching in America emerged out the convergence of social, political, and religious movements. Their sermons during the Great Awakening and American Revolution tended toward addressing cultural issues.[102] Specific examples of this type of preaching are found in John Leland, Oliver Hart, and Isaac Backus.[103] Oliver Hart's sermons were "primarily topical in the best sense of that word. He stayed with the biblical idea, but was extremely limited in the exposition of the text."[104] Nevertheless, the revivals of the mid- to late eighteenth century had a profound impact on Baptists. As Kidd and Hankins note,

> But the new, radical Baptist movement emerging de novo from the Great Awakening transformed American's religion landscape. The spawning of the radical evangelical Baptists was reminiscent of the way that the English Puritan and Separatist movement had helped create the original English Baptists.[105]

The distinction between the Separatist and Regular Baptists groups in the early Republic had less to do with diverging theologies and more to do with differing attitudes toward confessionalism and ecclesiological practices.[106] Both groups were Calvinistic in their theology to varying degrees.[107] McBeth writes, "Perhaps the most distinctive feature of the Separates was their emotional style of preaching and worship."[108] The evangelistic impulse of Separates' preaching is reflected in their use of what is commonly called an "invitation."[109]

Andrew Fuller

A considerable influence in shaping Baptist preaching is Andrew Fuller. Bebbington states, "Although he had died in 1815, Fuller remained the

---

102. Walker, *Let the Text Talk*, 156.

103. For more information on Leland, Hart, and Backus see Todd, *Let Men Be Free*.

104. Fasol, *With a Bible in Their Hands*, 22.

105. Kidd and Hankins, *Baptists in America*, 29.

106. McBeth, *Baptist Heritage*, 229. McBeth writes, "Differences between Separate and Regular Baptists centered partly in doctrine but perhaps more in manner of preaching, evangelism, and overall style of churchmanship." The Separate Baptists can be traced back to the revivalism of New England in the wake of the First Great Awakening. The Regular Baptists are associated with the Philadelphia Association.

107. Noll, *History of Christianity*, 103.

108. McBeth, *Baptist Heritage*, 230.

109. O'Kelly, "Influence of Separate Baptists," 130.

touchstone of orthodoxy over half a century later.... Fuller had done the most to shape the characteristics of modern Calvinism."[110] This embrace of evangelical Calvinism was, in some sense, a return to the Reformed orthodoxy found in the late seventeenth-century Baptist preaching.[111] Fuller was confident that his preaching was located within the larger Reformed tradition.[112] While cold hyper-Calvinism contributed to the decline, it was warm evangelical Calvinism that brought the denomination back to life by the end.

As it relates to preaching, he penned a series of letters titled "Thoughts on Preaching," in which he articulates a method for preaching that demonstrates a Claudian and evangelical influence.[113] Fuller states, "I believe it is the duty of every minister of Christ plainly and faithfully to preach the gospel to all who will hear it."[114] Fuller divides preaching into two categories: "The work of a Christian minister, as it respects the pulpit, may be distinguished into two general branches; namely, expounding the Scriptures, and discoursing on Divine subjects."[115]

Fuller argues the experiential nature of the Christian faith changes how the minister preaches the gospel. Thus, "Beware that you do not preach an unfelt gospel.... We may get into a habit of talking for the truth, and pleading for holiness, and yet be dead ourselves; and if so, we shall be sure to be despised."[116] For Fuller, the Pauline ambassador language was a primary way he described the task of preaching. He tied the function of an ambassador to the free offer of the gospel.[117] He says, "We may form some idea of the manner in which the gospel ought to be received, from its being represented as an *embassy*. 'We are ambassadors for Christ.'"[118]

The efficacy of the Spirit in the proclamation of the gospel plays an important role in Fuller's understanding of preaching. He states the "promise of the Spirit" is "the grand encouragement in promoting the

---

110. Bebbington, *Baptists Through the Centuries*, 104.
111. McKibbens, *Forgotten Heritage*, 16–19.
112. Clary, "Centre of Christianity."
113. See Fuller, *Complete Works*, 1:712–25.
114. Quoted in Haykin, *Armies of the Lamb*, 279.
115. Fuller, *Complete Works*, 1:712.
116. Fuller, *Complete Works*, 1:489–90.
117. Fuller, *Complete Works*, 3:769.
118. Fuller, *Complete Works*, 2:353.

spread of the gospel."[119] In Fuller's understanding, the Spirit makes the gospel effectual. He argues, "The Holy Spirit gave testimony to the word of his grace and rendered it effectual. The more sensible we are, both as ministers and Christians, of our entire dependence on the Holy Spirit's influences, the better."[120] Furthermore, the Spirit empowers the preacher to fulfill the "two main objects" of Christian ministry, "enlightening the minds and affecting the hearts of the people. These are the usual means by which the work of God is accomplished."[121]

Probably the clearest expression of Fuller's theology of preaching is *The Gospel Worthy of All Acceptation*. McMullen and Whelan note, "Fuller first put down his thoughts on this topic c. 1776, revised them in 1781, and finally prepared them for the press in 1784–1785."[122] The progress of composition is helpful in showing Fuller's adoption of evangelical preaching. The work is perhaps the most important defense on the subject during the eighteenth century.[123] As Morden states, "Its publication was a 'watershed' in Baptist history, as well as being an important landmark in the history of Christianity in the modern world."[124] Additionally, the work must be read considering Fuller's concern for the nature and application of preaching. Grant asserts, "*The Gospel Worthy of All Acceptation* was essentially concerned with pastoral theology."[125] This is especially true in the second edition (1801), in which he makes more explicit references to the evangelical nature of preaching.[126] Fuller was "clear that the need of the hour was not caution—rather, it was committed gospel preaching."[127] The work is not technically a preaching manual. Yet, it could possibly be deemed a theological justification for preachers. In this sense, *The Gospel Worthy of All Acceptation* reveals an evangelical theology of preaching.

In the work Fuller argues two major points. First, that it is the duty of every individual who hears the gospel proclaimed to respond in faith. Fuller claims,

119. Fuller, *Complete Works*, 3:359.
120. Fuller, *Complete Works*, 3:711.
121. Fuller, *Complete Works*, 1:479.
122. McMullen and Whelan, *Diary of Andrew Fuller*, 14.
123. Bebbington, *Evangelicalism in Modern Britain*, 64–65.
124. Morden, "Andrew Fuller," 151.
125. Grant, *Andrew Fuller*, 23.
126. Morden, "Andrew Fuller," 146.
127. Morden, "Andrew Fuller," 146.

> He that cometh to Christ must believe the gospel testimony, that he is the Son of God, and the Saviour of sinners; the only name given under heaven, and among men, by which we must be saved: he must also believe the gospel promise, that he will bestow eternal salvation on all them that obey him; and under the influence of this persuasion, he comes to him, commits himself to him, or trusts the salvation of his soul in his hands.[128]

This leads Fuller to conclude, "Now the grand designs of the salvation of Christ are the glory of God, the abasement of the sinner, and the destruction of his sins. It is God's manifest purpose, in saving sinners, to save them in this way; and can any sinner be excused from cordially acquiescing in it?"[129] He maintains that duty faith is required of all that hear the gospel.

Secondly, Fuller argues that gospel ministers must exhort everyone to believe in Christ. As Morden remarks, "Fuller struck, quite deliberately, at the two pillars of High Calvinist orthodoxy, contending that it was the duty of all to believe, and the duty of ministers to offer the gospel to all."[130] Fuller remarks on the role of the minister related to preaching,

> The work of the Christian ministry, it has been said, is to *preach the gospel*, or to hold up the free grace of God through Jesus Christ, as the only way of a sinner's salvation. This is, doubtless, true; and if this be not the leading theme of our ministrations, we had better be anything than preachers.[131]

From this, the author makes two polemical claims. First, he emphatically argues, "If by *preaching the gospel* be meant the insisting solely upon the blessings and privileges of religion, to the neglect of exhortations, calls, and warnings, it is sufficient to say that such was not the practice of Christ and his apostles."[132] His striking claim insinuates that those who fail to extend the free offer of the gospel do not follow the pattern of New Testament preaching.

Secondly, Fuller roots himself in the classical Reformed preaching tradition by appealing to John Owen's comment, "It is the duty of ministers to plead with men about their sins."[133] By doing so he explicitly

---

128. Fuller, *Complete Works*, 2:340–41.
129. Fuller, *Complete Works*, 2:350.
130. Morden, *Offering Christ to the World*, 27.
131. Fuller, *Complete Works*, 2:386.
132. Fuller, *Complete Works*, 2:386.
133. Fuller, *Complete Works*, 2:390.

challenges the high Calvinists who lauded their place in the Reformed tradition. He amplifies his claim by stating,

> Neither Augustine nor Calvin, who each in his day defended predestination, and the other doctrines connected with it, ever appear to have thought of denying it to be the duty of every sinner who has heard the gospel to repent and believe in Jesus Christ. Neither did the other Reformers, nor the puritans of the sixteenth century, nor the divines at the synod of Dort, (who opposed Arminius,) nor any of the nonconformists of the seventeenth century, so far as I have any acquaintance with their writings, ever so much as hesitate upon this subject.[134]

Fuller's polemical argument asserts that those who do not freely offer the gospel to sinners are outside of the Reformed tradition. At this point, he then draws out a few implications. He claims, "If the foregoing principles be just, it is the duty of ministers not only to exhort their carnal auditors to believe in Jesus Christ for the salvation of their souls; but it is at our peril to exhort them to anything short of it, or which does not involve or imply it."[135] Fuller's statement reveals that absolute necessity of evangelical preaching. Thus, preaching does not merely include the free offer. Rather, preaching by its very nature must extend the exhortation to believe to sinners. Therefore, "If we inculcate *this* doctrine, we need not fear exhorting sinners to holy exercises of heart, nor holding up the promises of mercy to all who thus return to God by Jesus Christ."[136] In this manner is preaching truly consistent with the preaching of the New Testament.

Haykin writes, "This epoch-making book sought to be faithful to the central emphasis of historic Calvinism."[137] Thus, *The Gospel Worthy of All Acceptation* provides theological justification for an evangelical theology of preaching. Fuller's evangelical Calvinism was brought to the forefront of English Calvinistic Baptist pulpits. As McKibbens notes, "Without rejecting their Calvinistic theology, Baptists managed to change the whole course of preaching."[138] It is easy to see, then, that Fuller's preaching contributed to the radical paradigm shift in Baptist preaching among English and American Baptists.

---

134. Fuller, *Complete Works*, 2:367. Jeffrey K. Jue argues that Fuller viewed himself in conformity with the Reformed tradition. See Jue, "Andrew Fuller."
135. Fuller, *Complete Works*, 2:387.
136. Fuller, *Complete Works*, 2:393.
137. Haykin, *Armies of the Lamb*, 29.
138. McKibbens, "Disseminating Biblical Doctrine," 45.

Eighteenth-century Baptist preaching in England experienced significant challenges. On one hand, hyper-Calvinism influenced a stream of Baptist preaching, which in turn resulted in a diminished evangelical offer. On the other, a renewal occurred that furthered the gospel cause. At the heart of these streams are theo-homiletical convictions.

NINETEENTH-CENTURY BAPTIST PREACHING

J. L. Dagg

J. L. Dagg published his *Manual of Theology* in 1857–1858. In the second part, *A Treatise on Church Order*, he specifically mentions the role of ministers and their preaching. Of the minister he says, "The special qualifications which the Holy Spirit bestows, bind him on whom they are bestowed to use them in the service of Christ."[139] While the responsibility to spread the gospel is given to all Christians, "special gifts are conferred on some, accompanied with special obligations. These constitute a special call to the ministry of the word."[140] This call "is the preaching of the word."[141] Preaching is made effectual by the work of the Spirit.[142] He adamantly advocates for the free offer of the gospel.[143] For Dagg, preaching is a higher office than the other ordinances, though he sees an important liturgical relationship between them and the preached word.[144]

Francis Wayland

As far as a codified work on preaching, Francis Wayland's work *Letters on the Ministry of the Gospel* in 1864 advocates for expositional preaching. Wayland begins his expository preaching discussion by stating, "As I have said before, in preparing to preach, the minister should ascertain, as far as possible, the very idea communicated by the Spirit in the text which he has chosen. If he has done this, the text will fasten itself upon the mind of the hearer, the sermon will enable him to understand the

---

139. Dagg, *Treatise on Church Order*, 242.
140. Dagg, *Treatise on Church Order*, 243.
141. Dagg, *Treatise on Church Order*, 243.
142. Dagg, *Treatise on Church Order*, 253.
143. Dagg, *Treatise on Church Order*, 325.
144. Dagg, *Treatise on Church Order*, 254.

text, the text will enable him to remember the sermon, and both will be treasured up for spiritual instruction."[145] He continues by elucidating the benefits of expository preaching. He writes, "In the first place, the particular passage, with its connections, the scope of the thought, with the special force of its individual expressions, are laid open to the mind of the hearer."[146] Wayland argues that "the hearer learns to do it himself. . . . Following the example of his minister, he seeks for the leading thought of the passage."[147] And "at last, a line of light shines upon this announcement of divine truth by which each portion is made severally luminous, and each casts its light upon every other."[148]

John Broadus

Following Wayland's work, Broadus wrote his *Treatise* in 1870, which influenced evangelical preaching for the next half century.[149] Broadus states, "Preaching is characteristic of Christianity. . . . The great appointed means of spreading the good tidings of salvation through Christ is preaching."[150] For Broadus, the preacher must possess four prerequisites for effective preaching: piety, natural gifts, knowledge, and skill.[151] Thus, message and messenger are related. He writes, "Piety furnishes motive power; nature gifts cultivated as far as possible, furnish means; knowledge gives material" and skill is related to "construction and in the delivery of discourse."[152]

These specific requirements provide the preacher the ability to perform the primary function—namely, to explain the Scriptures. Broadus argues, "To explain the Scriptures would seem to be among the primary functions of the preacher. . . . What nobler work than that of opening the Scriptures as Paul did at Thessalonica."[153] This explanatory element of preaching is deeply embedded within the Reformed tradition of

---

145. Wayland, *Letters on the Ministry*, 82–83.
146. Wayland, *Letters on the Ministry*, 84.
147. Wayland, *Letters on the Ministry*, 85.
148. Wayland, *Letters on the Ministry*, 86.
149. McKibbens, "John A. Broadus," 18.
150. Broadus, *Treatise*, 17.
151. Broadus, *Treatise*, 22. It should be noted that these characteristics are similar to the Reformed concept of "experiential preaching." See Beeke, *Reformed Preaching*.
152. Broadus, *Treatise*, 24–25.
153. Broadus, *Treatise*, 146.

explicatio verbi Dei.[154] The first and primary function of preaching is explaining the Biblical text. Broadus states, "To interpret and apply his text in accordance with its real meaning, is one of the preacher's most sacred duties. He stands before the people for the very purpose of teaching and exhorting them out of the Word of God."[155] Additionally, "A preacher of the gospel certainly ought not to preach morality apart from the gospel. He may present other than strictly evangelical motives, but these must be manifestly subordinate to the great motive of grateful love to Christ, and consecration to his service."[156] He affirms, "The facts and truths which belong to the Scripture account of Sin, Providence, and Redemption, form the staple of all Scriptural preaching."[157]

Charles Spurgeon

In 1875, Charles Spurgeon published his *Lectures to My Students*.[158] He also speaks directly to the role of preaching throughout his sermons. Spurgeon states, "I call your attention to this that you may be earnest in preaching the gospel. It is through the gospel that God is glorified. By the poorest gospel sermon that was ever preached, God through his Holy Spirit, gets to himself a glory."[159] Likewise, "The preaching of the gospel is like the setting up of a throne of judgment, 'for the Word of God is quick, and powerful, and sharper than any two-edged sword, piercing even to the dividing asunder of soul and spirit, and of the joints and marrow, and is a discerner of the thoughts and intents of the heart.'"[160]

Spurgeon's experiential view of preaching parallels the Reformed preaching tradition. He claims, "Let us always remember this in preaching the gospel, and never depend upon the man, or upon the word alone, but be this our prayer, 'Oh God, do thou work, for thou alone canst do so effectually.'"[161] He also uses the ambassador metaphor in relationship to Christ, speaking, "And, now, then, as God's ambassadors, we come to

---

154. Carrick, *Imperative of Preaching*, 14. Also see Nettles, "Enduring Impact," 203.
155. Broadus, *Treatise*, 32.
156. Broadus, *Treatise*, 86–87.
157. Broadus, *Treatise*, 76.
158. Spurgeon, *Lectures to My Students*.
159. Spurgeon, *Metropolitan Tabernacle Pulpit Sermons*, 16:21.
160. Spurgeon, *Metropolitan Tabernacle Pulpit Sermons*, 41:23.
161. Spurgeon, *Metropolitan Tabernacle Pulpit Sermons*, 11:639–40.

treat of peace.... Let the preacher vanish for a moment. Look and listen. It is Christ speaking to you now. Methinks I hear him speak to some of you."[162] Spurgeon calls Christ "the essential Word" and preaching of Christ "the operative Word."[163] Furthermore, the Spirit makes the word effective. He says, "God the Holy Ghost makes the preaching of Christ to you to be the opening of the prisons to them that are bound."[164] Additionally, "The true minister of God speaketh not apart from the Word of God, and when he speaks the Word of God, the God of the Word is himself there to make it effectual."[165]

Spurgeon sees a close relationship between preaching and the ordinances: "Cleave to the simple teaching of God's Word in doctrine, in practice, in the ordinances, and in everything. Cling, in fact, to the pure Church of Jesus Christ."[166] He speaks of the means of graces as a way to partake of Christ: "Faith is the first and grandest way of tying the scarlet line in the window, but let your faith follow on *in the use of the ordinances and means of grace*, for these assist her in laying hold upon Jesus.... The ordinance itself will not give you Christ, but often does the symbol blessedly enable the soul to realize Jesus and contemplate him so as to partake of him."[167]

Spurgeon is unashamed to give a full free offer to sinners. He proclaims, "Come to Jesus ye vilest of men! Labouring ones, heavy laden ones, come to Jesus! Black, foul, filthy, hard-hearted ones, come to Jesus! He is able to save unto the uttermost them that come unto God by him."[168] His appeal is immediate: "If there be a poor soul here who has never believed in Jesus, but is burdened with sin, I invite him, and I pray God the Holy Spirit to make the invitation effectual,to come now to Jesus Christ.... May he give you power to lay your hand on Jesus! Lean on him, soul; lean on him.... Trust him, rest in him."[169]

---

162. Spurgeon, *Metropolitan Tabernacle Pulpit Sermons*, 7:599.
163. Spurgeon, *Metropolitan Tabernacle Pulpit Sermons*, 11:640.
164. Spurgeon, *Metropolitan Tabernacle Pulpit Sermons*, 16:38.
165. Spurgeon, *Metropolitan Tabernacle Pulpit Sermons*, 42:359.
166. Spurgeon, *Metropolitan Tabernacle Pulpit Sermons*, 55:232.
167. Spurgeon, *Metropolitan Tabernacle Pulpit Sermons*, 55:520-21.
168. Spurgeon, *Metropolitan Tabernacle Pulpit Sermons*, 11:168.
169. Spurgeon, *Metropolitan Tabernacle Pulpit Sermons*, 18:252.

TWENTIETH- AND TWENTY-FIRST-CENTURY BAPTIST PREACHING

This survey shows that Baptists have offered their thoughts on preaching since the seventeenth century. However, unlike other traditions such as the Church of England and Presbyterianism, Baptists do not have a codified theology of preaching.[170] The irony is that when one surveys the homiletical landscape in the twentieth and twenty-first centuries, Baptist writers have produced important works, many of which have shaped the homiletical trajectory to the present. However, a substantial theology of preaching is often neglected. This does not mean that aspects of a Baptist theology of preaching are completely absent.

Homiletical Textbooks

For example, the Baptist homiletical textbook *Steps to the Sermon* spends roughly fifteen pages discussing the *nature of preaching*.[171] The authors write,

> The Word of God cannot be separated from its proclamation; the gospel is in fact a preached gospel; preaching is a redemptive event in contemporary time; the act of preaching is part of God's encounter with a contemporary listener; preaching is not merely a means of conveying content but is in a real sense bound up with the content; it is part of God's saving activity; and it is God's means of giving life to us. If these statements are true, all must admit to the supreme importance of preaching.[172]

Steven Smith's book *Recapturing the Voice of God* introduces a theology of preaching.[173] He links theology to a method. He claims, "We re-present the text; The text re-presents Christ; Christ re-presents the Father."[174] Additionally, Smith's work *Dying to Preach* addresses the spiritual nature of proclamation.[175]

---

170. Cranmer, *Certayne Sermons*. Westminster Assembly, "Directory for the Public Worship of God."

171. Brown et al., *Steps to the Sermon*, 4–18. Also see Brown et al., *Steps to the Sermon* (rev. ed.), 5–18.

172. Brown et al., *Steps to the Sermon* (rev. ed.), 7–8.

173. Smith, *Recapturing the Voice of God*, 11–15.

174. Smith, *Recapturing the Voice of God*, 14.

175. Smith, *Dying to Preach*.

Mohler's chapter in the *Handbook of Contemporary Preaching* is a helpful contribution.[176] Particularly, he directly mentions the external and internal minister. He writes, "The preacher stands before the congregation as the external minister of the Word, but the Holy Spirit works as the internal minister of that same Word. A theology of preaching must take the role of the Spirit into full view, for without an understanding of the work of the Spirit, the task of preaching is robbed of its balance and power."[177]

In the book *Text-Driven Preaching*, the claim is made that "God has spoken. God is not silent. He has revealed Himself in Jesus, who is the living Word, and in Scripture, which is the written Word. Therefore, the theological foundation for text-driven preaching is the fact that God has spoken!"[178] Ironically, chapter 1 does not lay a theological foundation but rather presents an Aristotelian model for preaching.[179] Chapter 4 explores the role of the Spirit in preaching.[180] There is no reference to the relationship between preaching and the ordinances. The word *ambassador* is not mentioned once. This does not discount the value of the work. Yet, it conceivably shows a transition in how preaching is taught to students.

John Piper's work *Expository Exultation* calls for a renewed spirituality related to preaching. He argues, "Preaching *is* worship and *serves* worship."[181] Thus, preaching possesses an experiential aspect. Additionally, the triune God takes an active role in proclamation.[182] The proclamation of the word is made effectual by the work of the Spirit.[183] Thus, "the preacher simultaneously *explains* the meaning of Scripture and *exults* over the God-glorifying reality in it."[184] In many ways, Piper's theology of preaching parallels elements found in the Reformed preaching tradition.[185]

---

176. Mohler, "Theology of Preaching," 12–20. Also see Mohler, *He Is Not Silent*, 40–48.

177. Mohler, "Theology of Preaching," 18.

178. Allen, introduction to *Text-Driven Preaching*, 3.

179. Patterson, "Ancient Rhetoric."

180. Bennett, "Secret of Preaching with Power."

181. Piper, *Expository Exultation*, 25.

182. Piper, *Expository Exultation*, 96.

183. Piper, *Expository Exultation*, 105.

184. Piper, *Expository Exultation*, 51.

185. While Piper grounds preaching in the context of worship, he fails to address how preaching relates to the ordinances. He does not explicitly call preaching a means of grace, though it is implied. Additionally, he does not draw from the depths of the Reformed preaching tradition (e.g., Bullinger or Calvin). Piper has also written another

In my research, the most extensive contemporary Baptist theology of preaching is found in *Power in the Pulpit* written by Jerry Vines and Jim Shaddix. They argue, "The entire preaching event must be built upon a certain theological foundation. . . . Four particular doctrines provide the groundwork for a proper understanding of biblical exposition—the Word of God, the call of God, the Spirit of God, and the gospel of God."[186] Preaching begins with a theology of the Bible. The written word is inspired by God, inerrant, authoritative, and sufficient.[187] Next, the Spirit of God has a particular role in preaching; he brings illumination and conviction. Additionally, the Spirit applies the sermon and empowers the preacher.[188] Furthermore, God calls men to preach. This calling is twofold: first, it's a call to serve the church and, second, to perform the work of an evangelist.[189] Last, a theology of preaching is concerned about the gospel, of which the primary focus is Christ. Therefore, all preaching must be Christ centered.[190]

In my opinion, chapter 2 in *Power in the Pulpit* is the clearest expression of a contemporary Baptist theology of preaching. Vines and Shaddix unfold much of what is written in this book. The fourfold theology of preaching presented in their work provides clarity and practicality to proclamation. In one sense, I attempt to substantiate the claims in their theology of preaching by appealing to Keach. In another sense, I believe Keach complements their proposed homiletical theology by nuancing their "four particular doctrines."

SUMMARY

I return to the question of this chapter—why. Why make the effort to retrieve a Baptist theology of preaching? Is it warranted? The answer is because Baptists have valued preaching throughout our history. In unique ways, Baptists have sought to articulate their doctrine through proclamation. Additionally, the earliest Baptists inherited a preaching tradition and modified it according to their understanding of Scripture.

---

book on preaching. See Piper, *Supremacy of God in Preaching*.
186. Vines and Shaddix, *Power in the Pulpit*, 60.
187. Vines and Shaddix, *Power in the Pulpit*, 60–69.
188. Vines and Shaddix, *Power in the Pulpit*, 70–77.
189. Vines and Shaddix, *Power in the Pulpit*, 78–85.
190. Vines and Shaddix, *Power in the Pulpit*, 86–93.

The theo-homiletical questions posed in chapter 1 are reflected in the Baptist preachers presented in this chapter in one way or another. We have wrestled (in a good way) with a homiletical theology from the seventeenth century to the present day. Thus, the role of preaching in the congregation, how preaching is made effectual, and the instrumentality of the minister are elements of one's homiletical theology. Our Baptist forebearers, though diverse, regarded preaching as a central aspect of Christ's church. Therefore, it is warranted to engage in the task of retrieval.

CHAPTER 3

The Religious Context of Benjamin Keach

IN HIS BOOK *PRIMITIVISM, Radicalism, and the Lamb's War*, Ted Underwood paints the picture well of 1640–1689 English history when he writes, "Civil war, the execution of a king, the establishing of a republican regime, the restoration of monarchy, plots against the government, and the Revolution of 1688 were among the political developments of the time. . . . The abolition and restoration of episcopacy, the repression of Nonconformists, and the 1689 Act of Toleration were significant features."[1] It was in this era of British history that Benjamin Keach was born and ministered in the heart of conflict. His preaching ministry is best understood within the broader English Reformation and Puritan impulse. In this chapter I am unable to deal with the particularities of the English Reformation. My goal, however, is to provide a general historical narrative.

THE ENGLISH REFORMATION

The English Reformation of the sixteenth century is a unique religious-political phenomenon that shaped much of Western culture.[2] Specifically,

---

1. Underwood, *Primitivism, Radicalism, and the Lamb's War*, 3.
2. For a historical overview of the English Reformation see Collinson, *Birthpangs of Protestant England*. Also, the classic work by Dickens, *English Reformation*. For a recent history, see Marshall, *Heretics and Believers*. Additionally, Ryrie has published a shorter history, *English Reformation*. Two recent scholarly works show the various streams of

the upheaval resulted in a nearly two-century-long religious and political battle that not only reshaped England but also the New World. The divorce that occurred between the pope and the crown altered the way individuals and the larger society viewed religious expression. In particular, the English Reformation helped to usher in the golden age of the English pulpit. What follows is a brief narrative of this critical period.

In the 1530s–1540s, King Henry VIII "consummated a dual revolution, severing the English Church from the Papacy and subjugating it to the control of the Crown in Parliament."[3] The move away from the Roman Catholic Church provided England the opportunity to become a Protestant nation.[4] After the death of Henry VIII, the aims of Protestantism advanced under King Edward VI, who took his Protestant faith more seriously than his father.[5] In particular, Edward was a diligent sermon note-taker of Protestant preachers.[6] By 1549, the Book of Common Prayer replaced the Latin Mass.[7] He passed laws that favored Protestant reforms.[8] Ryrie argues that Edward's "Protestant convictions were inchoate but unmistakable. His regimes threw themselves fully behind Archbishop Cranmer's project: to create a fully Reformed Protestant Church in England."[9]

However, Edward's reign was cut short by an illness in 1553. Enthroned as queen, the Catholic Mary I (1553–1558) was "determined to rip out England's shallowly rooted reformation."[10] Her terror caused an exodus of Protestant exiles to flee from England and find a home in the lower countries of Europe, specifically Switzerland.[11] It was during this exile period that Protestants became influenced deeply by Geneva's pastor-theologian, John Calvin.[12] Consequently, this introduced these exiles to the Geneva Service Book and Geneva Bible.[13] It further

---

Puritanism. See Winship, *Hot Protestants*, and Hall, *Puritans*.

3. Dickens, *English Reformation*, 106.
4. Collinson, *Birthpangs of Protestant England*, 1–27.
5. Winship, *Hot Protestants*, 11.
6. Winship, *Hot Protestants*, 13.
7. Winship, *Hot Protestants*, 12.
8. Dickens, *English Reformation*, 245.
9. Ryrie, *English Reformation*, 53.
10. Winship, *Hot Protestants*, 17.
11. Davies, *Worship of the English Puritans*, 25.
12. Davies, *Worship of the English Puritans*, 30.
13. Davies, *Worship of the English Puritans*, 33.

armed Protestants with the Presbyterian form of church polity.[14] Following the bloody reign of Mary I, her attempts were halted by Elizabeth I (1558–1603).

After Mary's death, Protestant exiles, radicalized with their newly minted Reformed ecclesiology, steadily made their way back to England. During this period The Elizabethan Settlement sought to bring peace to the religious warring in England.[15] For the most part, "Elizabeth I was indifferent if not hostile to Reformed principles."[16] The settlement commenced with a royal proclamation to forbid various types of preaching in 1558.[17] The queen continued by reestablishing the Church of England as the state church and the crown as the head of the church through the Act of Supremacy in 1559, reversing Mary's Catholic orders. Furthermore, The Act of Uniformity in 1559 made the Book of Common Prayer the official service book for the church.[18] Those who refused to conform with the act were fined.[19] These political actions provided the necessary ingredients for Dissenters to emerge.

In summarizing the religious/political movements, Hall concludes that the sixteenth-century English Reformation experienced three mishaps. First, the Church of England preserved the hierarchical structure that focused on bishops; second, the church preserved some aspects of the Catholic Mass and liturgy; and third, the church acknowledged the monarch as the supreme head or supreme governor of the church.[20] In this regard, Protestantism in England had not gone far enough. Winship argues, "If the English people were to be preached into committed Protestants, it would be men like the returning exiles who had the conviction, competence, education, and determination to accomplish that task. But the exiles wished to drive England to what they understood as wholehearted Protestantism, one free of any trace of Antichrist."[21]

---

14. Winship, *Hot Protestants*, 18.
15. Collinson, *Elizabethan Puritan Movement*, 29.
16. Hall, *Puritans*, 36.
17. Herr, *Elizabethan Sermon*, 11–13.
18. Winship, *Hot Protestants*, 28.
19. Cross and Livingstone, *Oxford Dictionary*, 1670.
20. Hall, *Puritans*, 35.
21. Winship, *Hot Protestants*, 28.

PURITANISM

Puritanism arose out of this desire to further Protestant commitments. Puritans were the "hotter sort of Protestants."[22] Winship writes,

> The term "puritan" first emerged in England in the 1560s as an insult thrown at ministers and laypeople who refused to conform to Church of England requirements that fell short of their high Protestant standards. Before long, the insult was being thrown not only at these law-breaking nonconformists, but at people who admired and worked with them and practiced the strict, activist piety they promoted. Anti-puritans who aggressively expanded this insult's range often acted in the fervent belief that puritanism threatened the foundations of church and state and that ripping it out of the Church of England required digging an ever wider, deeper hole around it.[23]

Historians are divided on how best to define English Puritanism. Patrick Collinson argues that the defining mark of Puritanism was not primarily its "fundamental principle" but rather "differences of degree, of theological temperature so to speak."[24] Alec Ryrie, in his book *Being Protestant in Reformation Britain*, states that "the division between puritan and conformist Protestants, which has been so important in English historiography almost fades from view when examined through the lens of devotion and lived experience."[25] Indeed, Puritanism cannot be defined by its theology. For half a century, "Reformed theology stood at the heart, not the edge, of the Church of England."[26] The Puritans in the Elizabethan Settlement were less Separatist in their mindset and more committed to preserving what they saw as the established church. For the purposes of this book, we will understand Puritanism as a Protestant renewal movement in England, which began within the Church of England under the Elizabethan Settlement in the late sixteenth century and continued until the end of the Restoration when the movement began to fracture. Puritanism was committed to furthering Reformed Protestant Christianity as evident in the desire to advance the attitudes and priorities of the

---

22. Winship, *Hot Protestants*, 1.
23. Winship, *Hot Protestants*, 1.
24. Collinson, *Elizabethan Puritan Movement*, 26–27.
25. Ryrie, *Being Protestant*, 6.
26. Moore, "Reformed Theology and Puritanism," 202.

Reformation in accordance with Scripture. This movement gave way to dissenting traditions out of which the Particular Baptists emerged.

Many religious and political factors precipitated the beginnings of Puritanism in sixteenth-century England. For example, one factor during the Elizabethan Settlement was the controversy regarding the ministerial vestments and church objects. The Vestarian Controversy of 1566 was the Puritan's proof that the church mirrored Catholicism in various ways, particularly in worship.[27] David Bebbington writes,

> The first clash between Puritans and the Elizabethan authorities took place over vestments, the clothes in which clergy dressed in church. The Prayer Book, as officially interpreted, required them to wear white surplices to conduct services. This distinctive form of dress, according to Puritans, had no scripture warrant. Furthermore, it marked off its wearers, the clergy, as different from the laity, and so formed a visible rejection of the priesthood of all believers that Protestants had held dear since Luther. Some Puritan ministers simply discarded the surplice, but in 1566, on the orders of the government, Archbishop Parker demanded that all should observe the church's rules.[28]

The Puritan preference for the Genevan Service Book and the Presbyterian form of church governance over against the Book of Common Prayer and the Episcopal order led many with Puritan tendencies to attack the Church of England. The Protestant Dissenters opposed the new reforms to conformity due to their Reformed influence. Another issue was the Puritan opposition to the Church of England's *Book of Homilies*.[29] Central to the popularity of Puritanism was the emphasis on preaching.[30] The second edition of the *Homilies* was written in 1562 and published in 1571. The Puritan's objection to the *Homilies* of the church was due in large part to the general nature of the sermons. It was argued that the *Homilies* were not tailored for the particular congregation in which the message was preached.[31] Moreover, the church lacked preachers educated enough to preach these messages as the parishes slowly embraced a word-centered theology over a sacrament-centered theology.[32] What

27. Davies, *Worship and Theology*, 46.
28. Bebbington, *Baptists Through the Centuries*, 17.
29. Church of England, *Second Tome of Homilees*.
30. Heal, "English, Scottish, and Irish Reformations," 242.
31. Edwards, *History of Preaching*, 358.
32. Hall, *Puritans*, 46.

started as a resurgence of the preached word in 1547 with the publication of Cranmer's *Homilies*, became a point of reformation contention for the Puritans. As a result, this gave rise to Puritan lectureships and the "prophesying" sessions. Queen Elizabeth I opposed these actions.[33] The Act Against Puritans of 1593 culminated as an attempt to repress Puritan tendencies. By restricting Puritan preaching, worship, and propaganda, the crown hoped to assert its power over the religious conscience of the Dissenters.

The complexities of the religious and political entanglements of the Elizabethan Settlement can be summarized: first, the Puritans were concerned about the nature of the church and, second, with royal supremacy.[34] To be more specific, the aims of Puritanism can be understood as both religious and political; religious in the sense that Puritanism sought to further Reformation principles regarding ecclesiastical worship, and politically the movement sought to challenge the authority of the established church, thereby challenging the crown.[35] The intense degree of the Puritan attitudes and priorities drove them to advance their Protestant aims. These Puritan Reformation attitudes and priorities continued under the reign of James I (1603–1625), Charles I (1625–1649), and the Commonwealth (1649–1660).

After the death of Queen Elizabeth, Puritans seemed eager to have King James preside over them as he did the Protestants in Scotland. However, "What puritans did not know, but would soon discover, was that James had grown thoroughly disillusioned with his insufficiently obedient church in Scotland and wanted nothing like it in England."[36] Even though James invited Puritans to Hampton Court to discuss reforms, his Protestant commitments were called into question. James I ushered in new laws that resulted in three hundred nonconformist ministers leaving their positions.[37] Additionally, he commissioned a new Bible translation, which became the King James Bible. The king warned, "I shall make them [Puritans] conform themselves, or I will hurry them out of the land."[38]

---

33. Hall, *Puritans*, 51.

34. Hall, *Puritans*, 54.

35. This does not mean that Puritans were anti-establishment. On the contrary, the Westminster Assembly from 1643 to 1653 shows the Puritan goal of reorienting the national church.

36. Winship, *Hot Protestants*, 59.

37. Winship, *Hot Protestants*, 59.

38. Quoted by Winship, *Hot Protestants*, 59. See Barlow, *Summe and substance*, 63.

After James's death, Charles I sought to emphasize the "catholic" aspect of the Church of England. Bebbington claims, "When, in the 1630s, the Church of England turned back toward Roman Catholic ceremonies, the undercurrent of hostility to false worship surfaced even more powerfully."[39] Strict conformity to the Book of Common Prayer along with newly instituted worship practices caused Puritan-minded ministers to either comply or resign.[40] Until the 1630s, Calvinism "provided a shared frame of reference for conformists and nonconformists."[41] However, the rise of Arminianism played a role in the destabilization of the church and government.[42] Laud's opposition of predestinarian teaching placed Puritans in the government's crosshairs. This theological reorientation drove the wedge deeper between conformists and nonconformists. Additionally, this would shape preaching and attitudes toward sermons.[43]

During this period, Puritanism burned hotter during the English Civil Wars. This led to political and religious resistance, whereby the crown and Parliament clashed. This clash resulted in the execution of the king in 1649. This act marked a defining moment for those who opposed the crown. However, in the eyes of those who were sympathetic to the king, he was viewed as a martyr.[44] Within the Commonwealth under Cromwell, nonconformity found political and religious power.[45] Cromwell, an Independent, advocated religious toleration for Protestant groups. The Westminster Assembly, driven by Puritan tendencies, sought to reform the religious/political environment once and for all.[46] Pederson notes, "Parliament's goal was to promote a 'further and more perfect reformation' of the English Church based chiefly on God's word, and to solidify its *sensus unitatis* with the Scottish and Reformed churches abroad."[47] This Assembly produced the Westminster Confession of Faith, the Directory of Worship, and the Larger and Shorter Catechisms.[48] While the Revolution ushered in dissenting toleration, Parliament's goal

---

39. Bebbington, *Baptists Through the Centuries*, 23.
40. Moore, "Reformed Theology and Puritanism," 210.
41. Tyacke, *Aspects of English Protestantism*, 216. Also see Tyacke, *Anti-Calvinists*.
42. Tyacke, *Aspects of English Protestantism*, 160–70.
43. Tyacke, *Aspects of English Protestantism*, 217.
44. Chadwick, *Reformation*, 237.
45. See Worden, *God's Instruments*.
46. Van Dixhoorn, *God's Ambassadors*, 172–73.
47. Pederson, *Unity in Diversity*, 62.
48. Morrill, "Puritan Revolution," 71.

was never achieved.[49] The debates during the Assembly revealed the fractures of Puritanism. While members had a common enemy in the rise of antinomianism, arguments over church polity could not be settled.[50]

The aforementioned fractures led to Charles II ascending to the throne. The king's Restoration included multiple laws repressing Protestantism. This ultimately sought to undermine Puritan reforms. The 1662 Act of Uniformity resulted in the ejection of Puritan ministers. Pederson states,

> The Act of Uniformity (1662) required Puritan ministers to renounce their ordinations and subscription to the Solemn League and Covenant and be re-ordained in what appears to have been a political repudiation of their ministerial credentials. Nearly 2,000 ministers refused to comply with these stipulations and were ejected from their pulpits on St. Bartholomew's Day, August 24, 1662. Two more acts of conformity were issued: The Conventicle Act (1664), which banned nonconformists from preaching in the fields or conducting services in homes; and the Five Mile Act (1665), which prohibited ejected ministers from coming within five miles of their former parishes or any city or town.[51]

This further resulted in "an anti-Puritan sea-change in the Church of England's pulpits, and a determination among most of the church's hierarchy to keep it that way."[52] The irony of removing the most committed Puritans from these prominent posts caused a groundswell of religious dissent. Thus, stronger religious communities slowly started to form in this period. The pressure upon nonconformists prompted them to meet in smaller conventicles. Despite the fallout from the Assembly, "the various elements of the Puritan movement reconstituted themselves as separate denominations."[53] As a result, Puritanism as a movement could not survive. Additionally, while Charles II's Restoration resulted in the reinstitution of bishops and the Prayer Book, the old Church of England would never return in full force.[54]

---

49. Pederson, *Unity in Diversity*, 65.
50. Moore, "Reformed Theology and Puritanism," 211.
51. Pederson, *Unity in Diversity*, 64.
52. Winship, *Hot Protestants*, 207.
53. Bremer, *Puritanism*, 27.
54. Chadwick, *Reformation*, 246.

BENJAMIN KEACH

Benjamin Keach was born to John and Joyce Keach on February 29, 1640. As one of seven children, Keach was baptized as an infant in the Stoke Hammond parish church, where his father served as a churchwarden. Crosby notes, "His parents were honest and pious persons, but not capable of giving him such a learned education."[55] Unfortunately, not much is known of Keach's childhood other than he was planning to enter the trade of being a tailor.[56] However, the little education he did receive was sufficient enough for him to read and study the Bible. This would establish the trajectory of his life and ministry for nearly fifty years.

Conversion and Early Ministry in Winslow

During the 1640s–1650s, religious toleration increased because of the English Civil War.[57] When Keach was nine years old, Charles I was executed in 1649. By the beginning of his teenage years, English citizens were no longer obligated to attend local parishes. Keach "dissented" from the established church. During his teenage years, under the Commonwealth and the Protectorate of Cromwell, Dissenters continued to experience a sense of religious freedom.[58] In 1655, at the age of fifteen, Keach had become convinced that the Bible did not teach infant baptism.[59] This led him to a minister who would be the "blessed instrument" in Keach's conversion.

Upon hearing the gospel through the ministry of Matthew Mead, who ministered in Great Brickhill, Keach was converted.[60] He was then baptized by immersion by John Russell, a General Baptist pastor.[61] As an unlicensed minister in 1658, Keach started preaching at eighteen years old as a General Baptist.[62] Two of Keach's brothers, Joseph and Henry,

---

55. Crosby, *History of the English Baptists*, 4:269.
56. Walker, "Tailor Turned Preacher," 25.
57. Mullett, "Radical Sects," 199.
58. Walker, "Tailor Turned Preacher," 27.
59. Nettles, *Beginnings in Britain*, 163.
60. Walker, *Excellent Benjamin Keach*, 24. Keach calls Mead the "blessed instrument in my conversion." See Keach, *Counter-antidote*, 3.
61. Nettles, *Beginnings in Britain*, 163.
62. Walker, *Excellent Benjamin Keach*, 23.

would both become active with the General Baptists.[63] While Keach remained active in ministry, there is no evidence that he actually served as a pastor of a local church in Winslow.[64] Keach also pursued marriage and a family. He married Jane Grove, "a woman of great piety and prudence, that dwelt at Winslow in Buckinghamshire," at the age of twenty.[65]

After the death of Cromwell in 1658 and his son's reluctance, Charles II rose to power.[66] Political and ecclesiological power was restored under the crown.[67] In London, the Great Ejection of 1662 forced dissenting ministers from their positions.[68] Subsequently, Keach fell prey to the Act of Uniformity in Buckinghamshire. Scholars note, "The 1662 Act of Uniformity and the other legislative measures of the Clarendon Code—the Corporation Act of 1661, the Five Mile Act of 1665, and the two Conventicles Acts of 1664 and 1670—outlawed Presbyterian, Baptist, Congregationalist and Quaker meetings, and subjected those who continued to attend them to harassment and persecution."[69] Although dissenting opposition was not uniform across the nation, the local authorities in Buckinghamshire were eager to enforce the new restrictions.[70] Crosby writes, "The reverend and famous Mr. *Benjamin Keach* had no small share in the sufferings of these times: He was often seized, when preaching, and committed to prison, sometimes bound, sometimes released upon bail, and sometimes his life was threatened."[71] In 1664, Keach was arrested and put on trial for publishing his book *The Child's Instructor*. Again, Crosby provides insight: "In this book were several things asserted, contrary to the doctrines and ceremonies of the *Church of England*: As that *infants* ought not to be baptized. That *Laymen* having abilities may preach the Gospel. That *Christ* should reign personally upon the earth in the latter day."[72] He was fined and sentenced to the pillory first at Aylesbury and

63. Arnold, *Reformed Theology*, 13.
64. Walker, *Excellent Benjamin Keach*, 89.
65. Crosby, *History of the English Baptists*, 4:271.
66. White, *English Baptists*, 91.
67. White, *English Baptists*, 96.
68. Coffey, *Persecution and Toleration*, 209. Also see Appleby, *Black Bartholomew's Day*.
69. Doran and Durston, *Princes, Pastors and People*, 133.
70. Walker, "Life of Benjamin Keach," 18–19.
71. Crosby, *History of the English Baptists*, 2:185. See Crosby for a detailed account of the trial.
72. Crosby, *History of the English Baptists*, 2:186.

then at Winslow.[73] As a married man with a family, Keach "became a marked man in Buckinghamshire."[74]

Pastoring in Southwark

The various circumstances of persecution and opposition in Buckinghamshire prompted Keach to move to London since "life for dissenters became difficult."[75] Societal life in London was not an easy one during this period. The capital had just experienced the Great Plague in 1665 and the Great Fire in 1666.[76] Personal trials came to Keach and his family when they were robbed by highwaymen on their way to London. Crosby records,

> This was no small trial, to be bereft of all that he had, and left to shift, with a wife and *three* children, in a strange place. Thus, he came to London, without any money, and almost without acquaintance. However, a man of such a publick character, and spotless conversation, was soon taken notice of; and *the Baptists*, who are as ready to acts of charity as any others, took care to supply his present necessities; and he joined with the rest of the passengers in suing the county, and so recovered the whole of their loss again.[77]

It is assumed that "the Baptists" who helped the Keach family also connected him to the congregation in Southwark who was without a pastor. In many ways, Southwark "was a stronghold of dissenting congregations."[78] He and his family lived near "St. Paul's, Shadwell," east of London Bridge on the north side of the River Thames.[79] Walker notes that by living in the same area where he ministered, Keach possibly faced greater opposition.[80] This makes sense as it was not until after the Act of Toleration in 1689 that his family moved closer to Southwark, settling on Freemans Street.

73. Walker, "Tailor Turned Preacher," 27.
74. Walker, "Tailor Turned Preacher," 27.
75. Nettles, *Beginnings in Britain*, 163.
76. Walker, *Excellent Benjamin Keach*, 84.
77. Crosby, *History of the English Baptists*, 3:144.
78. Walker, "Life of Benjamin Keach," 4.
79. Walker, *Excellent Benjamin Keach*, 86.
80. Walker, "Life of Benjamin Keach," 26.

Crosby notes that the church had a pastor named William Rider, who was a General Baptist. Though, "their pastor" had been "dead for some time," they nevertheless "unanimously chose Mr. Keach to be their elder, and he was solemnly ordained, with prayer, and laying on of hands, in the year 1668; being the 28th year of his age; and with this people did he continue to the end of his days."[81] This congregation would have a significant influence beginning with Keach and continuing through the nineteenth century.

Keach's new ministry and living arrangements proved to be significant for his ministerial relationships. He became friends with William Kiffen and Hanserd Knollys.[82] Kiffin pastored a congregation in Devonshire Square while Knollys's church met near Whitechapel.[83] He also became friends with John Norcott, who pastored a Particular Baptist congregation near Wapping.[84] Later in his ministry, he frequently gathered at a coffee house for associational meetings with Hercules Collins, Joseph Stennett, and Richard Adams.[85]

These relationships placed Keach in direct contact with the Particular Baptist tradition.[86] Most likely due to these various influences, Keach underwent a theological reformation that led him to become a Particular Baptist. Haykin speculates that Hanserd Knollys's influence played a significant role in Keach's move from General to Particular convictions.[87] Regardless of the exact details of Keach's theological change, by the time the Tooley Street congregation moved to Horsleydown, the new

---

81. Crosby, *History of the English Baptists*, 4: 272. Unfortunately, not much is known of William Rider.

82. For works on Knollys and Kiffen see Howson, *Christ Exalted*; Bustin and Howson, *Zealous for the Lord*; Kreitzer, *William Kiffen and His World*.

83. Walker, *Excellent Benjamin Keach*, 86. These locations are near to Shadwell.

84. Walker, *Excellent Benjamin Keach*, 87. Keach preached Norcott's funeral. See Keach, *Summons to the grave*.

85. Arnold, *Reformed Theology*, 23. Collins followed Norcott at Wapping and also authored *An Orthodox Catechism, being the sum of Christian Religion contained in the Law and Gospel*, a revision of the Heidelberg Catechism. Before his death, Keach requested that Stennett preach his funeral sermon. Adams was ordained by Hanserd Knollys, William Collins, and Hercules Collins. He also officiated the weddings of two of Keach's daughters.

86. Ironically, Keach was not aware of the First London Confession until sometime in 1692. See Keach, "To All the Baptized Churches," 109.

87. Haykin, *Kiffen, Knollys, and Keach*, 144. Knollys officiated the marriage of Keach and Susannah Partridge (second wife following the death of his first wife in 1670).

congregation was Calvinistic in its theology.[88] Keach says in a sermon, "And let me intreat you to study the Nature of the Covenant of Grace; for until I had that opened unto me, I was ignorant of the Mysteries of the Gospel."[89]

Keach regarded his former theological system as an error. It was not until he started studying the covenant of grace that he embraced Reformed theology. Perhaps this provides a reason why many of Keach's published sermons concern the covenant of grace. A central part of his theological reorientation became a critical aspect of his preaching. There is no evidence as to whether the Tooley Street Church split because of Keach's Calvinism. Before the new building near Horsleydown, the congregation was forced to meet in homes to avoid persecution from the authorities. According to Ivimey, the church was disrupted at least twice.[90] One of these times was due to Keach's child's catechism, like the one he was persecuted for while in Buckinghamshire.[91] Nevertheless, the church began to grow numerically. In 1672 the congregation obtained a license to build a new meeting house near Horsleydown and Goat-Yard Passage.[92] The meeting house was large enough to hold one thousand people.[93]

Personal Life and Theological Influences

Benjamin Keach arrived in London with his wife, Jane, along with their three children, Mary, Elias, and Hannah.[94] Sadly, his wife passed away in October 1670. Crosby records, "And as he had an extraordinary affection to his wife, so he took an uncommon method of expressing it at her death, by writing a poem to her memory, and entitling it, *A pillar*

---

88. Haykin, *Kiffen, Knollys, and Keach*, 145.
89. Keach, *Golden Mine Opened*, 314–15.
90. See Ivimey, *History of the English Baptists*, 2:363.
91. Ivimey, *History of the English Baptists*, 1:384.
92. Walker, "Tailor Turned Preacher," 28. Baptist historian Joseph Ivimey states, "The meeting-house in which Mr. Benjamin Keach preached, was situated in Goat-street, near St. John's church. It was a wooden building and stood at the north-west corner of Goat-Yard passage, now called Goat-Street. The front door came into a short cross street from Horsleydown Back-street to Free-school-street. The meeting-house was enclosed by a brick wall in front, with a court-yard, and lime trees on each side of the path leading to the principal door." See Ivimey, *History of the English Baptists*, 3:409.
93. Ivimey, *History of the English Baptists*, 3:410.
94. Walker, *Excellent Benjamin Keach*, 92.

set up.[95] Keach, a pastor and single father, remained a bachelor for two years until he married Susannah Partridge.[96] They remained together for thirty-two years, having four surviving daughters.[97]

When the family moved to Freeman Street, near the church, Keach operated a bookshop from his home. This gave him access to booksellers' catalogs, which in turn provided him the ability to read a wide range of theological works.[98] The works of the leading congregational minister John Owen proved to be influential in Keach's ministry.[99] Moreover, Keach had the "most respect" for John Cotton.[100] He frequently cited the Westminster Assembly and "our Annotators."[101] He drew from Calvin, Luther, Beza, Bullinger, and Perkins.[102] It was in the later part of his life, after 1689, that Keach would publish the majority of his works. The Act of Toleration granted Keach freedom to distribute his Baptist convictions. Due to the amount of his published material, Keach assumed an authoratative role among the Particular Baptist community.[103]

Baptist Networking and Controversies

As an established pastor in London he "was almost assuredly involved in the meeting that produced the *Second London Confession* in 1677."[104] He was a signer of the republished 1689 edition. He was also invited to Baptist associations and churches to aid their work.[105] Additionally, Keach was active in promoting the idea that local churches ought to financially support their ministers.[106] However, his denominational activity was not without issue.

---

95. Crosby, *History of the English Baptists*, 4:273.
96. Crosby, *History of the English Baptists*, 4:273.
97. Walker, *Excellent Benjamin Keach*, 95. Thomas Crosby married Keach's youngest daughter, Rebecca.
98. Walker, "Life of Benjamin Keach," 5–6.
99. Arnold, *Reformed Theology*, 36.
100. Arnold, *Reformed Theology*, 38.
101. Arnold, *Reformed Theology*, 39.
102. Arnold, *Reformed Theology*, 41–42.
103. Arnold, *Reformed Theology*, 41.
104. Arnold, *Reformed Theology*, 66.
105. MacDonald, *London Calvinistic Baptists*, 48–49.
106. MacDonald, *London Calvinistic Baptists*, 43.

Keach was active during the hymn-singing controversy in the late seventeenth century.[107] Keach already was advocating for congregational hymn singing by 1673.[108] At some point in 1689, Keach started introducing the practice of hymn singing at Horsleydown at the end of the services. This resulted in a firestorm of controversy within the congregation and the larger Particular Baptist community.[109]

Isaac Marlow, who was probably a member of Keach's church for a period, published works attacking Keach's views.[110] This did not prevent Keach from publishing hymnbooks.[111] It appears that by the turn of the century, Keach's idea of congregational hymn singing was the preferred expression in public worship.[112] Stanton also alludes that by introducing congregational hymn singing, Keach's Horsleydown congregation experienced numerical growth.[113] He writes, "The effect of his growth on the congregation's services of worship would have been unmistakable. Their singing—of up to one thousand people on Sunday mornings in pre-industrialized London—would have been very loud. Theoretically, assuming the congregational volume was roughly 70–80 decibels, they could have been heard up to half-a-mile away."[114] From his early children's primer to the hymn-singing debates, Keach was a "marked man." He wrote against Richard Baxter. Keach penned a single document titled *Mr. Baxter's Arguments for Believer's Baptism*.[115] In a somewhat ironic fashion, Keach collected statements from Baxter's work on baptism and

---

107. See a recent monograph on the hymn controversy, Stanton, *Liturgy and Identity*.

108. Stanton, *Liturgy and Identity*, 65.

109. Keach, *Breach repaired in God's worship*.

110. Arnold, *Reformed Theology*, 28. Marlow wrote in response to Keach; see Marlow, *Some Short Observations*, and Marlow, *Purity of Gospel Communion*.

111. Keach, *Spiritual Songs*. This work was originally published in 1696 under the title *Feast of Fat Things Full of Marrow*. This hymnbook was the first of its kind by an English Baptist. See MacDonald, *London Calvinistic Baptists*, 59.

112. Stanton, *Liturgy and Identity*, 207.

113. Stanton, *Liturgy and Identity*, 206.

114. Stanton, *Liturgy and Identity*, 72.

115. There are no known copies of this document, only referenced. Crosby notes, "Mr. Keach collected together [Baxter's arguments], and had them printed on a sheet, and called it as aforesaid, Mr. Baxter's arguments for believers baptism, and referred to the book and page, where he had the very words; and made some short remarks in the margin upon them." See Crosby, *History of the English Baptists*, 4:278–79. Also see Ivimey, *History of the English Baptists*, 2:365.

attempted to demonstrate that Baxter refuted himself.[116] The next conflict was over justification.[117] He published a work against the Quakers, *The Grand Impostor Discovered*.[118] Additionally, he argued against seventh-day Sabbatarianism.[119] The General Baptists attempted to censure Keach from attending their meetings.[120]

Perhaps some readers may conclude that Keach was purely polemical throughout his ministry while others may claim he was just convictional in his beliefs.[121] There is some truth to both conclusions. Keach had a way of finding himself in confrontation on important doctrinal matters that he believed were worth defending. However, attempting to assess motives is speculative. His public ministry did indeed have an *intensity* that caused his detractors to stir. Furthermore, he apparently believed it was incumbent upon him to add his voice to pressing issues impacting the religious and political climate of the late seventeenth century.[122] Nevertheless, whether it is his theological or polemical work, his pastoral impulse defined his ministry. Before he was a denominational statesman or doctrinal defender, his pastoral work within his local church was his primary calling.

KEACH'S PREACHING

What we know of Benjamin Keach's preaching is found only in his printed sermons and writings and from historians. We do not possess any handwritten copies of sermons or extracts on his homiletical thoughts. William Thomas Whitley claims that "Keach is thus a fair type of what Baptists were to be for long; earnest, self-educated, intensely evangelical and orthodox, the outlook narrowed to the denomination, and almost to the congregation."[123] Crosby recounts Keach's pastoral seriousness when

---

116. Ivimey, *History of the English Baptists*, 2:365.
117. Keach, *Marrow of True Justification*. Also see Hicks, "Analysis."
118. Keach, *Grand impostor discovered*.
119. Keach, *Jewish Sabbath abrogated*.
120. Whitley, *History of British Baptists*, 178.
121. For a summary of Keach's controversies see Copeland, *Benjamin Keach*, 17–69.
122. Keach wrote on the intersection of religious and political issues: Keach, *Distressed Sion relieved*. Also Keach, *God acknowledged*. Arnold has written on Keach's eschatology and how it influenced his view of seventeenth-century politics. See Arnold, "Radical, Baptist Eschatology."
123. Whitley, *History of British Baptists*, 178.

he states, "He [Keach], with unwearied diligence, did discharge the duties of his pastoral office, preaching both in season and out of season, visiting those under his charge, encouraging the serious, gently reproving the forward, defending the great truths of the Gospel, and setting them in the clearest light."[124] As for his preaching ministry, the intensity of his gospel proclamation is evident, as will be shown in chapter 5. Keach possessed a stern, yet gracious, pulpit demeanor. "He affected no unusual tones, nor indecent gestures in his preaching, his style was strong and masculine. He generally used notes, especially in the latter part of his life; and if his sermons had not all the embellishments of language, which some boast of, they had this peculiar advantage, to be full of solid divinity."[125] He viewed himself as an ambassador, standing in the stead of Christ, speaking the truth of the triune God. One can imagine the grave seriousness of Keach's exposition.

Benjamin Keach was "quintessentially Puritan" in his preaching.[126] This is indeed true in how Keach handled the exposition of Scripture and his manner of proclamation.[127] He claims,

> As I preach not to please men's ears, so but little regard ought to be had to the scoffing reflections of such men, who contemn everything of this kind, unless it consists of *a fancy-talking modulations of empty rhetoric . . . mixed with wit, learning, and philosophical notions.* . . . I am not for airy and florid orations in the ministration of the Word of God but for *the plain way of preaching* used by the Holy Apostles and our worthy modern Divines. . . . I may say of some men's orations, or elocutions, as Plutarch speaks of the Nightingale, who was at first taken with his delicate notes, but when he saw him said, "thou art a voice and nothing else."[128]

Keach's plain way of preaching contrasts "the fancy talking modulations of empty rhetoric . . . mixed with wit, learning, and philosophical notions." This was likely a direct attack on Archbishop John Tillotson, who

---

124. Crosby, *History of the English Baptists*, 4:304–5.
125. Crosby, *History of the English Baptists*, 4:305.
126. Deane, "Golden Mine Opened," 42.
127. Vaughn states, "Keach shared the structure which Perkins imparted . . . but Keach's style was distinctive and bore the mark of an age that was growing away from the Puritans." Vaughn, "Public Worship Practical Theology," 108.
128. Keach, *Display of Glorious Grace*, iii–iv.

practiced a "Metaphysical" manner of preaching.[129] Interestingly, Keach's mention of Plutarch's statement is a polemical remark and reveals what Keach thought about the ornate preaching of his day. According to Keach, the ornate preaching of the Church of England was merely a voice speaking, and nothing else. It is empty rhetoric. Additionally, he claims,

> The truth is, in preaching, to speak in a language the people understand not, it seems to serve for nothing, unless it is that the preacher would let them know he is a scholar. How ready is man to glory in his human attainments. . . . It ought to be the care of our churches to see that none but such men are allowed to preach, to whom God hath given competent gifts, and such also who are able to speak proper English, for the contrary exposes the Gospel to contempt.[130]

Keach advocates for plain and simple preaching, which, according to him, stands in contrast to other preaching styles. He was not impressed with pulpit scholarship or "human attainments." Thus, for Keach, the gospel must be preached with simplicity.

As for his method, Keach follows the threefold pattern of doctrine, reasons, and uses. He describes, "I have gone through the several Terms of the Text, by way of Explanation, and have taken Notice of several Propositions or Points of Doctrine that naturally arise therefrom."[131] He follows his usual method in his parable sermons, which follows Perkins's method: (1) open the scope of [the passage]; (2) explain the terms; (3) observe several points of doctrine and prosecute them distinctly; and (4) apply the whole.[132]

SERMONS AND WRITINGS

Dargan writes, "These [published sermons] show a fine insight into Scripture, a clear and convincing argumentation, a devout and earnest spirit, and a style usually simple and clear and not without graces of expression and occasional eloquence."[133] In all, Keach published 224 ser-

---

129. Tillotson, *Sermons, and Discourses*, 137. Tillotson quotes Plutarch and others in Latin. I discuss Metaphysical preaching in chapter 4.
130. Keach, *Exposition of the Parables*, vii.
131. Keach, *Golden Mine Opened*, 41.
132. Keach, *Exposition of the Parables*, 775. Deane, "Golden Mine Opened," 50.
133. Dargan, *History of Preaching*, 2:185.

mons. Holmes has done an exceptional job classifying and summarizing his sermons:[134]

> 4 Pastoral Sermons
> Sermon: A Summons to the Grave (1676)
> Sermon: The Everlasting Covenant (1693)
> Sermon: A Call to Weeping (1699)
> Sermon: God Acknowledged (1696)
>
> 68 Doctrinal Sermons
> Sermon Collection: The Marrow of True Justification (1692)
> Sermon Collection: A Golden Mine Opened (1694)
> Sermon Collection: Christ Alone the Way to Heaven (1698)
> Sermon: A Medium Betwixt Two Extremes (1698)
> Sermon Collection: The Display of Glorious Grace (1698)
> Sermon Collection: The Jewish Sabbath Abrogated (1700)
>
> 152 Parabolic Sermons
> Sermon Collection: The Counterfeit Christian (1691)
> Sermon Collection: An Ax Laid to the Root (1693)
> Sermon Collection: Exposition of the Parables (1701)[135]

Holmes further states,

> Keach's published sermons were almost entirely based on New Testament texts. Even without his 147 sermons on the parables of Jesus, the clear majority of Keach's other seventy-seven published sermons were taken from the New Testament. Other than his two sermon series, *The Display of Glorious Grace* and *Christ Alone the Way to Heaven or Jacob's Ladder Improved*, which contain a total of eighteen messages drawn from Isaiah 54:10 and Genesis 28:12, respectively, only three other individually published sermons were based on Old Testament passages.[136]

Keach's published sermons demonstrate pastoral sensitivity, robust Reformed theology, and evangelistic zeal. Additionally, his writings, particularly *Tropologia*, were most likely produced from sermon notes.[137] *Tropologia* gives scholars insight into Keach's hermeneutical and homiletical methodology. More will be said about this in chapter 5. The work

---

134. I will refer readers to Holmes's summary of Keach's sermons, "Role of Metaphor," 41–78.

135. Holmes, "Role of Metaphor," v.

136. Holmes, "Role of Metaphor," 43.

137. Walker, "Tailor Turned Preacher," 31–32.

titled *The Gospel Minister's Maintenance Vindicated* was published in 1689. The pamphlet argues that it is the responsibility of each congregation to support their ministers financially.[138] This document is significant for two reasons. First, it represents a consensus view among early Particular Baptists on the function of the minister. Second, it provides particular insight into Keach's view of preaching. He states, "Remember that your Pastors are the Ministers; nay, the Ambassadors of Jesus Christ; such who represent his Sacred Majesty, and have his Commission, for what they act and do in his Name, and dispense the Mysteries of God to you, according to their Duty."[139] While the document specifically argues for a minister's maintenance, Keach considers the duty of a preacher in the final section, "The Great and Weighty Work of a True Gospel Minister Opened." It is in this section where the author expounds on the preacher's role in preaching. The relevant statements will be analyzed in chapter 5.

SUMMARY

Benjamin Keach inherited a dissenting religious tradition that emerged out of Puritan attitudes and priorities. This does not mean that he embraced every aspect of the movement. It does, however, show Keach's sensitivity to nonconformity and anti-establishment religious expression. This background anticipates chapter 4, which explores the English homiletical setting of the sixteenth and seventeenth centuries.

---

138. Keach, *Gospel minister's maintenance vindicated*, 29.
139. Keach, *Gospel minister's maintenance vindicated*, 77.

CHAPTER 4

The English Homiletical Setting of the Sixteenth and Seventeenth Centuries

THIS CHAPTER PROVIDES THE homiletical milieu of the sixteenth and seventeenth centuries. In doing so, it grounds Keach within the larger stream of the Reformed preaching tradition. This is important to grasp as it relates to Keach's theo-homiletical convictions. First, I'll provide the homiletical background by noting highlights in the history of preaching from the Medieval era to early seventeenth-century England. Two critical observations are drawn that shape the remaining material presented in the chapter. These two observations are: (1) preaching ebbs and flows with cultural and political factors; (2) preaching renewals in the church's history are often connected to theological and methodological reforms.

Next, the focal point of this chapter, I'll discuss the Reformed preaching tradition from the sixteenth into the seventeenth century. The term *Reformed* has already been used throughout this work. For this chapter, the term is used in a way similar to Nimmo and Fergusson in their work *The Cambridge Companion to Reformed Theology*. They argue "that the Reformed tradition sets forth a particular agenda of theological discourse . . . an identifiable set of theological instincts, of doctrinal impulse."[1] The term *Reformed* is not exclusively used as another name for Calvinism. Reformed identifies a particular way of thinking about theology, the role of the church, and the nature of Scripture. This shapes theological discourse about the sacraments, preaching, and ministerial

---

1. Nimmo and Fergusson, introduction to *Cambridge Companion*, 4–5.

identity. Even among the diversity of Reformed authors, there are common themes that situate them within the Reformed tradition. While the Reformed preaching tradition is a broad-encompassing concept, the material presented in this chapter is divided into three major sections that identify significant contributions in homiletics. The first is a discussion of John Calvin's homiletical theology, and the second is a section on William Perkins's homiletical methodology. These two units shape the third section, which examines the birth of English Reformed plain preaching, commonly called Puritan plain. This exposes three Puritan theological commitments that have direct relevance to their preaching.

The breadth of seventeenth-century homiletics is vast, complex, and at times confusing. Yet, it represents a significant era in the history of preaching. As William Fraser Mitchell, in his book *English Pulpit Oratory*, claims, "The seventeenth century in England was *par excellence* an age of sermons."[2] Homiletical dynamics, such as methods and theories, gave rise to a golden era of English preaching. This is particularly true as it relates to the English Reformed tradition of preaching.[3] Therefore, it is important to provide historical highlights in English preaching that set the stage for sixteenth- and seventeenth-century homiletics.

HISTORICAL HIGHLIGHTS IN ENGLISH PREACHING

E. C. Dargan writes, "Since Christianity became an active force in human affairs there has been upward and onward movement, and one mighty

---

2. Mitchell, *English Pulpit Oratory*, 3.

3. Throughout this chapter, the phrases *English Reformed* and *English Reformed plain preaching* will be used as an identifying label for what is commonly called "Puritan plain preaching." As will be shown, Puritans were not the only ministers who used this method of preaching in the seventeenth century. Using this language perhaps runs the risk of being anachronistic since later sixteenth-century conformists and nonconformists shared similar Reformed theological frameworks. Nevertheless, by the early seventeenth century, conformist Arminianism was emerging, which shaped preaching and further distinguished them from Calvinistic nonconformist ministers. See Tyacke, *Anti-Calvinists*. The *English Reformed* nomenclature distinguishes that this manner of preaching is grounded in the larger Reformed preaching tradition. This language is drawn from Mary Morrissey. She claims that this term is an extension of the "new Reformed arrangement of Doctrines and Uses" coined by Blench. Morrissey, "Scripture, Style, and Persuasion," 687n1. In doing this, she identifies the homiletical method and the theory undergirding it. Scholars also use the term *New Reformed method* interchangeably with *English Reformed*. See Ford, "Preaching," 76.

factor in that progress has been preaching."[4] Preaching, as a central aspect of the church's worship and work, developed through significant stages. This section highlights some of these moments in the history of English preaching that set the stage for late sixteenth- and seventeenth-century homiletics.[5] While not much is known about Christian preaching in romanized Briton, the Anglo-Saxon invasion of the island led to the decline of the Roman church.[6] In the sixth century, Pope Gregory the Great sought to convert the island to Christianity by sending Augustine, a Benedictine monk, to establish the church among the Anglo-Saxons.[7] Through Augustine's preaching, by 597, King Ethelbert of Kent was baptized, and Augustine established Canterbury as "the center of his operations."[8] This launched a parish-planting movement. From 600 to 900, principal churches in England were established and staffed by monks and priests.[9] Parish priests rarely expounded the Bible, leaving monks to fill the gap in instruction from the Bible.[10] Thus, Benedictine monks sought to preserve preaching. Their preaching was expository in nature, missionary in impulse, and rigorously followed the lectionary.[11]

Yet, as Dargan observes, "We should not fail also to take account of the growth of liturgy and forms of worship. . . . Preaching was not vigorous and able enough to overcome the trammels of liturgy. More serious than this was the growth of the hierarchical spirit, the conception of the preacher as priest rather than prophet."[12] The ecclesiological development of the priesthood along with the elevation of the Eucharist tended to downplay the role of preaching among parishes. This issue

---

4. Dargan, *History of Preaching*, 1:8.

5. Highlighting significant homiletical developments requires a selective process. Admittedly, there are aspects of English homiletical history that cannot be mentioned in this section. The intent is to provide a general narrative. The writer agrees with Dargan: "In fact the great abundance of the material is one of the chief difficulties in the way of writing the history of preaching. Even allowing for all the helps and pressing the principle of selection as far as is admissible, there still remains a vast bulk of literature to go over, a deal of information to accumulate, study, digest, arrange, and finally set forth in writing." See Dargan, *History of Preaching*, 1:4.

6. Old, *Medieval Church*, 118–19.

7. Old, *Medieval Church*, 119.

8. Old, *Medieval Church*, 119.

9. Orme, *Going to Church*, 7.

10. Dargan, *History of Preaching*, 1:133–37.

11. Old, *Medieval Church*, 185–88.

12. Dargan, *History of Preaching*, 1:109–10.

will play a significant factor during the eleventh and twelfth centuries. The English monk the Venerable Bede (673–735), a student of the early fathers, sought to provide homiletical training for uneducated bishops and priests.[13] Bede states, "The pastors of the church have been ordained primarily for the task of preaching the mysteries of the word of God."[14] Despite some significant preachers, the homiletical decline continued until Alcuin (735–804) revised the Roman lectionary under Charlemagne (768–814), which occasioned a preaching revival.[15] Old writes,

> Emperor Charlemagne understood the importance of preaching. He knew it was going to take more than the sword to bring the Saxons into his empire, and more than politics to forge the rival barbarian tribes, the Franks, the Gauls, and what was left of ancient Rome, into the new Europe. Charlemagne was more than a statesman; he was the creator of a culture. He envisioned uniting the whole continent of Europe together, with everyone professing one Christian faith, speaking one Latin language, and claiming the heritage of classical civilization and the traditions of ancient Rome.[16]

Madigan, however, notes, "In the year 1000, almost none of the priests could have prepared a homily, none of their parishioners expected it, and few would have valued it."[17] Following the Norman conquest (1066), evidence suggests that preaching to the laity was not a prominent ministerial function among the priests in England.[18] Illiteracy was a significant cause for this. As Stansbury writes, "The administration of the sacraments did not require a particularly high level of academic learning; but preaching did."[19] The liturgical elements, particularly the Eucharist, tended to subordinate the role of preaching.[20] Pelikan observes, "For a denial of the sacraments was tantamount to a denial of the church itself. The sacraments were that important because each sacrament 'contains a certain spiritual grace,' and it was through the several sacraments that the

---

13. Old, *Medieval Church*, 122–27.
14. Quoted by Pelikan, *Growth of Medieval Theology*, 29.
15. Old, *Medieval Church*, 191–97.
16. Old, *Medieval Church*, 188–89.
17. Madigan, *Medieval Christianity*, 87–88.
18. Thomas, *Secular Clergy in England*, 329.
19. Stansbury, *Companion to Pastoral Care*, 26.
20. Gordan, "Late Medieval Christianity," 32.

grace of the forgiveness of sins, life, and salvation was communicated."[21] As a result, "sermons were exceedingly rare in the local parish church."[22]

As monastic communities gained strength in the Medieval period, preaching was vital in furthering Christian causes.[23] In particular, "with Bernard of Clairvaux (1090–1151) Christian preaching experienced a rebirth. . . . Bernard's preaching restored the art to something of the power and the beauty it had known in the days of Basil and John Chrysostom, Ambrose, and Augustine."[24] His preaching directly influenced Aelred of Rievaulx (1109–1167), a Cistercian monk in England.[25] Still, preaching was not a widespread phenomenon among local parishes.[26]

A momentous homiletical change occurred in the late twelfth century. Alan of Lille's *Summa de arte praedicatoria* was one of the first homiletical textbooks to demonstrate this new method of preaching that marked a move away from the patristic homily.[27] The thematic sermon structure was "a by-product of that distinct phase in the development of medieval thought and theology that we call scholasticism."[28] This sermonic structure was highly analytical, but its scholastic influence carried into sixteenth-century England. In addition to methodological developments, various political issues affected late Medieval preaching in England. For example, the rise and fall of papal authority shaped local parishes and the role of preaching in negative ways.[29]

Yet, as Edwards writes, "Seldom in the history of the church has there been such a rapid and widespread increase in the amount of preaching along with a corresponding proliferation of interest in that preaching as that which began early in the thirteenth century and continued through the fourteenth."[30] Scholars note that the Dominican and Franciscan friars

---

21. Pelikan, *Growth of Medieval Theology*, 204.

22. Madigan, *Medieval Christianity*, 87.

23. Old, *Medieval Church*, 254.

24. Old, *Medieval Church*, 289. For information on Bernard's preaching see Hoare, "Bernard of Clairvaux."

25. Old, *Medieval Church*, 287.

26. This is not to imply that preaching was nonexistent during this period. See Neale, *Medieval Preachers and Medieval Preaching*.

27. Alan of Lille, *Summa de arte praedicatoria*, 111–98.

28. Wenzel, *Medieval "Artes Praedicandi,"* 47. See part 2 of Wenzel's work for more details on the structure.

29. See Ozment, *Age of Reform*, 135–81.

30. Edwards, *History of Preaching*, 210.

were essential in the resurgence of preaching.[31] Old claims, "The new preaching orders brought the flowering orchard of medieval preaching to its fruition."[32] Specifically, the preaching tours of the friars significantly influenced England.[33]

Nevertheless, parishes in England still conducted the Mass in Latin, meaning regular teaching for the laity was lacking.[34] In the thirteenth century, local parishes adopted "quarterly sermons" to instruct converts.[35] Wabuda notes, "Four times a year, all priests were to expound in English a formidable list of essential subjects . . . the seven vices and seven virtues: the Creed, the Ten Commandments, the Two Precepts of the Gospel; the Seven Works of mercy, and the ultimate: the Seven Sacraments."[36] Preaching outside the Mass became a suitable option for those desiring further instruction, though this was less common due to the lack of skilled preachers.[37] As proto-Reformation movements formed, preaching served as an important function. For example, John Wycliffe's preaching in the fourteenth century helped pave the way for the flourishing of Reformation impulses in the sixteenth century.[38]

Although preaching was "a handmaid to the sacraments" for much of the Medieval church, it was not entirely a lost art.[39] This would change slowly as accessibility to the written word proved to be one of the greatest "Protestant victories."[40] Moving into the fifteenth and sixteenth centuries, outdoor preaching became an important English spectacle. Wabuda writes, "At the great outdoor pulpit crosses . . . any lack of parish sermons could be repaired."[41] Scholars have shown the religious and cultural impact of St. Paul's Cross.[42] Moreover, outdoor preaching also detached the sermon from the Mass.[43] Thus, preaching was being reshaped.

31. See Maier, *Preaching the Crusades*.
32. Old, *Medieval Church*, 341.
33. Maier, *Preaching the Crusades*, 111.
34. Orme, *Going to Church*, 247.
35. Wabuda, *Preaching*, 35–36.
36. Wabuda, *Preaching*, 34.
37. Orme, *Going to Church*, 250.
38. Edwards, *History of Preaching*, 247–55.
39. Wabuda, *Preaching*, 24.
40. Wabuda, *Preaching*, 99.
41. Wabuda, *Preaching*, 40.
42. See Maclure, *Paul's Cross Sermons*, and Kirby and Stanwood, *Paul's Cross*.
43. Carlson, "Boring of the Ear," 253.

John Colet had a direct impact on Reformation preaching.[44] Brown comments regarding Colet,

> His method was the same, for his discourses were not upon isolated texts, but continuous expositions of the facts of the Savior's life and of the substance of His teaching.... Colet's method of so dealing with the Scriptures as to make them living books to the men of his time, bringing out the richness and fullness of their teaching, starts again the question, often started before, as to the desirability or otherwise of continuous expository preaching.[45]

Edwards writes, "Thematic sermons were still the norm on the eve of the Reformation, but some preachers inspired by the humanists, such as Colet, had reverted to the patristic homily form."[46] This expository trajectory of Colet and those that followed him set the stage for Cranmer, who "preached Christ" under the reign of Edward VI (1547–1553).[47] This idea of "preaching Christ" was shorthand for the Reformer's doctrine of "justification by faith."[48] Reformation preaching slowly shaped England from the 1530s through the early 1550s. Through the publication of the *Book of Homilies* in 1547, the Church of England steadily experienced a resurgence of the word.[49]

Additionally, Hugh Latimer played a vital role in the preaching renewal of the English Reformation. His preaching paralleled the Reformed reorientation of the pastoral office.[50] His impact on the preaching of the English Reformation is also significant regarding his homiletical theology, which was influenced by Helvetic doctrine.[51] Latimer states, "For preaching of the gospel is one of God's ploughworks, and the preacher is one of God's ploughmen."[52] In another sermon he states, "This office of preaching is the office of salvation.... How can men then believe, but by and through the office of preaching? Preachers are Christ's vicars.... They are Christ's ambassadors.... The gospel is the power of God unto

---

44. Brown, *Puritan Preaching in England*, 36.
45. Brown, *Puritan Preaching in England*, 40.
46. Edwards, *History of Preaching*, 354.
47. Wabuda, *Preaching*, 85.
48. Wabuda, *Preaching*, 88. Also Davies, *Worship and Theology*, 35.
49. Cranmer, *Certayne Sermons*.
50. Zuidema, "Lords and Labourers," 185.
51. Zuidema, "Lords and Labourers," 185.
52. Latimer, "Sermon of the Plough," 60.

salvation for every believer. It is the mighty instrument of God."[53] We see in Latimer, and other Reformers, the high value placed upon preaching that was not seen in the Medieval era.

Last, the preaching resurgence in sixteenth-century England is also seen in church architecture and increased printed homiletical aids. By the 1550s, the English pulpit was moved away from the altar and located within the body of the church. Thus, "Now the preacher was elevated and displayed, more audible and visible than ever before, raised and exposed. . . . Pulpits grew grander and taller to compensate, and they were meant to fill the audience with a sense of awe as they listened."[54] Reformed homiletical materials were translated rapidly and printed. For example, Erasmus's work on preaching in 1535 introduced a shift away from the Medieval method of preaching to a *"rhetoricae eccleiasticae."*[55] Likewise, Melanchthon's four tracts on preaching between 1529 and 1553 catalyzed Protestant preaching in England.[56]

MID-SIXTEENTH- AND EARLY SEVENTEENTH-CENTURY PREACHING IN ENGLAND

These highlights are intended to support two general observations: (1) preaching ebbs and flows with cultural and political factors; and (2) preaching renewals in the church's history are often connected to theological and methodological reforms. In short, renewal is tied to retrieval. These factors set the stage for the late sixteenth- and seventeenth-century homiletical setting in England. Homiletical methods and theologies that developed during Elizabethan and Jacobean preaching would impact late seventeenth-century preaching. During the sixteenth and seventeenth centuries, there were four basic sermon forms: the homily, the thematic sermon, the classic oration, and the doctrine-use scheme.[57] These four forms can be divided into three structures: ancient, modern, and new Reformed; and two styles: plain and ornate style.[58] The ancient form de-

---

53. Latimer, "Sermon the Second," 349.
54. Wabuda, *Preaching*, 106.
55. Kneidel, "*Ars Praedicandi*," 12.
56. Kneidel, "*Ars Praedicandi*," 12–13.
57. Kneidel, "*Ars Praedicandi*," 17.
58. Pipa, "William Perkins," 40–41.

scended from the homilies of the early church fathers while the modern form was the product of the university schools.[59]

However, two streams of preaching emerged by the late sixteenth century: the Reformed plain and Metaphysical ornate.[60] As Davies writes, "the plain style of the Puritans . . . was the direct opposite of the Metaphysical style."[61] Concerning Metaphysical (ornate) preaching, Old states, "Not until the beginning of the seventeenth century do we find a distinctly Anglican school of preaching."[62] This school was known for being "witty" or "metaphysical."[63] Mitchell argues that many Anglo-Catholic divines embraced a larger classicist movement, which shaped their preaching. He states,

> The Anglo-Catholic divines of the close of the sixteenth century were turning from the barren logic of Calvin's "Institutes" to the beauty of classical oratory applied to religious subjects, to the tenderness and humanity of medieval poetry, and to that pictorialism which alike in description and painting, whether the emotion it suggested was charity or terror, was characteristic of the Middle Ages.[64]

Two significant Metaphysical preachers of the late sixteenth and early seventeenth centuries are Lancelot Andrewes (1555–1626) and John Donne (1571–1631).[65] Andrewes was "a superlative scholastic orator, the most celebrated of his age. . . . In purpose he was, above all else, a rhetorician."[66] It is said of Donne that "he brought to his sermons a public personality of ravishing charm; and second, a London Jacobean congregation came to church prepared to enjoy flesh-creeping thrills and theatrical rhapsodies as a legitimate part of a preacher's dispensation."[67] These preachers "loved to demonstrate their wit, to quote patristic and

59. Blench, *Preaching in England*, 71–72.

60. Plain preaching was "the plain easie way of *Doctrine* and *Use*." Wright, *Five sermons*, A3.

61. Davies, *Like Angels*, 47.

62. Old, *Age of the Reformation*, 331.

63. Edwards, *History of Preaching*, 369–70.

64. Mitchell, *English Pulpit Oratory*, 140.

65. The term *Metaphysical* does not mean these preachers were philosophical preachers, like the Cambridge Platonists of the seventeenth century. Rather, *Metaphysical* is connected to the term's usage as applied to the English Metaphysical poets and their use of wit, irony, and metric flexibility. See Davies, *Like Angels*, 7.

66. Chandos, *In God's Name*, 201.

67. Chandos, *In God's Name*, 242–43.

classical authors, to illustrate their points from natural history, and to use elaborate rhetorical forms, riddles, puns, paradoxes, and emblems."[68] Davies demonstrates eleven characteristics distinguishing Metaphysical preaching from the plain style:

> These characteristics may be listed as follows: (1) wit; (2) patristic citations and references; (3) the use of classical literature and history; (4) illustrations from "unnatural" natural history; (5) quotations in Greek and Latin, and etymology; (6) principles of biblical exegesis; (7) sermon structure and divisions; (8) the Senecan style; (9) paradoxes, riddles, and emblems; (10) speculative doctrines and arcane knowledge; (11) relating doctrinal and devotional preaching to the liturgy and the calendar of the Christian year.[69]

Davies is nuanced to say that not all Metaphysical preachers rigorously followed the style. This ornate style was also found among more than just the Anglo-Catholic divines.[70] However, contemporary scholarship has challenged the categories of *plain* and *ornate*.[71] It's argued that the distinction between the Metaphysical and Puritan preachers is built upon the false assumption that the Puritans were "logical and not emotional."[72] This assumption rests upon a simplistic and flawed dichotomy concerning the nature of rhetoric in the early modern era, particularly the application of rhetorical categories to preaching.[73] In summarizing the issue, Morrissey writes, "So it can be argued that underlying most discussion of seventeenth-century preaching is the distinction drawn from secular rhetoric between persuasion by the reason using a dialectical plain style or by the passions using the grand style. This is not, however, accurately descriptive of early seventeenth-century theories of preaching."[74] She concludes, "We must abandon the anachronistic distinction between the 'Puritan plain' and the 'metaphysical' styles."[75] She maintains that the distinction is largely due to the differences in homiletical theologies.[76]

---

68. Old, *Age of the Reformation*, 334.
69. Davies, *Like Angels*, 49; also see 50–88.
70. Davies, *Like Angels*, 133. Also see Mitchell, *English Pulpit Oratory*, 197.
71. Hunt, *Art of Hearing*, 81–94.
72. Hunt, *Art of Hearing*, 82.
73. Morrissey, "Scripture, Style, and Persuasion," 686.
74. Morrissey, "Scripture, Style, and Persuasion," 689.
75. Morrissey, "Scripture, Style, and Persuasion," 706.
76. Morrissey, "Scripture, Style, and Persuasion," 688.

Thus, homiletical historians argue that the distinction is neither accurate nor helpful.[77]

The *plain* and *ornate* distinction has been maintained by older scholars who suggest that the plain sermon was primarily Puritan. However, the plain method's popularity reveals that those outside the Puritan movement accepted it.[78] Hunt writes, "Its [plain sermon] popularity is indicative of a general respect for logical order and discipline in preaching, which was not exclusively Puritan any more than it was exclusively Ramist."[79] In actuality, the doctrine-use scheme was the dominant seventeenth-century sermonic model in England. Richardson states, "The sermons that were preached and heard and read with such general satisfaction were all built on virtually the same pattern."[80] Bishop John Hooper, particularly in his sermons on Jonah, used this doctrine-use method of preaching.[81] It was the method that was popularized by the Latin commentaries of Musculus.[82] By the mid-sixteenth century, many Elizabethan preachers already used the method.[83] Early Puritan preachers like Cartwright and Chalderton used the method before Perkins's codification.[84]

Ironically, Anglican preachers claimed to be the "true" exponents of the plain sermon.[85] Anglican minister Matthew Robinson's method was "exposition of the text, then a doctrinal observation, confirmed by reasons and demonstrations, next particular applications."[86] Arminian minister William Chappell, who wrote "The Preacher, or The Art and Method of Preaching" (1656), advocated for the doctrine-use method of preaching.[87] In 1621, Richard Bernard writes in *The Faithfull Shepheard*, "Preaching is, as you well know, *a sound and plainly laying open of holy Scripture*, by a public minister before the people, to their understanding and capacity,

---

77. Contra Miller, *New England Mind*, and Mitchell, *English Pulpit Oratory*.
78. Hunt, *Art of Hearing*, 95–96.
79. Hunt, *Art of Hearing*, 96. Peter Ramus will be discussed later in this chapter.
80. Richardson, *English Preachers and Preaching*, 70–71.
81. Davies, *Worship and Theology*, 243.
82. Blench, *Preaching in England*, 101.
83. Pipa, "William Perkins," 180–81.
84. Pipa, "William Perkins," 151.
85. Hunt, *Art of Hearing*, 397.
86. Mayor, *Autobiography of Matthew Robinson*, 70; also see Richardson, *English Preachers and Preaching*, 72.
87. See Chappell, *Preacher*, 3.

according to the analogy of faith, with the words of exhortation applied to the conscience, both to inform and reform."[88] Archbishop John Tillotson preached using the doctrine-use scheme.[89] In conclusion, Van Hof states,

> It [the plain sermon] was popular, to be sure—but it was carefully cultivated in the universities, ruminated about by doctors of divinity, and spelled out in detailed instruction manuals. It is the characteristic of the plain style, which is the one truly unique aspect about it, at least until its day—it was the only form of preaching to enjoy immense popular appeal among the common people while at the same time submitting to the scholarly attention of the academic and theological elite.[90]

Therefore, there is clear evidence to conclude that the plain method of preaching was not distinctively Puritan. Yet, those who tended toward Puritan tendencies did gravitate to the plain style. The question is, Why did they adopt this method? What is apparent is that there was indeed an obvious difference between the *plain* and *ornate* styles (if we can use these terms) that go beyond mere methodology. Perkins writes,

> Wherefore, neither the words of arts nor Greek and Latin phrases and quirks must be intermingled in the sermon. (1) They disturb the minds of the auditors, that they cannot fit those things which went afore with those that follow. (2) A strange word hinders the understanding of those things that are spoken. (3) It draws the mind away from the purpose to some other matter. Here also the telling of tales and all profane and ridiculous speeches must be omitted.[91]

The reason for Perkins's sharp statement is that "speech must be spiritual and gracious . . . it is both simply and perspicuous, fit both for the people's understanding and to express the majesty of the Spirit."[92] For Perkins, the concern was not specifically the nature of rhetoric. Rather, it was a difference in his view concerning the preacher's character, the audience's reception, and the role of the Spirit in preaching.[93] He states, "The demonstration of the Spirit is when the minister of the Word does in the

---

88. Bernard, *Faithfull Shepheard*, A3.
89. Smyth, *Art of Preaching*, 146–47.
90. Van Hof, "Theory of Sermon Rhetoric," 279.
91. Perkins, *Art of Prophesying*, 350.
92. Perkins, *Art of Prophesying*, 350.
93. Morrissey, "Scripture, Style, and Persuasion," 686.

time of preaching so behave himself that all, even ignorant persons and unbelievers, may judge that it is not so much he who speaks as the Spirit of God in him and by him."[94] The effectual work of the Spirit is central to the Reformed preaching tradition. If the Spirit's power is how the word becomes effectual unto salvation, it stands to reason that by negating various "witty" elements from preaching, the Spirit works inwardly to regenerate sinners. Morrissey again argues,

> There are two very important implications of this emphasis on the Word . . . that are central to the English Reformed theory of preaching: First, it makes the Bible more than a means of information. Scripture is not merely a record of the sayings of Christ; it is a revelation of God under the "veil" of its words. Consequently, preaching is more than merely informative on morality or godliness: the sermon was to make that particular part of Scripture operative for the hearers. For this reason, sermons were composed around a biblical text, and the preacher's role was partly the didactic one of showing the significance of the text to the hearers. In effect, the text delimited and defined the subject of the sermon. Second, if Christ was present in the Word and that presence made operative in preaching, it was not just because of the preacher's oratorical skills: the operative force in this encounter was the Holy Spirit, who gave the necessary grace to the hearers that enabled them to benefit from the sermon.[95]

Thus, the proclamation of a sermon is the means by which the Spirit saves sinners. In contrast, Andrewes and other conformist preachers subordinated preaching to other means of grace.[96] The difference between the preaching of conformist and nonconformist ministers in the late sixteenth and seventeenth centuries can be described as a distinction relating to a *theology of preaching*.[97] Their respective sermonic methods and styles were intrinsically connected to homiletical theories. The label "plain" does not mean that these sermons lacked rhetorical quality. Hence, "Notwithstanding the pastoral concern for simplicity, preachers who advocated and practiced the 'plain style' recognized the need to color their sermons with some rhetorical tropes. They saw the use of oratory

---

94. Perkins, *Art of Prophesying*, 349.
95. Morrissey, "Scripture, Style, and Persuasion," 689–90.
96. Morrissey, "Scripture, Style, and Persuasion," 698–700.
97. This is a central argument in Dahlman's dissertation. His chapter on the preaching manuals of Perkins and Bernard demonstrates this claim. See Dahlman, "Opening a Box," 124–87.

as a means to an end."[98] *Plain*, rather, is connected to theo-homiletical simplicity as it relates to the work of the Spirit and the hearers' ability to understand the sermon.

Morrissey argues that the "unique status of preaching in Reformed theology set it apart from other forms of oratory and shaped the theory of preaching" in the late sixteenth century and early seventeenth century.[99] Puritan preaching emerged from the Reformed preaching tradition, while popular Metaphysical preaching was shaped by cultural and theological factors.[100] Old argues, "Puritan preaching had a tendency to run counter to the prevailing baroque culture of the seventeenth century."[101] Additionally, "The doctrine-and-use method was ideal for these purposes, as it made it much easier for the hearer to visualize the sermon structure in diagrammatic form."[102]

The plain sermon, therefore, allowed the preacher to deductively preach and thereby educate the congregation as a means of theological catechesis. Heal argues, "For those who were already strongly committed to Puritan forms of piety, orality and literacy were self-reinforcing: sermons were heard and notes taken; passages of those notes were discussed among the godly and were related to appropriate scriptural texts."[103] This became an important aspect that stood in contrast to the ornate preaching of the conformist preachers. Uneducated laity profited from the plain sermon in practical ways.[104] The plain sermon sought to expound a text of Scripture according to its plain sense, so that the hearers could understand it clearly.

Therefore, English Reformed plain preaching stood in contrast to the ornate preaching of the conformists.[105] While scholars should be careful in using the *plain* and *ornate* rhetorical categories, it is noted

98. Ford, "Preaching," 74.

99. Morrissey, "Scripture, Style, and Persuasion," 687.

100. Old, *Age of the Reformation*, 332. Also, Morrissey, "Scripture, Style, and Persuasion," 694.

101. Old, *Age of the Reformation*, 333.

102. Hunt, *Art of Hearing*, 99.

103. Heal, "English, Scottish, and Irish Reformations," 243–44.

104. Van Hof, "Theory of Sermon Rhetoric," 304.

105. Dahlman, "Opening a Box," 164–73. The labels plain and ornate could be used, if nuanced, to maintain that there was a difference in their theories of preaching, which motivated a difference in pulpit styles. It should also be noted that the argument that the Puritans were "logical, not emotional" falls short when one reads Puritan sermons. See Kater, "Puritan Preaching and Pathos."

that different homiletical theories did indeed shape pulpit rhetoric. The English Reformed preaching tradition possessed unique characteristics that tended toward plainness in interpretation, sermon construction, and delivery. This will be discussed later in this chapter. It is argued that the Reformed preaching theology catalyzes such an approach. The theological and ecclesiological instability of the preceding generations prompted a seismic transition that resulted in the Reformed preaching tradition.

PREACHING IN THE REFORMED TRADITION

The significance of the continental Reformation and its influence on the English Reformation cannot be overstated, particularly the homiletical theology that emerged. The Reformed preaching tradition was birthed through the ministries of the Magisterial Reformers and continued to shape homiletics in England.[106] This preaching resurgence among the sixteenth-century Reformed went hand in hand with reorientating the church's liturgy. As a result, "The classical Protestant Reformation produced a distinct school of preaching. It was a preaching of reform, to be sure, but it was also a reform of preaching. . . . What happened was that with the Reformation came a refocusing of preaching, a rethinking of its purpose, and a reevaluation of its relation to the worship of the Church."[107]

The Reform of Ministerial Identity and Praxis

Preaching was the primary means by which ecclesiological reform and spiritual transformation occurred. Furthermore, the Reformed sermon was "pedagogical literature," providing the hearers the theological and practical tools to resist the church of Rome.[108] In a unique sense, Reformed preaching emerged out of an ecclesial context and in response to the Roman Catholic Church.[109] This is demonstrated in how the

---

106. Muller notes, "The teachings of no single theologian . . . can account for the development of the Reformed tradition." Muller, *Calvin and the Reformed Tradition*, 13. This work uses the *Reformed tradition* to refer to the ecclesiological traditions/theologies that emerged from various theologians such as Huldrych Zwingli, Heinrich Bullinger, and John Calvin.

107. Old, *Age of the Reformation*, 1.

108. Ford, "Preaching," 66–67.

109. Ford, "Preaching," 66. Catholic preaching was also affected. But as Old notes, "[Catholic] preachers simply refused to move in the direction the Reformers moved in

Reformers understood the role and identity of the minister. The Reformers' move away from the priest's mediatorial function to the minister's ambassadorial function marked a significant reorientation in pastoral work.[110] This is made clear in both Bullinger and Calvin.

Bullinger confronts the priest's ecclesiological authority in several of his sermons.[111] He argues that Catholic priests attempt to exercise authority by consecrating the Eucharist, administrating the sacraments, appointing ministers, preaching, and judicial correction.[112] Thus, "these things do these men teach concerning ecclesiastical power, not only foolishly, but also falsely."[113] He holds priests in contempt as agents of false doctrine. The priests are mocked as "sacrificers."[114] Bullinger argues that the "priests are ordained more to read, to sing, and say Mass" than to preach the Scriptures.[115] God did not appoint Christ as "a prince" or "a pope," so also "he appointed no princes in the church, but ministers and elders, who with the word of Christ should feed Christ's flock."[116] He contrasts the Catholic priests with Christ's ambassadors: "Therefore that thing which Christ, the Son of God, who is the greatest, the best, and the chief high priest of his church, worketh in his catholic church inwardly and in their minds, as the only searcher of the hearts; the very same outwardly he declareth and testifieth by his ministers, whom the

---

their reform of preaching. . . . For the most part Counter-Reformation preaching quite intentionally moved in the opposite direction." Old, *Age of the Reformation*, 160.

110. For information on Catholic preaching during the early modern period see Worcester, "Catholic Sermons." The Council of Trent addresses the role of preaching: "But whereas the preaching of the Gospel is no less necessary to the Christian commonwealth than the reading thereof; and whereas this is the chief duty of bishops; the same holy synod hath resolved and decreed, that all bishops, archbishops, primates, and all other prelates of the churches be bound personally, if they be not lawfully hindered, to preach the holy Gospel of Jesus Christ." See Buckley, *Canons and Decrees*, 26–27. Yet, nowhere in the canons or decrees does the word *ambassador* appear regarding priests. This does not suggest that Catholics did not use the ambassador metaphor elsewhere in their sermons or writings. The point is to show that, according to Bullinger and Calvin, they saw a difference in the functions of the priest and minister.

111. Bullinger, *Decades*. Evidence of this confrontation are found elsewhere in Bullinger's writings and sermons, yet, for the scope of this book sermons found in *The Fifth Decade* are noted.

112. Bullinger, *Decades*, 38–39.

113. Bullinger, *Decades*, 40.

114. Bullinger, *Decades*, 116.

115. Bullinger, *Decades*, 144.

116. Bullinger, *Decades*, 89.

scripture for that cause calleth witnesses, ambassadors, or messengers."[117] Likewise, the "keys of the kingdom" are operative through "the ministry of preaching the gospel."[118] He concludes, "The Lord, our high priest, speaketh unto us even at this day by the ministers preaching his word."[119] For Bullinger, Christ does not speak by the priests. God has not given the church a "prince or pope," but rather ministers, who are charged with the task of preaching the Scriptures. He places the ambassadorial function of the minister in opposition to the Roman Catholic priest. Therefore, it is through ministers, functioning as ambassadors, that Christ speaks through his word.

Calvin also condemns the priests, who consider "the Mass as the sacrificing of Christ."[120] He states that Rome teaches the office of Christ was transferred to priests, whom he defines as "persons who sacrifice to God."[121] He explicitly contrasts priests with the "ministers whom God has appointed as his ambassadors."[122] Calvin states, "The message of reconciliation was entrusted to ministers to act as ambassadors with Christ."[123] Those called as ambassadors are "interpreters of his secret will" and "represent his [Christ's] person."[124] In Calvin's commentary on 2 Cor 5:19–21, he labels the pope and his priests "dumb idols" who stand in contrast to "the ministers of the Church" who "are ambassadors."[125] Additionally, he makes the distinction between the "papist priests" and those commanded to be "stewards of the gospel."[126] Calvin argues that priests do not act on behalf of Christ since (1) the Mass itself is "blasphemy" and (2) Christ is the only perpetual priest.[127] In sum, he repudiates "the sacerdotal dignity" of the priests.[128]

Bullinger and Calvin juxtaposed the role of the Catholic priest and the Protestant minister. Consciously, they elevated the work of preaching

---

117. Bullinger, *Decades*, 97.
118. Bullinger, *Decades*, 146.
119. Bullinger, *Decades*, 103.
120. Calvin, *Institutes*, 2.15.6.
121. Calvin, *Short Treatise*, 184.
122. Calvin, *Short Treatise*, 184.
123. Calvin, *Institutes*, 3.5.5.
124. Calvin, *Institutes*, 4.3.1.
125. Calvin, *Commentaries*, 2:239.
126. Calvin, *Institutes*, 4.19.28.
127. Calvin, *Institutes*, 4.18.2.
128. Calvin, *Short Treatise*, 189.

over the Mass.[129] In doing so, they distinguish their view of an overseer by readily employing the term *minister*. A minister does not offer Christ's sacrifice to God in the Mass. Rather, a minister offers Christ's sacrifice to the congregation through the preaching of the word. They further define the preaching role of the minister as an ambassador. This metaphor expresses the proclamation function of the Reformed minister in contrast to the mediatorial role of the priest. A true minister of Christ, according to the Reformers, functions as an ambassador on behalf of Christ in the event of proclamation.[130] The ambassador metaphor carried significant weight within the Reformed preaching tradition of the sixteenth and seventeenth centuries.[131] This tradition subsequently shaped homiletics in early modern England.

The Reform of Preaching

Maag writes, "The Reformation's emphasis on the centrality of Scripture and its exposition in worship meant that preaching took on a greater role as the Reformation took hold."[132] "The roots of Reformed preaching lay," as Amy Nelson Burnett claims, "in the *lectio continua* approach to preaching on the Scripture text introduced by Zwingli in Zurich, as well as in the model of the patristic homily."[133] Zwingli viewed preaching as "most sacred." He states, "I believe that the work of prophesying or preaching is most sacred, so that it is a work most necessary, above all others. . . . Whithersoever, then, prophets or preachers of the Word are sent, it is a sign of God's grace, that He wishes to manifest a knowledge of Himself to His elect."[134] Zwingli's sermon "Of the Clarity and Certainty of the Word of God" is a clarion call to embrace the authority of the

---

129. Wandel, "Switzerland," 240–42. Wandel writes, "Preaching in Geneva was the centerpiece of the effort to make the Word of God living in the heart of each Christian. While the Consistory monitored, admonished, and, in extreme cases, disciplined, preaching, for Calvin, was the main vehicle for the reformation of character and conduct."

130. Calvin, "Genevan Confession," 32. He writes, "As we receive the true ministers of the Word of God as messengers and ambassadors of God."

131. Van Dixhoorn argues, "It is the metaphor of ambassador that seemed chiefly to inform the thinking of the [Westminster] divines when they considered preaching and preachers." Van Dixhoorn, *God's Ambassadors*, 116.

132. Maag, *Worshiping with the Reformers*, 58.

133. Burnett, "How to Preach," 112.

134. Dennison, "Zwingli, Fidei Ratio," 132.

word in preaching.[135] For it is in and through the word that God makes himself known.[136] In terms of his theology of proclamation, he held to a high view of Scripture, the absolute sovereignty of God in salvation, a Christocentric reading of the Bible, and the efficacy of the Spirit.[137] Following Zwingli's influence, the Reformed preaching tradition was shaped by Heinrich Bullinger and the Second Helvetic Confession (1566). The Second Helvetic was "the most widely received of the sixteenth-century Reformed confessions."[138] As a chief figure of the Reformed movement, the *Praedicatio verbi Dei est verbum Dei* theology is reflected in many seventeenth-century Reformed preachers.[139]

Additionally, various Reformed preaching manuals were published. For example, Andrew Hyperius's sixteenth-century work introduced an early modern expository structure to preaching.[140] Old writes, "Hyperius taught that in the preaching of a sermon, seven things should take place: the reading of the lesson, the invocation of God's blessing, the exordium or introduction, the division of the text, the confirmation of the message, the confutation of objections, and finally the conclusion."[141] Hyperius may have been an early forerunner to the plain sermon.[142] Also, Lambert Daneau's work *Method of Handling Holy Scripture* (1579) reveals "an important shift in how Scripture was being treated by contemporary Reformed preachers."[143] Daneau's method focused on one verse rather than a larger discourse of Scripture.[144] This resulted in the single verse being used "as a springboard to expound on the theological truth . . . contained in the verse."[145] This method is also reflected in William Perkins in the late sixteenth century and Richard Bernard in the seventeenth century.[146]

---

135. Old, *Age of the Reformation*, 48–50. See Zwingli, "Of the Clarity," 59–95.
136. Zwingli, "Of the Clarity," 61–62.
137. King, "Ulrich Zwingli," 303–7.
138. Dennison, "Second Helvetic Confession," 809.
139. Translation: *Preaching the word of God is the word of God*. For a brilliant work on Bullinger and the Second Helvetic Confession, see Halstead, "*Verbum Dei*."
140. Hyperius, *De formandis concionibus sacris*.
141. Old, *Age of the Reformation*, 371.
142. Pipa, "William Perkins," 140.
143. Burnett, "How to Preach," 115.
144. Burnett, "How to Preach," 115.
145. Burnett, "How to Preach," 115.
146. More will be included regarding Perkins's homiletical influence in this chapter. See Bernard, *Faithfull Shepheard*.

These factors would shape the homiletical trajectory of the English Reformed preaching tradition.

The Reformed view of preaching is codified in various confessional statements dating back to the sixteenth century. For example, the Bern Synod of 1532 states, "The preaching should be with great affection and fervent love to our hearers, and for correction and edification through God, such as takes place among the upright. Thus, the sheep of Christ hear the voice of their Lord, the true Shepherd, whom they know and whom they follow."[147] The 1563 Heidelberg Catechism asks, "What is the Office of the Keys?" The answer is, "The preaching of the Holy Gospel and Christian discipline; by these two, the kingdom of heaven is opened to believers and shut against unbelievers."[148] The Bohemian Confession of 1573 argues,

> Moreover, the preaching of the Word of God and of the gospel is the true ministry of grace instituted and commanded of Christ our Lord, in which the full and perfect will of God concerning eternal reconciliation necessary to salvation and made manifest in the Holy Scripture is declared and preached to all people. Christ charged His disciples with this doctrine in the words of this sentence: "Go into all the world and preach the gospel to every creature" (Mark 16:15).[149]

Additionally, the 1607 Confession of the Heidelberg Theologians states, "We believe furthermore that God has ordained the preaching of His gospel to that end that He is pleased to work in us faith in Christ, and that God the Lord is not insincere in this preaching, but rather, that it is His sincere will and intent that all men who hear such preaching would believe it and turn to Christ."[150]

Central to the 1618 Canons of Dort is the work of preaching. Preaching is mentioned in the third article under the heading of the doctrine of election: "And that men may be brought to believe, God mercifully sends the messengers of these most joyful tidings to whom He will and at what time He pleases; by whose ministry men are called to repentance and faith in Christ crucified."[151] In commenting on particular redemption, the

---

147. Dennison, "Bern Synod," 271.
148. Dennison, "Heidelberg Catechism," 788.
149. Dennison, "Bohemian Confession," 358.
150. Dennison, "Confession of the Heidelberg Theologians," 34.
151. Dennison, "Canons of Dort," 4:121.

authors maintain "the promise of the gospel is that whosoever believes in Christ crucified shall not perish, but have eternal life. This promise, together with the command to repent and believe, ought to be declared and published to all nations, and to all persons promiscuously and without distinction."[152] Additionally, all who come and believe in Christ through the word find rest and eternal life.[153] The Spirit illuminates the mind and regenerates the heart through the preaching of the word.[154] Furthermore, the Father preserves his elect by his word and Spirit unto the end.[155] Last, "And as it has pleased God, by the preaching of the gospel, to begin this work of grace in us, so He preserves, continues, and perfects it by the hearing and reading of His Word."[156]

Preaching was vital in furthering God's purposes among Reformed churches and pastors. Emerging out of ecclesiological conflict, Reformed preaching was pivotal in the life of the local church and the larger community. Furthermore, the preaching tradition would have a significant impact on English homiletics. As it specifically relates to the Reformed preaching of seventeenth-century England, two major factors gave rise to its prominence: John Calvin's homiletical theology and William Perkins's homiletical methodology. The following two sections explore the nuances of each factor.

THE FIRST MAJOR FACTOR: CALVIN'S HOMILETICAL THEOLOGY

As the Marian exiles returned to England during Elizabeth's reign, they were armed with John Calvin's theology and ecclesiology. Additionally, they possessed a Reformed homiletical theology. As such, the theological precursor to mid-sixteenth- and early seventeenth-century Puritan preaching was Calvin's theology of preaching.[157] Edwards argues, "Most English clergy operated out of an essentially Calvinist theological

---

152. Dennison, "Canons of Dort," 4:131.
153. Dennison, "Canons of Dort," 4:136.
154. Dennison, "Canons of Dort," 4:137.
155. Dennison, "Canons of Dort," 4:145.
156. Dennison, "Canons of Dort," 4:147.
157. Manetsch notes that Calvin's homiletic was shaped by Renaissance humanism, the homilies of Chrysostom, and his own reflection on the content and style of biblical writings. He further shows how Melanchthon's work influenced Calvin. See Manetsch, *Calvin's Company of Pastors*, 156–62.

framework. As a result, Calvin's highly exegetical understanding of the work of the preacher inevitably had its influence, especially among the more thoroughgoing Calvinists, those called Puritans."[158] Thus, Calvin was "the dominant theological influence in Elizabethan England."[159] Calvin summarizes his thoughts on preaching in the *Summary of Doctrine Concerning the Ministry of the Word and Sacraments*: "The end of the whole Gospel ministry is that God, the fountain of all felicity, communicate Christ to us who are disunited by sin and hence ruined, that we may from him enjoy eternal life; that in a word all heavenly treasures be so applied to us that they be no less ours than Christ's himself."[160] Calvin's proclamation theology can be summarized in four major elements supported by three theo-homiletical commitments.

First, he was an expositor of Scripture.[161] For Calvin, preaching was "formally bound to the Scriptures."[162] His understanding of the Bible as the word of God resulted in biblical exposition. Manetsch notes, "At the heart of Calvin's hermeneutic and theory of preaching stands a particular understanding of the nature and authority of the sacred text."[163] As a result, he confined "himself to the continuous exposition" of the text, thus, "the form of this [style of] preaching is determined by the movement of the text."[164] Calvin would focus on a clause or sentence within the context of that given text, resulting in a sermon form that was flexible.[165] His expository method was less refined stylistically than the Scholastic sermon and reflected a more patristic model of preaching. However, what is foundational for Calvin, therefore, became foundational for the Puritans who followed the Reformer—namely, an emphasis upon the word. The text of Scripture was the sole basis for the Reformed sermon.[166]

Second, he advocates for a Christocentric model of preaching. For Calvin, Christ was the apex of divine revelation in the Scripture.

---

158. Edwards, *History of Preaching*, 362.

159. Hall, *Puritans*, 17.

160. Calvin, "Summary of Doctrine," 171.

161. Broadus, *Lectures*, 115. Broadus states, "But Calvin gave the ablest, soundest, clearest expositions of Scripture that had been seen for a thousand years, and most of the other great Reformers worked in the same direction."

162. Parker, *John Calvin*, 117.

163. Manetsch, *Calvin's Company of Pastors*, 158.

164. Parker, *Calvin's Preaching*, 132.

165. Parker, *John Calvin*, 119.

166. Beeke, *Reformed Preaching*, 41.

Additionally, he said, "The Scriptures should be read with the aim of finding Christ in them."[167] This resulted in a sermon that brought the hearer to Christ. Moreover, Christ draws near to the hearer through the proclamation of the word. Parker concludes that "redemption of God in Christ" was heard daily from Saint Pierre's pulpit.[168] Additionally, the Christ-centeredness of the English Reformed sermon is evident. This Christocentric element of the Puritans parallels the notion of "preaching Christ," firmly rooting this sermonic style in the Reformed tradition. As Perkins states, all preaching is "preach one Christ, by Christ, to the praise of Christ."[169]

Third, his preaching can be described as "sacramental preaching."[170] As Leith states, "Calvin thought of preaching as the primary means by which God's presence becomes actual to us and by which God's work is accomplished in individual life and in the community."[171] Also, Yuille asserts, "Perkins adopted Calvin's view [sacramental preaching], stressing the efficacy of God's Word, preached in the power of the Holy Spirit. And it is this conviction that led him to formulate a method of preaching that would . . . best achieve its experiential end."[172]

Last, Calvin preached experientially. Beeke argues that "Calvin believed that the truth of Scripture is foundational to Christianity, yet truth must be experienced in the form of experimental knowledge."[173] The truth of Scripture must be experienced personally. Thus, those who communicate the word must also experience the transforming reality of

167. Manetsch, *Calvin's Company of Pastors*, 161.
168. Parker, *John Calvin*, 122.
169. Perkins, *Art of Prophesying*, 356.
170. John Calvin, *Institutes*, 4.14.4. In particular, see Beach, "Real Presence of Christ," 92n38. Beach's explanation of "sacramental preaching" is assumed in this book. He writes, "Sacramental is used to express the reality of God's presence through human instrumentation or divine activity through human labor. God is agent; humans are instruments. Although the notion of a sacramental word might more immediately be associated with the 'word character' of the sacraments, as when Augustine calls a sacrament 'a visible word,' this phrase refers to the sacramental character of the word itself—that is to say, it refers to the presence of Christ in, with, and through the word proclaimed. The sacramental character of the word means that God's word genuinely belongs to God, that it is from God and of God; it is his speech. Therefore God, through the Holy Spirit, is speaking and is the agent of grace. 'Sacramental Word,' therefore, has no sacerdotal connotations. God does not transfer his work to humans or cloth human beings (or a human institution) with his power to dispense grace ex opere operato."
171. Leith, "Calvin's Doctrine," 29.
172. Yuille, "Simple Method," 225.
173. Beeke, *Reformed Preaching*, 24.

the word. Beeke also states, "The Puritan preachers, who learned from the Reformers, were masters of the art of application."[174] This art of application is foundational to experiential preaching.

Three Theo-Homiletical Commitments

Three *theo-homiletical* commitments ground Calvin's high view of preaching. First, in preaching there is a *minister externus* and *minister internus*. Calvin claims,

> When we say that the Holy Spirit uses an *external minister* (*minister externus*) as instrument, we mean this: both in the preaching of the Word and in the use of the sacraments, there are two ministers, who have distinct offices. The (*a*) external minister administers the vocal word. . . . But the *internal minister* (*minister internus*), who is the Holy Spirit, freely works internally, while by his secret virtue he effects in the hearts of whomsoever he will their union with Christ through one faith. This union is a thing internal, heavenly and indestructible.[175]

There is a synergetic relationship between the two ministers in the act of preaching. As a result, "We believe this communication to be (*a*) mystical, and incomprehensible to human reason, and (*b*) spiritual, since it is effected by the Holy Spirit."[176] Also, "Christ does not otherwise dwell in us than through his Spirit, nor in any other way communicates himself to us than through the same Spirit."[177] For Calvin, union with Christ by means of the Spirit is the key that unlocks the experiential nature of preaching. Preaching is participatory. This conviction is found throughout the Puritan preachers and Benjamin Keach, as will be demonstrated.

Second, Calvin proposed that the preached word by the Spirit in human communication is indeed the word of God. He remarks, "For among the many noble endowments with which God has adorned the human race, one of the most remarkable is, that he deigns to consecrate the mouths and tongues of men to his service, making his own voice to be heard in them."[178] God is so closely identified with his preached word

---

174. Beeke, *Living for God's Glory*, 260.
175. Calvin, "Summary of Doctrine," 173.
176. Calvin, "Summary of Doctrine," 171.
177. Calvin, "Summary of Doctrine," 172.
178. Calvin, *Institutes*, 4.1.5.

that "it may be said that the mouth of the prophet was the mouth of God himself."[179] This is akin to Calvin's theological mentor, Augustine. Central to an Augustinian theology of proclamation is the relationship between the words of Scripture, Christ the embodied Word, and the words of the preacher. Augustine's sermons were "built on the bedrock on the intimate relationship between the sermon and Scripture."[180] It is in the words of the preacher, in so far as those words are faithful to Scripture, that Christ becomes present.[181] Morgan writes, "Christian speech, for Augustine, possesses its own embodiment. Words are humble, they do not draw attention to themselves; and they are humble to the extent that they reveal what they seek to speak of. . . . Christian speech thereby becomes the transaction point for the embodied eschatological future."[182] It is in preaching that "Christian speech both emerges from God's participation in humanity and aspires to human participation in God."[183] For Augustine, words are not static. Rather, they are made performative by means of the Spirit.[184] Augustine was convinced that mere human words do not possess the power to transform.[185] The sermon was the "transaction point" by which God's word is revealed through human words. In this way, the preached word is the means through which the incarnate-risen Word communicates. Augustine maintained that Christ spoke through the biblical text mediated by the words of the preacher.

Likewise, Calvin is theologically nuanced, clarifying that the preacher's words are not replacing the biblical word proclaimed. Yet, when the Spirit accompanies the preached word, the word spoken is indeed the word of God.[186] Calvin states that God, "the author of preaching connects his Spirit with it, and then promises a beneficial result."[187] Wallace asserts that this "sacramental action" is a union that "takes place between the divine element—the Spirit or action of God—and the human activity."[188]

---

179. Wallace, *Calvin's Doctrine*, 82.
180. Glowasky, *Rhetoric and Scripture*, 30.
181. Turley, "Theology of Preaching," 12.
182. Morgan, *Incarnation of the Word*, 90.
183. Morgan, *Incarnation of the Word*, 99.
184. Morgan, *Incarnation of the Word*, 97.
185. See Cary, *Outward Signs*. Also, see Cary, "Inner Word."
186. See Cunnington, *Preaching*, 88–89.
187. Calvin, *Institutes*, 4.1.6.
188. Wallace, *Calvin's Doctrine*, 159.

Third, in Calvin's understanding of preaching there is an intrinsic relationship between the word of God and the presence of God. Leith acknowledges this relationship, stating, "In doctrine he [Calvin] knew that the words of the sermon are at best frail, human words, but words which can by the power of the Holy Spirit become the occasion of the presence of God."[189] Preaching is a "sign of God's presence."[190] Gerrish notes, "The word is not simply information about God; it is the instrument through which union with Christ is effected and his grace is imparted.... In this sense, it is the sacramental word."[191] Calvin ties together God's sacramental presence and preaching in his commentary on Isa 50:2. He writes, "Now, the Lord is said to 'come' when he gives any token of his presence. He approaches by the preaching of the Word."[192]

The proclamation of the word, in the power of the Spirit, becomes a pledge of God's presence among his gathered people. Calvin's sacramental preaching emphasis flows from his larger Eucharistic theology.[193] Again, drawing from Augustine, Calvin states that the sacrament is a "visible sign of a sacred thing or a visible form of an invisible grace."[194] As such, "Sacraments ... present Christ the more clearly to us."[195] They are a "seal of the promises of God" in Christ.[196] The sacraments are "evidences of divine grace" to be received by faith.[197] The means of grace are made effective by the agency of the Spirit in the same way the word is made effective.[198] Calvin would conclude, "Let it be a fixed point that the office of the sacraments differs not from the word of God; and this is to hold forth and offer Christ to us, and in him, the treasures of heavenly grace."[199] Parker draws the conclusion, "Just as Christ is present at the Supper spiritually, that is, by the working of the Spirit, so he is present in the preaching spiritually—by the working of the Spirit."[200]

189. Leith, "Calvin's Doctrine," 32.
190. Wallace, *Calvin's Doctrine*, 84.
191. Gerrish, *Grace and Gratitude*, 76.
192. Wallace, *Calvin's Doctrine*, 85.
193. Gerrish, *Grace and Gratitude*, 82.
194. Calvin, *Institutes*, 4.14.1.
195. Calvin, *Institutes*, 4.14.22.
196. Calvin, *Institutes*, 4.14.20.
197. Calvin, *Institutes*, 4.14.7.
198. Calvin, *Institutes*, 4.14.9.
199. Calvin, *Institutes*, 4.14.17.
200. Parker, *Calvin's Preaching*, 42.

Additionally, for Augustine, the risen Christ speaks by means of his Spirit. In the same way that the Spirit is active in the mystery of the Eucharist, he is operative in preaching. Yet, unlike the Eucharist, "it is through the preaching of the church . . . that our temporal engagement with this mystery first occurs."[201] As the elemental properties of the sacrament (bread and wine) cannot within themselves become efficacious, preaching also lacks the ability. As Carroll notes, "For Augustine, Scripture, sacrament, and sermon formed an indissoluble unity . . . an all-embracing allegory. This element unites his celebration of the Mystery in Word and Sacrament with his preaching."[202] In and through the proclamation of the word, Christ is present in the church and remains in heaven. Morgan again notes,

> Preaching, that is, inasmuch as it gives insight into the nature of God, lifts human persons out of 'this world' and locates them somewhere between the world into which the light of God came without being recognized, and the next world where God will be fully visually apparent. Words, in short, form the bridge between this world and the next, creating the possibility of the mind's cognition of eternal reality.[203]

For Calvin, following Augustine, these realities are efficacious for believers because of their union with Christ. He claims, "The whole comes to this that the Holy Spirit is the bond by which Christ effectually binds us to himself."[204] He adds, "By the same grace and energy of the Spirit we become his members, so that he keeps us under him and we in our turn possess him."[205] Calvin writes, "For this is the design of the gospel, that Christ may become ours, and that we may be ingrafted into his body. Now when the Father gives him to us in possession, he also communicates himself to us in him; and hence arises a participation in every benefit."[206] Preaching communicates Christ, as Parker states: "Thus Christ, the substance of the gospel, offers in it his broken body and shed blood."[207] Additionally, there is a Trinitarian basis: "We believe the Holy

---

201. Morgan, *Incarnation of the Word*, 137.
202. Carroll, *Preaching the Word*, 182.
203. Morgan, *Incarnation of the Word*, 139.
204. Calvin, *Institutes*, 3.1.1.
205. Calvin, *Institutes*, 3.1.3.
206. Calvin, *Commentaries*, 1:60.
207. Parker, *John Calvin*, 123.

Spirit to effect this union rests on a certain ground, namely this: Whatever (*a*) the Father or (*b*) the Son does to bring the faithful to salvation, Holy Scripture testifies that each operates through the Holy Spirit."[208]

As is clear, Calvin's language in discussing the act of preaching is like that of the sacraments. He claims, "The Lord offers us his mercy, and pledge of his grace, both in his sacred word and in the sacraments."[209] In his commentary on 2 Cor 3:6 he states, "The nature of the gospel is to teach *spiritually*, because it is the instrument of Christ's grace."[210] Calvin, in his *Short Treatise of the Lord's Supper* writes, "But just as God has placed all fulness of life in Jesus, in order to communicate it to us by his means, so he ordained his word as the instrument by which Jesus Christ, with all his graces, is dispensed to us."[211] To be more explicit, in his biography of the Reformer, Parker asserts, "[For Calvin] the sermon, we might say, is the audible Eucharist. . . . Calvin was fond of saying that in the pulpit Christ must preside."[212] Therefore, the end goal of Calvin's preaching was "union with Christ."[213]

Calvin's homiletical theology is established in his deep admiration for the Bible as God's word and the mysterious working of God's Spirit. Calvin applies the function of the sacraments often found in Medieval theology to preaching, thereby viewing proclamation as a means of grace.[214] For Calvin and those that followed, a rich and robust theology of preaching grounded biblical exposition. This homiletical theology grounds the English Reformed preaching tradition as reflected in the Puritans.

THE SECOND MAJOR FACTOR: WILLIAM PERKINS'S HOMILETICAL METHODOLOGY

Stephen Holmes states, "There was, in the seventeenth century, a distinctive Puritan/Nonconformist tradition of preaching, classically illustrated in Perkins' famous *Arte of Prophesying*."[215] William Perkins is

---

208. Calvin, "Summary of Doctrine," 172.
209. Calvin, *Institutes*, 4.14.7.
210. Calvin, *Commentaries*, 2:173.
211. Calvin, *Short Treatise*, 166.
212. Parker, *John Calvin*, 123.
213. Gerrish, *Grace and Gratitude*, 82.
214. Gerrish, *Grace and Gratitude*, 76.
215. Holmes, "Nonconformist Preaching and Liturgy," 253.

considered "the principal architect of Elizabethan Puritanism."[216] In *The Art of Prophesying*, Perkins "articulated the new Reformed Method and the plain style in a concise fashion, bringing together the fruits of homiletic principles developed earlier in the century in England and on the continent."[217] Also,

> Perkins's *The Arte of Prophesying* was not revolutionary in its presentation of interpretive method. . . . Though his preaching manual addressed the preparation and delivery of sermons, which included sustained attention to proper exegetical method, his contributions to homiletics and biblical interpretation were not new. . . . He offered a usable, understandable, and repeatable summary of a Reformed method of interpretation.[218]

The concise manual demonstrates a Reformed hermeneutic and its application to homiletics. Perkins's homiletical presuppositions are thoroughly Reformed, as has already been demonstrated. Nevertheless, Perkins's work proved to be important for the English Reformed preaching tradition. The following is a summary of his work.[219]

First, Perkins establishes two parts to *prophecy*: preaching the word and public prayer.[220] These ministerial actions echo the Old Testament prophets and the New Testament apostles. Perkins's use of the word *prophesying* is related to his understanding of Jesus, for he says that "the art of prophecy" is "preaching the Word in the name and room of Christ."[221] Old argues, "We understand that to mean that Christian preaching is a continuation of the teaching ministry of Jesus. . . . The fact that Perkins uses the word 'prophesying' in the title of his preaching manual makes it clear that he is purposely trying to use the vocabulary of the New Testament."[222] Preaching is, therefore, prophetic because it declares the word of God in the name of Christ.

Perkins grounds the act of prophesying/preaching in 1 Cor 14:3, 1 Cor 14:24, and Rom 1:9, further arguing that this act "is a solemn public

---

216. Pipa, "William Perkins," 4.
217. Ford, "Preaching," 76.
218. Ballitch, *Gloss & Text*, 56–57.
219. Milioni, "William Perkins."
220. Perkins, *Art of Prophesying*, 290.
221. Perkins, *Art of Prophesying*, 290.
222. Old, *Age of Reformation*, 263. It is important to note that the idea of "prophesying" was used within Puritan circles as homiletical conferences were called "prophesyings" in 1564. See Davies, *Worship and Theology*, 297–98.

utterance by the prophet, related to the worship of God and the salvation of our neighbors."[223] For Perkins, the act of preaching was both doxological and evangelistic.[224]

The high view of Scripture permeated Perkins's view of preaching. He writes, "The perfect and equal object of preaching is the Word of God."[225] He articulates that the nature of Scripture can be described in terms of its perfection, purity, and eternity.[226] By perfection, Perkins argues that the Scripture is sufficient and complete. The purity of Scripture means, according to Perkins, that the word does not contain errors. Last, Perkins states that the word is eternal, in that it "cannot pass away until everything it commands has been fully accomplished."[227] As a result, the word has the power to "discern the spirit of man" and "to bind the conscience is to constrain it either to accuse us or to excuse us of sin before God."[228]

This leads Perkins to discuss the issue of interpretation.[229] He develops the importance of the literal meaning and various exegetical means to obtain this meaning. He states, "Preparation has two parts: interpretation, and right division (or cutting). Interpretation is the opening of the words and sentences of the Scripture that one entire and natural sense may appear."[230] Again, the emphasis is on obtaining the literal and plain meaning of Scripture. After establishing the principles for interpreting Scripture, Perkins states there are two more interpretive elements: resolution/partition, and application.[231] First, the resolution/partition is the unfolding of the passage into its various doctrines.[232] For Perkins, the deduction of the biblical doctrine follows the interpretation of Scripture. He notes "that collections ought to be right and sound, that is to say, derived from the genuine and proper meaning of the Scripture."[233]

---

223. Perkins, *Art of Prophesying*, 289.
224. Old, *Age of Reformation*, 261.
225. Perkins, *Art of Prophesying*, 291.
226. Perkins, *Art of Prophesying*, 291–92.
227. Perkins, *Art of Prophesying*, 292.
228. Perkins, *Art of Prophesying*, 292.
229. Perkins, *Art of Prophesying*, 301. For a more detailed look at Perkins's interpretative method, see Lea, "Hermeneutics of the Puritans," and Gane, "Exegetical Methods."
230. Perkins, *Art of Prophesying*, 303.
231. Perkins, *Art of Prophesying*, 329.
232. Perkins, *Art of Prophesying*, 329.
233. Perkins, *Art of Prophesying*, 331.

He continues to discuss application/uses. He writes, "Application is that whereby the doctrine rightly collected is diversely fitted according as place, time, and person do require."[234] The basic principle of application is whether the doctrine is a statement concerning the law or the gospel. As a result, application can be both mental and practical. In this regard, Perkins lists seven basic ways of applying doctrine, which are related to seven different spiritual conditions.[235] He concludes, "Thus, any place of Scripture ought to be handled, yet so as that all the doctrines are not propounded to the people, but those only which may be fitly applied to our times and to the present condition of the church. And they must not only be choice ones, but also few, lest the hearers are overcharged with their multitude."[236]

In delivering the sermon, Perkins identifies two specific requirements. First, "Human wisdom must be concealed, whether it is in the matter of the sermon or in the setting forth of the words, because the preaching of the Word is the testimony of God and the profession of the knowledge of Christ and not of human skill."[237] Second, "The demonstration of the Spirit is when the minister of the Word does in the time of preaching so behave himself that all, even ignorant persons and unbelievers, may judge that it is not so much he who speaks as the Spirit of God in him and by him."[238] This leads Perkins to conclude with the plain method. He states:

> The order and sum of the sacred and only method of preaching: 1) To read the text distinctly out of the canonical Scriptures; 2) To give the sense and understanding of it, being read, by the Scripture itself; 3) To collect a few and profitable points of doctrine out of the natural sense; 4) To apply (if he has the gift) the doctrines rightly collected to the life and manners of men in a simple and plain speech.[239]

Yuille summarizes Perkins's theology of preaching as experiential in the end, methodological in approach, and supernatural in effect.[240]

---

234. Perkins, *Art of Prophesying*, 334.
235. Perkins, *Art of Prophesying*, 335–43.
236. Perkins, *Art of Prophesying*, 347.
237. Perkins, *Art of Prophesying*, 349
238. Perkins, *Art of Prophesying*, 349.
239. Perkins, *Art of Prophesying*, 356.
240. Yuille, "Simple Method," 230.

Through his influence, the *plain sermon* became the dominant sermon method during the seventeenth century.[241] Perkins's homiletical methodology is grounded in two influences.

Philosophical Influences in Perkins's Preaching

Scholarship has demonstrated that one of the motivating factors for Perkins and the articulation of his homiletic was the guidance of Ramus.[242] Peter Ramus was a French philosopher-logician (1515–1572) who sought to reorganize dialectic and logic, which subsequently influenced rhetoric.[243] McKim argues,

> Ramus wished to liberate logic from the highly formalized, scientific structure of its medieval heritage.... For Ramus this meant the simplification of Aristotelian "categories" into "arguments" or "concepts." A logician's task was one of classification, arranging concepts in such a fashion as to make them understandable and memorable. "Method" was Ramus' term for the orderly presentation of a subject.[244]

Ramus divided dialectic into three parts: a natural origin, a theory of discourse, and a practical application.[245] The Ramus method is seen in the way Perkins structures the plain sermon, a sermonic movement of doctrine, reason, and application.

Furthermore, Ramism sought to bring unity between theology and ethics, which further established the doctrine-use scheme that Perkins followed.[246] Among the Puritans, the classical canons of rhetoric were minor aspects of their sermons. Kater posits, "Ramus proposed that invention and arrangement belong to logic, while style and delivery are considered as 'rhetoric.' In this method, the sermon is designed primarily with a clear and logical argument."[247] The lack of rhetorical effect in some of the Puritans' preaching was not due to their negative disposition of

---

241. Hunt, *Art of Hearing*, 96.
242. McKim, "Functions of Ramism."
243. McKim, "Functions of Ramism," 504–5.
244. McKim, "Functions of Ramism," 504.
245. Hunt, *Art of Hearing*, 96.
246. McKim, "Functions of Ramism," 508.
247. Kater, "Puritan Preaching and Pathos," 47.

its persuasive uses but rather due to their emphasis upon the nature and function of the sermon itself.

Ramus also influenced Perkins regarding a "general to specific" approach to discourse. This is reflected in Perkins's emphasis on application or uses. Puritan sermons were highly practical as the application was both mental and ethical/practical. Last, the Ramist influence upon Perkins appears primarily in the way he organized his material.[248] Nevertheless, the Puritan preacher did not "slavishly follow Ramus."[249] Perkins retained Aristotelian rhetorical concepts (logos, ethos, pathos) and Augustinian aspects.[250]

Hermeneutical Influences in Perkins's Preaching

Writing on the Reformed hermeneutic, Richard Muller, in *Post-Reformation Reformed Dogmatics*, shows:

1. In order to get at a right interpretation the interpreter must be a person with saving faith, must have a right heart, and must pray to the Holy Spirit for illumination.
2. There is "a single literal and grammatical meaning of the text of Scripture and . . . [they] argue that no extrapolated allegorical, tropological, or anagogical sense of the text can ever be a firm basis for theological formulation."
3. "Words . . . can have only a single sense in any particular place—otherwise there is ambiguity of meaning and ambiguity breeds errors in interpretation," and this sense can be either simple or mixed.
4. The simple sense can be either "proper and grammatical" or "figurative or tropical."
5. An important interpretive rule was that of the analogy of Scripture.
6. The analogy of faith included the "practice of the church, the decrees of the sounder councils, and the expositions of the fathers" as long as they agreed with Scripture and the analogy of Scripture.

---

248. Pipa, "William Perkins," 167.
249. Pipa, "William Perkins," 164.
250. Van Hof, "Theory of Sermon Rhetoric," 287.

7. The text of Scripture was accommodated and revelation was progressive.[251]

These elements are reflected in Perkins. The Puritan hermeneutic was grounded in understanding the literal meaning of a particular text. This led them to reject the Catholic fourfold sense of Scripture. As Perkins notes, "There is one only sense, and the same is the literal. An allegory is only a certain manner of uttering the same sense. The anagoge and tropology are ways whereby the sense may be applied."[252] Franks notes that for Perkins, these other "meanings" are located within the literal meaning of a text. Thus, the Puritans indeed valued the literal sense, but viewed allegory, tropology, and analogy as "aspects" of the literal meaning.[253]

Franks demonstrates that the Puritans exhibited the most mature expression of premodern exegesis.[254] This affected the way the Puritans preached Christ from the Old Testament. In *The Art of Prophesying*, Perkins proceeds to discuss "subordinate means to help" interpret a passage of Scripture, the analogy of faith, the circumstances of the particular passage, and comparison with other passages.[255]

Historically, the emphasis on the literal meaning of the text is derived from Calvin's hermeneutic.[256] James Thomas Ford provides insight when he claims, "Instrumental in the development of biblical hermeneutics and homiletics was the *prophezei* of Zurich . . . and Geneva . . . where Reformed expositors displayed the same basic hermeneutic principles in their sermons as in their commentaries . . . avoiding the use of allegory . . . and favoring the literal historical method."[257] This resulted in the Puritans adopting an interpretation method grounded in the inerrancy and sufficiency of Scripture.

This hermeneutic was a defining mark between many Puritans and Anglicans. Erwin Gane clearly reveals, "It was a hermeneutical difference, based not on different concepts of Bible inspirations, but on different understandings of the interpretation and application of specific spiritual

---

251. Muller, *Holy Scripture*, 479–87; 505.
252. Perkins, *Art of Prophesying*, 303.
253. Franks, "Rightly Handling," 46.
254. Franks, "Rightly Handling," 52.
255. Perkins, *Art of Prophesying*, 303.
256. Manetsch, *Calvin's Company of Pastors*, 160.
257. Ford, "Preaching," 69.

passages."[258] He continues, "The results of the Puritan hermeneutic were theological as well as practical."[259] While Anglican preachers generally valued the Reformed principle of *sola Scriptura*, it appears they were more comfortable with a hermeneutic that balanced both Geneva and Rome. Thus, the English Reformed plain sermon was simply the exposition of the plain sense of a biblical text. Therefore, this theologically oriented hermeneutic affected the homiletic of these Puritans.

THE THIRD MAJOR FACTOR: ENGLISH REFORMED PLAIN PREACHING

Calvin's homiletical theology and Perkins's homiletical method meshed into the Reformed plain preaching of the Puritans. Reformed plain preaching did not follow strictly the patristic homiletical form of Calvin. Rather, it was closely akin to a more scholastic or analytical form. Old writes, "English Puritanism is an expression of Protestant scholasticism," which sought to be "expository."[260] The Reformed plain preaching of the Puritans was unique in its hermeneutical and theological rigor while seeking to be expository and plain. Most Puritans broadly adopted this doctrine-use scheme.[261] Puritans believed that plain preaching aided in the conversion of individuals.[262] This opposed Catholicism, which held the sacraments as the means for obtaining salvation. For the faithful, preaching was the means of grace.[263] Winship notes, "The Reformation's message of justification by faith alone succeeded all too well in 'Protestantizing' the laity who heard it away from an anxiety-ridden, priest-driven rigorous Christianity."[264] Nothing proved more successful in reforming the heart and mind of Protestant ideology than the pulpit. Old argues, "If the Reformation institutionalized in the sixteenth century was to have its full effect, it needed to be carried into the hearts and minds of Christians and transform the life of the whole congregation . . . for the preaching of the Word of God was the means God had given for

258. Gane, "Exegetical Methods," 22–23.
259. Gane, "Exegetical Methods," 23.
260. Old, *Age of Reformation*, 326.
261. Pipa, "William Perkins," 177.
262. Ryrie, *Being Protestant*, 352–62.
263. Ryrie, *Being Protestant*, 352.
264. Winship, "Weak Christians," 468.

the reforming of the heart."[265] Thus, "The sermon was the defining event of early modern Protestant worship. The preacher, duly called to his . . . vocation by God and recognized by the Church, spoke the word of God to the people."[266]

Three Theological Convictions

By the mid-seventeenth century, *The Directory for the Public Worship of God* states, "Preaching of the word being the power of God unto salvation, one of the greatest and most excellent works belonging to the ministry of the gospel, should be so performed that the workman needs not be ashamed but may save himself and those that hear him."[267] The sermon was central to advancing the aims of late sixteenth- and seventeenth-century Puritanism. As Davies argues, "For the Puritan, the proclamation of the Gospel through preaching brought men to the existential crossroads, where the way led either to life everlasting or to destruction, and the aim of his preaching was to convert his hearers from worldliness to godliness. He wished to transform, not merely to inform."[268]

The Puritan emphasis on preaching in a Reformed plain manner was practical and theological. First, it was practical to the extent that the pure truth of the word should be expounded plainly for their hearers. Second, it was theological in that the truth of the word possessed the power to bring the hearers to Christ. In summarizing the Reformed plain preaching of the Puritans, Davies writes,

> The Puritan sermon was simple. . . . It did not provide a vehicle for the richer resources of rhetoric, with set pieces of sustained eloquence, grandiose comparisons and contrast, tirades, apostrophe, and so forth. . . . Nor did the sermon form lend itself to brilliant word analysis, patristic erudition, metaphysical and far-fetched conceits, and sheer sparkle of Lancelot Andrewes. Such elaborate rhetoric, "taffeta terms," and ornate diction were suitable for sermons on state occasions, but it meant that the Word of God, which is sharper than any sword, and which could pierce to the quick of the conscience, remained sheathed in a jeweled scabbard. The Puritan sermon was no ceremonial sword; least

---

265. Old, *Age of the Reformation*, 252.
266. Ryrie, *Being Protestant*, 351.
267. Westminster Assembly, "Directory for the Public Worship of God," 485.
268. Davies, *Worship and Theology*, 294–95.

of all was it like the painted, wooden sword of a homily officially prescribed. It was a lithe, lean, sharp instrument, poised to strike the soul. Thus, a simple, straightforward form for the sermon was felt to be appropriate to the Gospel itself, a reminder that the preachers were after all clay vessels, yet containers of the Gospel, that the greatest preacher of Christ the world had seen, St. Paul, had insisted that the Gospel was to be preached not by words of eloquence but by the integrity of conviction.[269]

While diverse, the Puritans shared at least three theological convictions that motivated their attitudes and priorities, particularly related to their preaching. First, the Puritans sought to carry forth the Reformed principle of *sola Scriptura*.[270] Van Dixhoorn argues that while the Puritans did not hold a monopoly on a high view of Scripture, it was nevertheless the very heart of Puritanism and Puritan preaching.[271]

This meant that the Puritans desired the whole of the Christian life and the church to be ordered according to Scripture. As a result, "Every area of life came under the influence of God and the guidance of the Word."[272] The national church during the early seventeenth century held the conviction that various Catholic traditions should be retained, while the Puritans argued that the Scriptures should govern the Christian life and church.[273]

The Puritans believed that the Bible was God's word in that it was of divine origin. John Owen writes, "The whole authority of the Scripture . . . depends solely on its divine original origin. . . . The Scripture hath all its authority from its Author."[274] Unequivocally, the Puritans believed in the inspiration of Scripture. Ryken states, "The Puritans' line of reasoning on biblical authority is impeccable: if God is the author of Scripture, it cannot lie, and if it does not deceive, it must be inerrant and infallible."[275]

Furthermore, the Puritans believed that the Bible was sufficient. As Baxter states, "The Scripture sufficiency must be maintained, and nothing

---

269. Davies, *Worship and Theology*, 307–8. While there are some nuances that could be made in Davies's description, there is general agreement with his assessment.

270. See Thompson, "*Sola Scriptura*."

271. Van Dixhoorn, *God's Ambassadors*, 16.

272. Lewis, *Genius of Puritanism*, 12.

273. Davies, *Worship and Theology*, 51.

274. Owen, *Works*, 16:297; see also 309.

275. Ryken, *Worldly Saints*, 141. Ryken argues that Rutherford, Ames, Baxter, and Owen all expressed their belief in the inspiration, inerrancy, and infallibility of Scripture.

beyond it imposed on others; and if papists, or others, call to us for the standard and rule of our religion, it is the Bible that we must show them, rather than any confessions of churches, or writings of men."[276] The Scripture, as the word of God, is the source of power because the word brings transformation. Watson exclaims, "Conform to Scripture, let us lead Scripture lives. O that the Bible might be seen printed in our lives!"[277]

Second, for the Puritans, the role of the pastor was foundational to the church and the Christian life. John Flavel writes, "Let us so study and preach, let us so pray and converse among our people, that we may both save ourselves and them that hear us."[278] Bickel stresses that the pastoral ministry of the Puritans was comprised of catechizing, counseling, comforting, and communing with those under their spiritual care.[279] These pastoral responsibilities defined Puritan pastors. *The Directory of Public Worship* states that the minister should perform his task:

1. Painfully, not doing the work of the Lord negligently
2. Plainly
3. Faithfully
4. Wisely
5. Gravely
6. With loving affection
7. As taught of God, and persuaded in his own heart, that all that he teacheth is the truth of Christ[280]

Preaching is the central function of the Puritan pastoral office. John Owen writes, "The first and principal duty of a pastor is *to feed the flock* by diligent preaching of the word."[281] Again, Owen states, "A man is a pastor unto them whom he feeds by pastoral teaching, and to no more, and he that doth not so feed is no pastor."[282] For Owen, the pastoral office was a teaching office. A pastor who did not preach was "no pastor." Owen also claims that the work and duty of pastoral preaching require five elements: spiritual wisdom and understanding; experience of the power of

---

276. Baxter, *Reformed Pastor*, 132.
277. Watson, *Body of Practical Divinity*, 29.
278. Flavel, "Character," 583.
279. Bickel, *Light and Heat*, 71.
280. Westminster Assembly, "Directory for the Public Worship of God," 487–88.
281. Owen, *Works*, 16:74.
282. Owen, *Works*, 16:75.

the truth; skill to divide the word; prudent and diligent consideration of the church; zeal for the glory of God and compassion for souls.[283]

Third, the Puritans believed that the preacher possessed a significant ambassadorial role in preaching. This is drawn from the ministerial reorientation that occurred in the early sixteenth century.[284] Davies notes, concerning Puritan proclamation, "Preaching was, in short, the declaration of the transforming revelation of the living God confirmed in the hearts of the believers by the interior witness of the Holy Spirit."[285] Van Dixhoorn writes, "It is the metaphor of ambassador that seemed chiefly to inform the thinking of the divines when they considered preaching and preachers."[286]

For the Puritans, ambassadorial preaching possessed an authoritative and representative function. Jeremiah Burroughs (1599–1646) draws out various implications regarding the ambassadorial role of the minister.[287] He says "that a Minister of the Gospel when he comes, is an Ambassador; he comes in Christ's stead, and what he shall deliver (according to his Commission) is to be looked at as if God, and as if Jesus Christ did preach unto you." Burroughs amplifies this when he says, "Ministers of the Gospel, they come to you in the name of the King of Heaven, in the name of Jesus Christ. . . . There is a kind of a representation even of the person of Christ in them."[288] He further explains,

> So just thus it is with people, they come [now] to hear the ministry of the word; they heart a sound in their ears, and what they hear is very good; but they look only at a man; the man speaks . . . but they do know it is God's voice. . . . And when he pleads with you, you should think that it is Christ that is pleading with you; when he is opening of any scripture to you, you should think that Jesus Christ is opening that Scripture to you, and when you come with such a heart, then God opens all his mind to you.[289]

---

283. Owen, *Works*, 16:75–77.

284. See the section "The Reform of Ministerial Identity and Praxis" of this chapter for this argument.

285. Davies, *Worship and Theology*, 295.

286. Van Dixhoorn, *God's Ambassadors*, 116.

287. Burroughs, *Gospel Reconciliation*, 280–91.

288. Burroughs, *Gospel Reconciliation*, 282.

289. Burroughs, *Gospel Reconciliation*, 287–88.

Additionally, Thomas Brooks (1608–1680) states, "Witness his continuing the ministry of reconciliation among poor sinners in all ages; witness the constant treaties, that by his ambassadors and Spirit he still hath with poor sinners about the things of their peace."[290] Again, "Kings and princes have their ambassadors in very high account: so has God his."[291] Last, John Owen (1616–1683) argues, "The names of 'ambassadors,' 'stewards,' and the like, wherewith they are often honoured, are figurative, and given unto them by allusion only."[292] The ambassador metaphor, in some sense, was a Reformed identity marker.

ASPECTS OF A REFORMED THEOLOGY OF PREACHING

Calvin's homiletical theology and Perkins's homiletical method provided the foundation for the Reformed plain preaching of the Puritans. This is demonstrated in the Puritan's view of the Scriptures, the pastor's vocation, and the ambassador's preaching function. There is a unique vitality that is expressed in English Reformed preaching. In commenting on the Westminster Assembly's role in seventeenth-century homiletics, Van Dixhoorn writes,

> What was true of pulpit theology at the assembly was true for Presbyterians and Congregationalists for the next two centuries. Preaching held a central place in services of worship and in personal piety, thus providing a unifying principle among English dissenters.... Preaching was regarded as central to Christian life and worship, and the preaching of God's ambassadors was still seen as the ordinary means that God extraordinarily blessed.[293]

Schuringa identifies "four critical dimensions of Reformed preaching" that are helpful when considering the broad scope of the tradition. First, the subject of preaching. Second, preaching as a means of grace. Third, the administration of the word. Fourth, the preacher's own experience.[294] Reformed preaching was thoroughly scriptural. The tradition sought to expound the Bible with a particular experiential emphasis. Thus, in the

---

290. Brooks, *Complete Works*, 245–46.
291. Brooks, *Complete Works*, 225.
292. Owen, *Works*, 13:20.
293. Van Dixhoorn, *God's Ambassadors*, 179.
294. Schuringa, "Vitality of Reformed Preaching."

public administration of the word, Christ brings transformation by his Spirit, thereby communicating grace to the hearers. This has a definitive impact on the life of the preacher and congregation. Nimmo further nuances some of these dimensions. Specifically, he highlights the external proclamation of the word and the internal work of the Spirit in the preaching event.[295] Joel Beeke, in his work *Reformed Preaching*, sets forth a contemporary understanding of this preaching tradition. He writes, "Reformed experiential preaching is preaching that applies the truth of God to the hearts of people to show how things ought to go, do go, and ultimately will go. . . . We could say that the Reformed experiential preacher receives God's Word into his heart and then preaches it to the minds, hearts, and lives of his people."[296]

Thus, those within the Reformed preaching tradition saw themselves standing as Christ's ambassadors speaking to God's people. As opposed to the Catholic priest, there was a prophetic and authoritative function in their proclamation. The Reformed preacher was a minister, a steward of the sacred mysteries of God. He was not merely a pastor, but a believing Christian who had experienced the transformative power of the gospel. Preaching was empowered by the Spirit, the instrumental means of regeneration. As the external word goes forth, the Spirit ministers grace to those who believe.

SUMMARY

The Puritan use of the plain sermon was the result of hermeneutically and theologically informed presuppositions. It was the preferred method that fit their view of preaching as a means of grace to sinners. We can conclude that *the hotter degree* to which the Puritans sought to further their Reformation attitudes and priorities lead them to champion the plain method of preaching. It was, therefore, the method of preaching that enhanced the word as the center of worship. This monograph agrees with Pipa: "The structure and style of Puritan preaching arose from their theology and purpose of preaching."[297] It is proposed that the plain approach to preaching as reflected in the Puritans was more of a theologically driven model rather than a particular form of sermon. It was the

---

295. Nimmo, "Theology of Preaching."
296. Beeke, *Reformed Preaching*, 41.
297. Pipa, "William Perkins," 61.

Swiss historian J. H. Merle d'Aubigne who said, "The only true reformation is that which emanates from the Word of God."[298] It is asserted that this is the impulse that drove the Puritans in their plain preaching. The frequency and intensity by which the Puritans preached their sermons stands as a testimony to the enduring nature of the primacy of the word in worship and the Christian life. This is the tradition inherited by Particular Baptist Benjamin Keach. We turn to the next chapter to consider Keach's homiletical theology.

---

298. D'Aubigné, *History*, 134.

CHAPTER 5

Benjamin Keach's Theology of Preaching

THIS CHAPTER EXPLORES KEACH'S theology of preaching using the six questions that were established in the first chapter. The following methodology will be applied to analyze the sermons and writings of Keach for a homiletical theology. Statements directly and indirectly related to preaching will be categorized using the six theo-homiletical questions. *The basis* explores God's revelation and the nature of the Bible. *The object* of preaching explores the gospel and its nuances. *The subject* investigates the role of the human preacher and the divine preacher. The third question, *the means*, aims at understanding the role of the Spirit and rhetoric in preaching. *The context* details the ecclesiological setting of preaching with other liturgical elements, particularly baptism and the Lord's Supper. Last, *the goal* examines the intended purpose of proclamation for Christians and non-Christians. To provide this synthesized homiletical theology, the sermons and writings are not analyzed independently of each other. Rather, they are harmonized under each question. Due to the amount of material, the content cannot be exhaustive. Perhaps the research opens the door for additional academic inquiry. However, the data demonstrates a mature theology of preaching.[1]

The thesis of this book is once again stated: It is maintained that Benjamin Keach's sermons and writings reflect a mature theology of preaching that is grounded biblically and informed theologically. Therefore, his

---

1. When necessary, the language, spelling, and sentence construction are modernized for the reader's convenience.

theology of preaching can serve as a theological-homiletical framework for contemporary expressions of preaching. His homiletic is epiphanical, expositional, experiential, effectual, ecclesial, and evangelical.

QUESTION ONE (BASIS): WHAT IS THE BASIS FOR PREACHING?

The first question delves into the rationale behind preaching. This section elucidates Keach's comprehension of divine revelation as recorded in Scripture. His preaching was meticulously Bible-centric, emphasizing the exposition of biblical doctrines. The bedrock of his theology of preaching lies in the authority of Scripture. He frequently associates the Bible's authority with its efficacy. Furthermore, this leads him to assert that the Bible is both sufficient and indispensable for conversion. Consequently, his preaching is centered around the revelation of God as expounded in the Scriptures.

The Authority, Efficacy, Sufficiency, and Necessity of the Bible

The basis for Keach's theology of preaching is his conviction that God has spoken in his word to reveal himself to humanity. Revelation is the basis for preaching. Keach writes, "The history of the Gospel, and principles of Christianity and Godliness, could not be known without revelation; had not God afforded us the written Word, what should we, or could we have known of these mysteries?"[2] This revelation is first made known in creation and is amplified in the person of Christ. God's divine glory and power are fully revealed in Christ.[3] The revelation of the Son is made known in two ways: first, in the word and second, in the preaching of the gospel. The creator God, who forms the universe by his word, has revealed himself in the Bible. For Keach, preaching is part of God's continual revelation of himself to human beings. It is through preaching that God reveals his Son to sinners.[4]

---

2. Keach, *Tropologia*, 932.

3. Keach, *Exposition of the Parables*, 31. The work was originally titled, *Gospel mysteries unveil'd: or an exposition of all the parables, and many express similitudes contained in the four evangelists, spoken by our Lord and Saviour Jesus Christ*. The 1858 edition is used for accessibility and readability purposes.

4. Keach, *Exposition of the Parables*, 846.

He presents his detailed views on the Bible in his work *Tropologia: A Key to Open Scripture Metaphors*. In the preface, "The Divine Authority of the Bible," he claims, "The divine wisdom treasured up in the Bible, although unadorned with the paint of human eloquence, gives us a rich profusion of a grave, genuine, and majestic dignity of elocution, suitable to those sacred mysteries it unfolds."[5] He emphatically states "that the Scripture or book called the Bible, is of divine original, inspired by the Spirit of God, and therefore of infallible truth and authority."[6] In this section of the work, Keach presents a series of arguments defending the authority and efficacy of Scripture. In particular, he argues that the Spirit of God speaks in and through the simplicity of the Bible.[7] This plainness is evidence of the divine origin and authority. He writes, "The more plain therefore the word and law of the great God is, it is, we say, the more becoming the Author thereof, and evidence of his divine stamp and authority."[8] This leads Keach to conclude,

> Of all writings in the world, the sacred Scriptures assume most unto themselves; they tell us, that they are the "Words of eternal life"; . . . that they are by the inspiration of the Holy Ghost, the testimony of Jesus Christ, the faithful Witness; that they shall judge the world; that they are able to make wise unto salvation; . . . that they are the immortal seed, of which the sons and daughters of God must be begotten.[9]

The words of Scripture are inspired by the Spirit and are the testimony of Jesus Christ. The plainness of the Scriptures makes the hearers of the preached word "wise unto salvation." For Keach, the Scriptures are the only rule for faith and practice.[10] Thus, the Bible is authoritative.

Additionally, Keach maintains that the Scripture's efficacy in transforming individuals is another evidence of its divine authority. "But besides these outward and more visible trophies of the sacred Scriptures how marvelous is their empire, efficacy, and power within, upon the hearts and consciences of men."[11] He argues that Scripture is not like any other book.

---

5. Keach, *Tropologia*, v.
6. Keach, *Tropologia*, ix.
7. Keach, *Tropologia*, xi.
8. Keach, *Tropologia*, xi.
9. Keach, *Tropologia*, xii.
10. Keach, *Short confession of faith*, 5–6.
11. Keach, *Tropologia*, xvii.

Rather, the power of the Bible in changing those who receive the word is evidence of its supernatural character. As Keach states, "These things are evident from the experience of thousands that have felt and undergone such power of the word... because the Almighty Author has endued them with such virtue through the Spirit, whereby they become the power of God unto salvation."[12] The written word, he says, "is more sure than in the voice that came from the excellent glory in the holy mount" and "the holy Scripture is of the greatest authority and hath most power and efficacy in it to bring men to believe."[13] Keach connects authority and efficacy. Because the Bible possesses authority from God, when preached, the Bible is efficacious to lead people to Christ. Thus, he claims,

> Know this first, ... the rule of your faith and practice, or first and principally above all things, as the great article of your faith, that the holy Scripture is of divine authority, and is to be preferred above that glorious voice heard in the mount; and so far above all pretended visions, new inspirations, spirits, or any other way or means whatsoever, that any can pretend unto.[14]

Therefore, the Bible "as read—especially as preached and opened in the ministry of such men Christ has sent or authorized to preach—has far more efficacy to bring men to believe, than any pretended immediate revelation, or than if one should rise from the dead."[15] Indeed, the preaching of the word is the "means God has ordained . . . for the effecting of his own gracious design and purpose."[16]

Related to the authority and efficacy of Scripture are its sufficiency and necessity. In a sermon on the parable of the rich man and Lazarus, Keach establishes the doctrine "that it is no small blessing and privilege for a people to have the written word of God, especially the Gospel or New Testament . . . the writings of the evangelists, and holy apostles of our Lord Jesus Christ."[17] The main argument of the sermon sets forth that the written word is the means of God's revelation to humanity. Specifically, he argues, "The Word of God is of such great use that without the knowledge of it what can men know in any nation of the world concerning

---

12. Keach, *Tropologia*, xvii.
13. Keach, *Exposition of the Parables*, 855.
14. Keach, *Exposition of the Parables*, 854–55.
15. Keach, *Exposition of the Parables*, 848.
16. Keach, *Exposition of the Parables*, 854.
17. Keach, *Exposition of the Parables*, 846.

God . . . but only mere natural religion, or what is made known by the light of natural conscience, through the help of the visible things of the creation."[18] Keach is clear that without the word, humanity has no savable knowledge of God. Thus, the Bible is God's special revelation and sufficient to draw sinners to salvation.

He claims "God saw it was necessary" for the church to have the Scriptures.[19] Keach asserts that the written word is sufficient for saving knowledge concerning Christ. Again, he says, "This shows the absolute necessity of the writings of the New Testament."[20] Moreover, "God being pleased this way only to reveal or make known the blessed Saviour, and to make his Word as it is written and opened in the ministration of the Gospel his ordinary way to work faith through the spirit in the souls of men."[21] It is through the ministration of the Gospel (i.e., preaching) that this knowledge is proclaimed. In this way, the word of salvation is made known to humanity. This leads Keach to apply the doctrine in multiple ways:

1. O, prize God's holy Word, esteem the law of his mouth above thousands of gold and silver.

2. Labor to believe the truths contained therein, never doubt of the verity of God's word.

3. Expect no new revelation from God, for God hath established his Word for ever.

4. O, take up and read, search the Scripture, neglect not reading your holy Bible, and pray that God would give you wisdom to understand what you read; pray over the Word which is the immortal seed, by which the babe of grace is begotten and nourished.

5. Know that the Word of Christ remains just as you find it written, even every precept every ordinance, every promise, without any alteration, additions to it, or diminution from it: therefore have no regard to any who press things upon you as truths of Christ that are not written.

6. Be aware of those men who contemn the holy Scripture.[22]

---

18. Keach, *Exposition of the Parables*, 846.
19. Keach, *Exposition of the Parables*, 846.
20. Keach, *Exposition of the Parables*, 846.
21. Keach, *Exposition of the Parables*, 846.
22. Keach, *Exposition of the Parables*, 847.

In the sermon, he gives the final exhortation: "Take heed you do not receive the Word of God's grace in vain, but strive to mix faith with it, for otherwise it would not profit you anything, or at least not be made an instrument of God's power to the salvation of your souls."[23] Keach encourages his hearers to receive the preached word with faith for the message to be profitable.

He also details specific functions of the Scripture. In the sermon "The Trial of the False Professor," Keach poses the question, Why is the word of God called good? He replies with a series of statements. First, it brings good news to sinners. Second, it is an announcement of "the good and gracious Counsel and Purpose of God in saving poor Sinners by Jesus Christ." Third, it is good in its effects. Fourth, as a shining light it enlightens the eyes and it illuminates dark minds. Fifth, it revives the dead soul. Sixth, it enriches the soul. Seventh, it has a transforming impact on men's souls to regenerate. Eighth, it is offensive against enemies of the gospel and defends against spiritual attacks. Ninth, it is the revelation of God's Son. Tenth, it brings comfort and strength to the believer. Last, it is "our food . . . food for our souls."[24] He concludes with the exhortation, "Sirs, if you have never tasted how good the Word of God is, your State doubtless is bad; but it is not enough to have a taste of it, but you must feed upon it: Eat, O Friends; drink, yea drink abundantly, O Beloved."[25]

Summary

Why preach? Because the Bible is God's revelation of himself to humanity. In general, Keach preached the Bible as the word of God because he believed that God revealed himself in the word. For Keach, the Bible is sufficient and necessary to make one wise unto salvation. He rigorously maintains the Reformed doctrine of Scripture.[26] However, the mere preaching of the word is not enough. It must be heard with faith.[27] Additionally, the word is intended to transform those who believe its testimony. Keach's theology of preaching rests on the authority, efficacy, sufficiency, and necessity of the written word. He honored the word and

---

23. Keach, *Exposition of the Parables*, 847.
24. Keach, *Golden Mine Opened*, 335–37.
25. Keach, *Golden Mine Opened*, 336–37.
26. Bush and Nettles, *Baptists and the Bible*, 75–81.
27. Keach, *Exposition of the Parables*, 856.

sought to expound its teaching to his congregation. God reveals himself in creation, in Christ, and in the Scriptures. His preaching was epiphanical, grounded in God's divine revelation of himself in the Bible.

QUESTION TWO (OBJECT): WHAT IS BEING PREACHED?

In analyzing Keach's theo-homiletical convictions, the second question centers on the subject matter of the sermons. The section is divided into two distinct units. The first unit examines the content of Keach's Christ-centered gospel proclamation. The second unit focuses on his articulation of the covenant of grace. According to Keach, as he expounded the Scriptures, he believed Christ was the mediator of the covenant and the pinnacle of divine revelation. Furthermore, he refined his exposition of the gospel in a Reformed manner.

Preaching Christ

Since the Bible affirms the salvific work of Jesus, Keach perceived no distinction between preaching the Bible and preaching Christ. To preach the Bible is to preach the gospel, as the culmination of Scripture is Christ himself. In other words, if a minister preaches the Bible, they must also preach Christ. Frequently, Keach would employ the Scriptures, the gospel, and the word interchangeably. Moreover, he condensed these phrases into the statement, "preach Christ." He asserts, "Faith comes by hearing the word of God preached; but when the gospel goes from a people, they lose the instrument of God's power."[28] In an exhortation to the congregation he encouraged, "Be also frequently under the ministry of the word and hear such who preach Christ; Christ being the great Subject they continually insist upon. Faith comes by hearing. But it is Christ then that must be preached."[29]

He insists that preaching Christ is the fundamental role of the preacher.[30] "Ministers may learn from hence to see to the nature of that spiritual food with which they feed Christ's family . . . it must be Christ;

---

28. Keach, *Exposition of the Parables*, 497–98.
29. Keach, *Exposition of the Parables*, 536.
30. Deane explores the nuances of Keach's Christocentric preaching. See Deane, "Golden Mine Opened."

he is only the bread of life; it is Christ he must preach; Christ must be the subject of all his preaching, we preach Christ, and him crucified."[31] Ministers must feed the congregation Christ, the bread of life, as they expound the Bible. Furthermore, he says, "They must in all things exalt Jesus Christ, or seek the Honor alone of their Blessed Sovereign: The whole of their Work is to magnify Christ, exalt Christ; To Preach Christ the Lord, and themselves but Servants for Jesus sake."[32]

Keach's proclamation is rigorously Christocentric, extending to his theology of preaching. Christ is not merely the subject of his preaching but also the source of empowerment for the ministry of the word. Keach elucidates four ways in which Christ is "all in all" through the ministry of preaching:

> Christ is All in all in the ministry of the word. (1.) It is Christ that is preached: "We preach Christ crucified. . . . " (2.) It is Christ that gives grace and gifts to preach: "To me is the grace given, that I should preach among the Gentiles the unsearchable riches of Christ" (3.) It is he that ordains and appoints men to this work and puts all true preachers into the ministry. (4.) It is he that opens the mouth to speak, and the ear and heart to hear and receive the word. Take Christ away, and what Gospel can be preached? &c. What is Paul? and what is Apollos? I am nothing. Gospel ministry and ministers are nothing without Christ.[33]

According to Keach, preaching is thoroughly Christ centered. Christ is the primary object of proclamation. Jesus equips and appoints individuals to preach. Christ also "opens the mouth" and "the ear and heart" to understand the word. For Keach, the totality of preaching begins and ends with Jesus's Lordship. In his sermon "Christ Alone the Way to Heaven," he identifies what it means to *preach Christ*. He claims,

> I have formerly showed you what it is to preach Christ, so as to exalt him and lift him up in the ministration of the gospel. First tis' to preach the excellencies of his person. . . . To preach that he is God, God by nature . . . but the most high God, the eternal God, coessential, coequal, and coeternal with the Father. . . . To preach that he is man, truly man. . . . That he is God and man, in one person, both natures making but one Christ, by a wonderful, and hypostatical union. . . . To preach Christ is to preach

---

31. Keach, *Exposition of the Parables*, 270–71.
32. Keach, *Display of Glorious Grace*, 142–43.
33. Keach, *Tropologia*, 489.

his incarnation, his birth, his life, his death, his resurrection, his ascension, and his intercession.... To preach Christ, is to preach his holy doctrine.... To preach the preciousness of Christ.... To preach Christ, is to preach the necessity of Christ and of his death.[34]

Keach advocates a full Christ-centered gospel, rather than a reductionistic version. It involves the entirety of Christ's person, his redemptive work, and his current session. He describes the work of Christ as a victory: "Lord Jesus, having conquered Satan, and the powers of hell, rode as it were in triumph through their kingdom, the air, and made a show of them openly, as a glorious victor."[35]

This christological proclamation is grounded in Keach's stated Christology.[36] He argues:

1. He [Jesus] came down from Heaven to fix his Foot in our Nature upon the Earth.
2. He was Incarnate, or assumed a Body prepared for him by the Father.
3. He was Born of a Virgin, tho' without Sin: That's the third Gradation.
4. He lived a Holy and Spiritual Life.
5. He died the Cursed death of the Cross to satisfy divine Justice for us; and in our stead.
6. He Rose again from the Dead the Third Day, for our Justification.
7. He Ascended up into Heaven.
8. He makes Intercession, pleading the Merits of his Blood for us.[37]

A central theme in his Christology is the eternal generation of the Son. He asserts that God the Father eternally begets the Son, who is eternally and unchangeably begotten and cannot beget the Father. Similarly, the Holy Spirit proceeds from the Father and the Son, and neither Father nor Son can proceed from the Holy Ghost.[38] Specifically, Keach empha-

---

34. Keach, *Christ Alone the Way*, 49–51. In the context of the sermon, he continues to elucidate other aspects of preaching Christ. For example, Keach shows eighteen ways to preach the types of Christ from the Old Testament.

35. Keach, *Tropologia*, 739.

36. Also see Keach, *Beams of divine light*.

37. Keach, *Christ Alone the Way*, 19.

38. Keach, *Golden Mine Opened*, 92.

sizes that Christ bore witness to the unity of the Father and the Son, asserting that they are one in essence.[39] He proclaims that Christ is the only-begotten Son of God, by eternal generation. Keach proclaims the doctrine of Christ's hypostatic union. Jesus Christ "is both God and Man, the Eternal God; not God by Office, but God by Nature, the most High God who made Heaven and Earth, and yet truly Man, taking our Nature into a mystical Union with his Holy Deity, being made like unto us in all things, Sin only excepted; and thus both God and Man in one Person."[40]

Keach's Christocentric proclamation also addresses the offices of Christ as prophet, priest, and king. As a priest, he is the propitiation for our sins. As a king, he is invested with kingly authority and serves as the mediator. As a prophet, he is the minister of the new covenant.[41] These threefold offices collectively express Christ's work in the redemption of the elect. In summary, Keach maintains orthodox views regarding the person and work of Jesus.

The Content of the Gospel

Keach's Christ-centered proclamation is grounded in the salvific work of the triune God. "The Father, Son, and Holy Ghost, are concerned in our Salvation; the *Father elects*, this is principally ascribed to the *first Person* in the Godhead; the *Son purchases*, he redeems; and the *Holy Spirit renews*, calls, and sanctifies."[42] It is "in the Gospel" that the "full Declaration" of the triune God is made known: "The Father sending the Son as a Mediator, the Son dying for our Sins, and the Spirit sanctifying our Souls: the Father by eternal Generation begetting the Son, the Son begotten of the Father, and the Spirit proceeding from the Father and the Son; yet all Three are but one and the same God."[43] He also uses various metaphors to describe this Trinitarian work:

> Salvation is called a Garment; *He hath clothed me with the Garments of Salvation, he hath covered me with the Robe of Righteousness.* The Father may be said to prepare the Matter which this Robe is made of; the Son wrought it, he made the Garment,

---

39. Keach, *Exposition of the Parables*, 93.
40. Keach, *Golden Mine Opened*, 93.
41. Keach, *Display of Glorious Grace*, 67–71.
42. Keach, *Golden Mine Opened*, 174.
43. Keach, *Everlasting Covenant*, 24.

and the Holy Spirit puts it on the Soul; the Garment of Salvation is Christ's Righteousness. Again, the Father sought out or chose the Bride, the Son espouses and marries her, but it is the Holy Ghost that inclines her Heart and stirs up, nay, that causes the Soul to like and to love this Blessed Lover and brings it to yield and consent to accept heartily and willingly of Jesus Christ. We were sick of a fearful and incurable Disease, and the Father found out the Medicine; the Blood of Christ is that Medicine, and the Holy Spirit applies it to the Soul. We were in Debt, in Prison, and bound in Fetters and cruel Chains, and the Father procured a Friend to pay all our Debts; The Son was this our Friend, who laid down the infinite Sum; and the Holy Spirit knocks off our Irons, our Fetters and Chains, and brings us out of the Prison-house. The Father loved us and sent his Son to merit Grace for us; the Son loved us, and died, and thereby purchased that Grace to be imparted to us; and the Holy Spirit works that Grace in us. O what is the Nature of this Salvation; how Great, how Glorious! That the whole Trinity, both the Father, and the Son, and the Holy Ghost, are thus employed in and about it, that we might have it made sure to us for ever.[44]

In this way, "the love of the Father, and of the Son, and of the Holy Spirit, is the same in nature, and of like extent."[45] Theologically, Keach is affirming the inseparable operations of the Godhead in the work of salvation. Yet, Keach is operating within a larger theological framework. God's triune work is related directly to the covenant of grace. Austin Walker writes, "In his sermons, it [covenant of grace] is not only a repeated theme, but it is the underlying theme and basis for his understanding of the way in which the triune God works out his salvation."[46] The covenant of grace is the "organizing principle" for Keach's theological framework and his preaching.[47] The covenant of grace provides for him the basis to articulate various elements of God's redemptive message in a logical manner.[48] Additionally, the covenant of grace is personal to Keach. He

---

44. Keach, *Golden Mine Opened*, 382–83.

45. Keach, *Exposition of the Parables*, 34.

46. Walker, "Tailor Turned Preacher," 30.

47. Arnold, *Reformed Theology*, 123. Also see Renihan, *From Shadow to Substance*, 299–319.

48. Other seventeenth-century Baptists wrote on the nature of the covenant. See Coxe, *Discourse of the covenants*. For a historical theology of seventeenth-century Baptist federalism see Denault, *Distinctiveness*.

confesses that he "was ignorant of the Mysteries of the Gospel" before studying the covenant.[49]

Scholars assert that Keach's articulation of federal theology was not unique to him.[50] Specifically, he follows other theologians, collapsing the covenant of redemption and the covenant of grace into one covenant.[51] In doing so, he seeks to mitigate antinomian accusations and notions of eternal justification.[52] However, it seems that the *uniqueness* of Keach's covenant scheme was his analogous use of "two warring parties whose relationship had suffered a major breach."[53] He says, "I must confess, divers Worthy and Learned Men have wrote most excellently upon the Covenant of Grace, yet perhaps hardly any in the Method here used, nor under the Notion of a Covenant of Peace."[54] Indeed, in *The Display of Glorious Grace*, he calls the covenant of grace "the covenant of peace."[55] This leads him to describe the gospel as the *proclamation of peace*.[56] This innovation in Keach's covenant scheme was equally homiletical as it was theological.[57] By defining the covenant as the *covenant of peace*, he highlights the work of reconciliation as a foundational aspect to salvation.

The homiletical usage of peace serves as an analogous bridge from Keach's context into the biblical text. For example, he introduces sermon I referencing the "peace lately concluded betwixt the French King and the Confederate Princes."[58] Walker notes that this "is probably referring to the Treaty of Ryswick signed by France, United Provinces, England

---

49. Keach, *Golden Mine Opened*, 314–15.

50. Riker, *Catholic Reformed Theologian*, 107. Riker understands Keach to say that his collapse of the covenant of redemption and covenant of grace was unique. Riker disagrees, which is correct. Keach's collapse was not unique. However, Arnold shows that Riker misunderstood Keach's intent. Keach was not claiming his collapse of the two covenants distinguished his federal theology from others. Rather, it was the method of teaching and particularly the nomenclature of the covenant of peace that marked Keach. See Arnold, *Reformed Theology*, 142n201.

51. Keach, *Everlasting Covenant*, 6.

52. Keach, *Everlasting Covenant*, 6–7. Also see Keach, *Display of Glorious Grace*, 205.

53. Arnold, *Reformed Theology*, 142.

54. See Keach, *Display of Glorious Grace*, iv.

55. Keach, *Display of Glorious Grace*, 8.

56. Keach, *Display of Glorious Grace*, 120.

57. Brown alludes to Keach's homiletical use of the *peace* image. See Brown, "Baptist Preaching," 15.

58. Keach, *Display of Glorious Grace*, 1–2.

and Spain and the Emperor in 1697."[59] This introduction prompts him to transition, "My Brethren, *Peace* made between Kingdoms and Nations may soon be broken or removed: But there is a *Peace* which being made shall be lasting, and never be removed: And this brings me to the Words of my Text."[60] He uses the imagery of war and peace in various ways. For example, he calls original sin the first cause of the "breach and war" between God and humanity.[61] The covenant of peace is the "treaty."[62] The "terms of peace" are extended to sinful individuals through the proclamation of the gospel.[63] This announcement happens through ambassadors of peace (e.g., preachers).[64] Keach uses the national and political setting to illustrate aspects of his covenant scheme. In this sense, the metaphor is a homiletical aid highlighting the war/peace relationship that an individual has with God.[65] This is part of his method in teaching about the covenant.

Keach's preaching on the covenant of peace is vital in understanding the object of his pulpit ministry. He explains what the gospel of peace means by highlighting five key essentials.[66] First, the gospel shows how sinful humanity can be reconciled to God. Second, it reveals that God is the one who performs this work. Third, the basis of reconciliation is the death of Christ. Fourth, individuals are only reconciled when they place their faith in Christ. Fifth, the gospel is the instrumental means, through the Spirit, which affects one's reconciliation to God.[67] For Keach, the Spirit's role in the covenant of peace is foundational to the believer. By the Spirit, the blessings of the covenant are made a reality.[68]

In Keach's proclamation of the covenant, reconciliation is a prominent emphasis. Since the covenant is one of peace, God's work in Christ is the means of reconciliation.[69] However, Keach is clear to say that reconciliation with God does not occur until the Spirit unites the

---

59. See Walker, *Excellent Benjamin Keach*, 252n8. The sermons were published in May 1698.
60. Keach, *Display of Glorious Grace*, 4.
61. Keach, *Display of Glorious Grace*, 11.
62. Keach, *Display of Glorious Grace*, 26.
63. Keach, *Display of Glorious Grace*, 94.
64. Keach, *Display of Glorious Grace*, 130.
65. See Holmes, "Role of Metaphor," 154.
66. Keach, *Display of Glorious Grace*, 120–22.
67. Keach, *Display of Glorious Grace*, 121.
68. Keach, *Display of Glorious Grace*, 116.
69. Keach, *Display of Glorious Grace*, 122.

individual to Christ by faith.⁷⁰ Therefore, the "terms of peace" are faith in the redemptive work of the Son. Reconciliation brings the believer into the "Mystical Union with him [Christ] by the Spirit."⁷¹ This union is the "possession of the Sacred Blessings of this Covenant."⁷²

Additionally, since the covenant of peace is an organizing principle, this allows Keach to touch on the "grand blessings and privileges" of redemption.⁷³ These include:

1. Adoption, to as many as received him to them gave he power to become the Sons of God
2. Righteousness and Justification from all things
3. Sanctification
4. Pardon of all Sins, and that forever, and not only forgiven forever, but they also are forgotten forever
5. Peace
6. Communion with the Father and the Son
7. Godly Zeal
8. Spiritual Strength and Courage
9. All Ordinances are given, yea, Fat and Green Pastures, Bread and Water of Life
10. The Ministers of Christ are given
11. All the Promises of God, are given in the Covenant
12. Yea, a Right to Eternal Life also is given and granted to all in this Covenant
13. Final Perseverance is given by this Covenant⁷⁴

Likewise, the proclamation of the covenant affords Keach the framework to proclaim related aspects of God's redemptive work. First is the love of the Father. He claims, "God's Love to us in Christ is an amazing and wonderful Love, our Peace shall be made, tho it cost God the Blood of his own dear and beloved Son."⁷⁵ Second is sovereign election.⁷⁶ For Ke-

---

70. Keach, *Display of Glorious Grace*, 121.
71. Keach, *Display of Glorious Grace*, 165.
72. Keach, *Display of Glorious Grace*, 171.
73. Keach, *Display of Glorious Grace*, 238.
74. Keach, *Display of Glorious Grace*, 238–39.
75. Keach, *Display of Glorious Grace*, 63.
76. Arnold shows that Keach subscribed to an infralapsarian view of the fall and

ach, "God's special Love and Election" is not the result of the Father's knowledge of faith or man's good works "but from and of God's mere Mercy, Sovereign Grace and Favor."[77] Third is the free grace of God. He proclaims that God's covenant "is wholly in a way of Free Grace and Favor."[78] Specifically, he states, "The Covenant of Peace is alone of God's Free Grace."[79] Fourth is the substitutionary death of Christ.[80] His death is an "atoning sacrifice" whereby "his Precious Blood quenched the Fire of God's Wrath, and so it is the only way by which we come to be delivered from Hell: Our *Jonah* was cast over-board to make a Calm and caused the Storm of Divine Vengeance to cease."[81] He encourages his congregation to celebrate Christ's propitiatory sacrifice. Thus,

> We may also from hence see cause to admire the Love of Jesus Christ, who bore the Wrath of God for us: Certainly had he not had the Power of the Deity to uphold him, he could not have born that Wrath that was so heavy upon him. . . . His Blood has quenched this flaming Fire, so that you shall never feel what the Wrath of God is. Brethren, remember we could not be delivered from the Wrath of God, unless Jesus Christ did bear it in our stead.[82]

Fifth, Keach proclaims Christ as the representative, surety, and mediator for the elect. The Son acts "for and in behalf of all the Father gave unto him."[83] Christ "entered into Covenant with the Father, as the great Surety of all the Sheep."[84] As the elect's surety, the Son "struck Hands with God for us in this Covenant."[85] As the mediator, the Son "is a middle Person" who stands "betwixt God and Man . . . he being God and Man in one Person, he is a meet and a proper Reconciler of God to Man, and of Man

---

God's decree of election. Also, he demonstrates that Keach held to single predestination. See Arnold, *Reformed Theology*, 162–64.

77. Keach, *Display of Glorious Grace*, 19.

78. Keach, *Display of Glorious Grace*, 172.

79. Keach, *Display of Glorious Grace*, 174.

80. Keach argues against general atonement in favor of particular redemption. See Keach, *Golden Mine Opened*, 249–56.

81. Keach, *Display of Glorious Grace*, 115–16. Keach maintains the doctrine of particular redemption. See Keach, *Display of Glorious Grace*, 10.

82. Keach, *Golden Mine Opened*, 482.

83. Keach, *Golden Mine Opened*, 202.

84. Keach, *Golden Mine Opened*, 126.

85. Keach, *Display of Glorious Grace*, 86.

to God."[86] In Keach's own homiletical way, he expresses his convictions through a rhetorical parallelism:

> Christ in the Covenant of Grace, is the Mediator, *we are those he mediates for*; Christ is the Head, we are the Body, *the covenanted for*; Christ is the Surety, we the Poor Debtors and Criminals, *he struck hands to satisfy God's Justice for*; Christ is the Redeemer, *we the Redeemed*; Christ the Savior, *we the Saved*; Christ is the Purchaser, *we are the Inheritance he purchased.*[87]

Based on the covenant of peace, Keach provides the practical benefits of what God has done for the believer. In a sermon, he poses the question, "What ground of Comfort and Consolation to Believers is here?"[88] Because of the covenant of peace, sins are fully forgiven. All the accusations from the law, sin, and Satan are silenced and answered by Christ's intercessory work. The believer's wants and needs are supplied. Reconciliation is accomplished. Every affliction works together for the good of the believer. Last, the believer stands firmer than Adam.[89] Keach summarizes the various themes in his sermon "The Everlasting Covenant." He declares,

> *God's Divine Love, Mercy and Goodness to lost Man, to admiration is displayed hereby, God so loved the World, that he gave his only begotten Son, &c.* Joh. 3:16. Rather than Mankind should be utterly lost, he will enter into a Covenant with his own Son, and substitute him our Mediator, Head and Surety to satisfy for our Sins; *and be made a Curse for us*: that so by his own Free-Grace through the Redemption that is in Jesus Christ, we might be reconciled, justified and eternally saved *i.e.* by his Merits and Righteousness imputed to us: there was nothing in Man to oblige God to pity him, we were his Enemies, when Christ died for us; and he offered and propounded this glorious Contrivance of his Wisdom to his Beloved Son in the Covenant of our Peace, out of his infinite Love and Goodness, as seeing us fallen, *and lying in our Blood*, it was as we were in that woeful Condition he first loved us, and as the Effects of that Love entered into a Covenant *with the Son* for us.[90]

---

86. Keach, *Display of Glorious Grace*, 45–46.
87. Keach, *Everlasting Covenant*, 6; emphasis added.
88. Keach, *Display of Glorious Grace*, 302.
89. Keach, *Display of Glorious Grace*, 302–4.
90. Keach, *Everlasting Covenant*, 22–23.

Therefore, the covenant of peace gives Keach the theological framework for his gospel articulation. In this framework, he can speak about love, grace, and atonement while also providing a theological relationship to these elements. For Keach, the covenant was more than just a theological topic open for speculation. Rather, it was the basis for the "main design in all" his preaching.[91] While the covenant of grace was by no means the only homiletical topic found in Keach's pulpit, it did serve as a vital aspect of his preaching ministry.

Related to the covenant of peace is justification by faith.[92] In the publication *The Marrow of True Justification*, he states that a preacher must preach the doctrine, since "he cannot omit if he would truly Preach the Gospel of Jesus Christ."[93] This doctrine "tends so much to the Honor of God, and the magnifying of his infinite Wisdom, and his Free Grace, and Mercy in Jesus Christ."[94] Keach's articulation of justification is consistent with the broader Reformed community.[95] In the first sermon, he defends two truths. First, human works do not justify sinners in the sight of God. Second, justification is achieved through the free grace of God.[96] Specifically, justification is the result of "the Imputation of the perfect Personal Righteousness of Christ, received only by the Faith of the Operation of God."[97] Justification is grounded in the death of Christ, who fulfilled the law of God and satisfied divine justice.[98]

In the second sermon, Keach argues against "mixing" obedience to the law and faith.[99] Thus, he makes a law and gospel distinction. He says, "The difference betwixt the Law and the Gospel . . . that the one requires doing, *Do this and live*; but the other, no doing but believing for Life and Salvation: their Terms differ not only in degree, but in their whole

---

91. Keach, *Display of Glorious Grace*, v.

92. The background of Keach's articulation of justification is his conflict with Richard Baxter. The *Baxterian* doctrine of justification maintained that "obedience to the law, in addition to the application of Christ's blood, must be present for justification." See Arnold, *Reformed Theology*, 152–54. Also see Keach, *Medium Betwixt Two Extremes*.

93. Keach, *Marrow of True Justification*, 1.

94. Keach, *Marrow of True Justification*, 2.

95. Arnold, *Reformed Theology*, 156.

96. Keach, *Marrow of True Justification*, 8.

97. Keach, *Marrow of True Justification*, 8.

98. Keach, *Marrow of True Justification*, 5.

99. Keach, *Marrow of True Justification*, 21.

Nature."[100] Justification is not the result of obedience but of faith in Christ. He concludes the sermon, "We hold forth Christ to be your whole Savior ... whom if you close with, and believe in, you shall be justified: We tell you God justifies the Ungodly, *i.e.* that they are so before justified."[101]

Summary

Keach claims, "The Gospel is an instrument, prepared and made fit by the Almighty, to break or plough up the fallow ground of our hearts."[102] Central to his theology of preaching is the covenant of peace, particularly the doctrine of justification by faith alone. The covenant of peace provides Keach with a coherent theological scheme to touch on various salvific elements. Therefore, Keach's preaching is Christ centered because it is theo-centered. It is theo-centered because it is Bible centered.

QUESTION THREE (SUBJECT): WHO IS DOING THE PREACHING?

In question three, *who is doing the preaching* is explored. Focusing on the human and divine elements of preaching, this section is divided into two major units. A brief overview of Keach's thoughts concerning pastoral ministry is warranted. This is followed by a discussion of the minister's preaching according to Keach. The second major unit will explore the divine preacher. The interrelationship between the human and the divine is part of one's theology of preaching. As Greenhaw notes, "The connection between the biblical texts and the preacher's words becomes a central focus in theologies of preaching."[103] Keach provides a glimpse into this, as will be demonstrated. In sum, this question exposes the *experiential* nature of Keach's preaching.

---

100. Keach, *Marrow of True Justification*, 22.
101. Keach, *Marrow of True Justification*, 35.
102. Keach, *Tropologia*, 589.
103. Greenhaw, "Theology of Preaching," 479.

A Minister's Pastoral Labors

In Keach's exposition on Matt 13:52, he directly addresses the minister's pastoral responsibilities. He articulates the doctrine "A good and faithful minister of the gospel ought to be like a rich householder, ever have a store of spiritual provision."[104] Keach employs the metaphor of a faithful steward to illustrate the minister's role within the local church. He elaborates on ten specific ways in which a minister is expected to be faithful in fulfilling his duties:

1. They must seek to steward their responsibility for the glory of God.
2. Mind their Lord's concerns and business.
3. Faithfully dispense the word of truth (fundamentals of Christianity).
4. Preach the whole counsel of God.
5. Preach frequently.
6. Provide care over the church.
7. Deal impartially with everyone.
8. Keep good discipline.
9. Defend the truth.
10. Act with humility.[105]

Throughout his sermons, Keach emphasizes the essential role of ministers. He identifies two crucial components that define a true minister: the internal workings of the Spirit and the external call of a local church.[106] The minister is entrusted with a significant responsibility, which entails preserving the purity of the gospel. The church's purity is closely tied to the proper constitution of the congregation, ensuring its congregational nature. This order is maintained through genuine discipline. As overseer, the pastor cares for the entire church. The pastoral work is further amplified through the administration of the ordinances, with preaching serving as the primary function.[107] Consequently, Keach

---

104. Keach, *Exposition of the Parables*, 261.
105. Keach, *Exposition of the Parables*, 262–64.
106. Keach, *Exposition of the Parables*, 266.
107. Keach, *Exposition of the Parables*, 266.

believes that the elder holds a crucial position within and over the local congregation, adopting a "single-elder" model of church leadership.[108]

Keach states, "For the power of the keys is given to the church, but a pastor is a ruler or governor therein."[109] However, he distinguishes between pastors and teachers, recognizing them as distinct types of ministers.[110] An elder was formally ordained and held a stewardship or ruling function over the local congregation.[111] This function encompasses guiding the work of deacons, caring for souls, and maintaining order within the congregation. Therefore, the elder must be a teacher, but it is not necessary for a teacher to be an elder. At the heart of this distinction lies the elder's authority to administer the ordinances and minister the gospel. Regarding preaching, the elder is lawfully called by the church to exercise his gifts. Since the gospel is entrusted to his care, the minister must steward it faithfully to the glory of God.

The Human Preacher

It is Keach's conviction that the primary work of the minister is the proclamation of the Bible:

> The work of a pastor is to preach the Word of Christ, or to feed the flock, and to administer all the ordinances of the gospel, which belong to his sacred office, and to be faithful and laborious therein, studying to show himself approved unto God . . . because he is to feed the people knowledge and understanding. He must be faithful and skillful to declare the mind of God and diligent therein, also to preach in season and out of season. . . . Moreover, he must make known the whole counsel of God to the people.[112]

---

108. Renihan, *Edification and Beauty*, 73–78. Renihan states, "The judicial power of the keys is in the church, and the execution of power is in the elder(s)."

109. Keach, *Exposition of the Parables*, 327.

110. See Keach, *Exposition of the Parables*, 636. Also see Renihan, *Edification and Beauty*, 107–14. The Second London Confession also says, "Although it be incumbent on the Bishops or Pastors of the Churches to be instant in Preaching the Word, by way of Office; yet the work of Preaching the Word, it not so peculiarly confined to them; but the others also (a) gifted and fitted by the Holy Spirit for it, and approved, and called by the Church, may and ought to perform it." *Confession of Faith Put Forth*, 91.

111. Keach, *Tropologia*, 855. He writes, "So Ministers are to rule the house and Church of God by the rule of God's word."

112. Keach, *Glory of a true church*, 8–9.

The preaching function holds paramount importance within the local church. It constitutes an integral aspect of the minister's sacred office, necessitating their unwavering faithfulness and diligent labor to nourish the congregation. This conviction is not exclusive to Keach. His assertion bears similarities to that of John Owen, who posits, "The first and principal duty of a pastor is to feed the flock by diligent preaching of the word."[113] In delineating the specifics of pastoral preaching, Owen contends,

> Sundry things are required unto this work and duty of pastoral preaching; as—(1) Spiritual wisdom and understanding in the mysteries of the gospel. . . . (2) Experience of the power of the truth which they preaching in and upon their own souls. . . . (3) Skill to divide the word aright. . . . (4) A prudent and diligent consideration of the state of the flock over which any man is set. . . . (5) All these, in the whole discharge of their duty, are to be constantly accompanied with the evidence of zeal for the glory of God and compassion for the souls of men.[114]

Keach delineates three pivotal characteristics of a genuine gospel minister. Firstly, they are regenerate individuals who have received divine grace and ministerial gifts from Christ. Secondly, they are regularly summoned and empowered to preach by the church. Thirdly, they preach Christ, as he represents the essence of their ministry.[115] Consequently, a minister must be a Christian. For the preacher to effectively proclaim Christ, they must possess an experiential knowledge of Christ. In his commentary on the regeneration of the minister, Keach states, "He that ministers the word, ought principally to experience the grace of God in his own heart, and the power of it, in that grand and evangelical work of regeneration."[116] The preacher is regenerated, called, and empowered to preach Christ. The minister's experience, through union with Christ, is intrinsically linked to proclamation. Consequently, union with Christ serves as the foundation for ministerial giftedness and activity. This is evident in Keach's utilization of the ambassador metaphor. The metaphor serves as the primary image that governs Keach's comprehension of the minister's preaching ministry.

---

113. Owen, *Works*, 16:74–96.
114. Owen, *Works*, 16:74; see also 75–77.
115. Keach, *Exposition of the Parables*, 60.
116. Keach, *Tropologia*, vii.

Ambassador Metaphor in *Tropologia*

Foundational to Keach's theology of preaching is the *ambassador* metaphor, drawn from 2 Cor 5:20. This metaphor frequently appears throughout his corpus, particularly in *Tropologia*. He states, "The term [ambassador] is applied to the ministers of the Gospel; and it sets forth, 1. The dignity, 2. The duty of Ministers."[117] He then identifies the parallels:

Metaphor[118]	Parallel
I. Ambassadors are authorized and sent abroad by princes, about the great affairs of their kingdoms.	I. Ministers are authorized, empowered, and sent by the Lord Jesus, the Prince of the kings of the earth, on the great affairs of his glory, and man's good.
II. Ambassadors usually are persons of eminency; it is an office that a prince will not confer upon any of his subjects, but on such as are of great esteem in his court, such as are fitly qualified for that great trust confided in them; in a word, great honor and dignity is conferred upon them.	II. Faithful Ministers of Christ, such as are Ministers indeed, are eminent persons, such as are great favorites to the court of heaven. What higher dignity doth Christ confer upon any of his saints here below! They also are men fitly qualified for this great employment; and what their qualifications are, and must be, you may see in 1 Tim. 3:1–7, and Tit. 1:7–9, viz., "Blameless as the stewards of God, not self-willed, not soon angry, not given to wine, no striker, not given to filthy lucre, a lover of hospitality, a lover of good men, sober, just, holy, temperate, holding forth the faithful word, able by sound doctrine to stop the mouths of gainsayers, &c., not a brawler, not covetous, one that rules well his own house."
III. The dignity of Ambassadors appears in the greatness of their prince from whom they come: they have usually respect according to the rank and quality of their master.	III. Now true faithful Ministers are sent as Ambassadors from the great God, who is King of heaven and earth: "By whom kings reign, and princes decree judgment," Prov. 8:15. "With him is terrible majesty, he rules and reigns over all, and who can say unto him, What doest thou?"

---

117. Keach, *Tropologia*, 850. He also lists angels (thirteen nuances), stars (nine nuances), labors (six nuances), watchmen (eight nuances), trumpeters (eleven nuances), spokesmen (six nuances), clouds (six nuances), fathers (ten nuances), stewards (five nuances), planters (fourteen nuances), builders (ten nuances), pillars (three nuances), shepherds (eight nuances), and rulers (ten nuances) as metaphors for the minister.

118. Keach, *Tropologia*, 850–54.

Metaphor[118]	Parallel
IV. An Ambassador appears according to the dignity of the person whom he represents, and whose place he supplies.	IV. True and faithful Ministers represent the Person of Jesus Christ. O! and what honor is this! They are employed in his stead, they are his deputies: He is the chief Ambassador, called therefore the "Messenger of the Covenant"; Mal. 3:1, from him they receive their authority.
V. The Excellency of the message Ambassadors are sent about, shows further the dignity of the officers. Now there are three sorts of embassies in the world: 1. Embassies of peace. 2. Embassies of Marriage. 3. State embassies, which respect trade and commerce, &c.	V. Ministers come with a threefold embassy:— 1. Of peace. 2. Of Marriage. 3. Of heavenly commerce and trades, &c.
1. An Ambassador is welcome, when he comes from a prince about peace; and that especially.	1. Christ's Ministers are welcome when they come with an embassy of peace; and needs they must be so, if we consider the things following:
(1.) When he comes from one that is formidable, mighty in power, and whose armies are irresistible; now to a poor, weak, and naked people, how welcome is his approach!	(1.) These Ambassadors come from that great God that is dreadful in power, that if he speak but in his wrath, the earth trembles, whose armies are also ready; who offers not peace, because he cannot make war, or stands in need of our friendship, but merely from his great love wherewith he hath loved us, &c. What can sinners do to withstand his power? Doth he fear their hostility? Can they shoot their arrows as high as heaven? If they strike at him, he makes their swords turn into their own bowels. O how gladly should these Ambassadors be received! Who would not tremble to think of this God!
(2.) An Ambassador is welcome, when he is sent to a people that have felt already the impression of his power, and are pining under the bleeding miseries of his anger.	(2.) So a Minister of Christ is welcome to poor sinners, who find the arrows of divine vengeance sticking in their very hearts, and the curse of God cleaves to every faculty of their souls, who lie bleeding under his heavy anger.

Metaphor[118]	Parallel
(3.) An Ambassador is welcome, when the terms he offers are honorable and easy: not like the peace that Nahash offered to the men of Jabesh-Gilead, viz., that they should have every one his right eye thrust out, and lay it as a reproach to Israel.	(3.) Now the Ministers of the Gospel offer honorable and easy terms: God might require the perfect keeping of the whole law, he might demand satisfaction for all the wrongs and injuries we have done to his justice; but they offer terms of peace and pardon, upon the acknowledgment of sin, and laying down our arms, and to hold no league or secret friendship with sin and Satan any longer, to take hold of Christ, and plead the atonement of his blood: "Believe on the Lord Jesus, and thou shalt be saved."
(4.) An Ambassador is welcome, when he offers peace from a prince that is real to his word, and gives good security for the performance of what he promises.	(4.) Now God doth by his faithful Ministers give the greatest assurance imaginable of the performance of whatsoever he offers to poor sinners; he hath past his word, nay, more, it is upon oath, Heb. 6.
2. Ambassadors sometimes offer an alliance, by marriage, between one state and another.	2. And this is one great part of a Minister's embassy, he is sent to let sinners know what good will the God of heaven and earth bears to them, and that he is desirous to bestow his own dear Son, the heir of all things, in marriage upon; what favour and grace is this! Can sinners be so sottish, foolish, and ungrateful, as not readily to receive and embrace this offer?
3. Sometimes, as we minded before, Ambassadors come with an embassy for trade, that there may be an open trade and commerce between such and such princes and states, &c.	3. The Ministers of the Gospel come with embassies for commerce; God is willing in Christ's name, to trade with man again: for no sooner had Adam sinned, but a war was commenced, and all trade forbidden: but now through Christ there is a free trade opened again to heaven; convinced and repenting sinners may be stored with all things they need, as pardon, peace, union, and communion with God, and eternal life, even all the riches of grace and glory: "Ho every one that will,—Come, buy;—and you that have no money, come, buy, and eat; yea, come, buy wine and milk without money, and without price," Isa. 55:1.

Metaphor[118]	Parallel
VI. Those that honor an Ambassador, honor the prince that sent him; but those that abase, slight, or despise him, do also despise the prince or state that sent him. We cannot despise this messenger, and yet honor his master, saith Mr. Gurnal.	VI. So those who receive and show all due respects to Christ's faithful Ministers, honor Christ, whose deputies they are, and whose Person they represent. "Few are so bold, as to say with that proud king, 'Who is the Lord, that I should obey him?'" Exod. 5:2. Yet many dare say, "Who is the Minister, that I should obey his message, or repent at his summons, or tremble at the words he speaks?" What is he? Do I not know him? What is he better than us? Shall I mind what he says? A rush for his doctrine, &c. But let such read that word, "He that heareth you, heareth me; and he that despised you, despised me; and he that despised me, despised him that sent me," Luke 10:16.
VII. An Ambassador should take heed he cast no indignity upon his office, by any base or unworthy practice; he should behave himself with all wisdom and gravity, and avoid all dirty and unseemly actions; for in so doing, he would bring much honor and renown not only to himself, but to his master also that sent him.	VII. So Ministers must be holy men, that they bring not themselves, and the dignity of their function, into contempt. A wise, grave and gracious behavior exceedingly becomes a Minister. Paul saith, he magnified his office. O then let others take heed they do not vilify and debase it. That which another man may do without much reproach, you cannot do, but it will be to your great blemish and dishonor, nay, and to the dishonor of Christ, and of his truth also.

Metaphor[118]	Parallel
VIII. An Ambassador is to do his uttermost endeavor to negotiate and accomplish such matters he is sent about; he must see to his charge: for if the treaty of peace, or marriage, or embassy for commerce and trade, succeed not, the Ambassador is sure to be called to an account, how he hath discharged his place, &c.	VIII. So Ministers must see the work of their place and function. "They are," saith Gurnal, "called Ambassadors, in regard of their duty, as well as dignity; where there is honor, there is *onus*, places of honor are places of trust. Many like well enough to bear the Ministers' dignity; with Diotrephes, they love pre-eminence, yet would willingly be excused the work that attends it. None have a greater trust reposed in their hands, than Ministers; it is *tremendum onus*, a weight that made the apostle tremble under it: 'I was among you, (saith Paul,) with much fear and trembling.'" They have the charge of souls committed to them, one of which is more worth than all the world, no less than the price of blood, the precious blood of Jesus Christ. To them is committed the Word of reconciliation. Hence they pray and beseech, and use all means imaginable to bring the souls of men to terms of peace and reconciliation with God, through Christ; they knowing the sad and dreadful effects, if they speed not in their embassy. "Knowing the terror of the Lord, we persuade men." And in another place, "We pray you in Christ's stead, be you reconciled to God," 2 Cor. 5:11, 20. For if the treaty of peace between God and sinners doth not succeed, the Minister is sure to be called to an account, how he discharged his trust in the business, &c.
IX. An Ambassador is to keep close to his instructions; he is in nothing to act contrary to, or derogate from his commission.	IX. So Ministers must see they Keep close to the Word of God; they had need to take their errand well before they come into the pulpit, or assembly of God's people. "I have received of the Lord, what I delivered unto you." They must speak nothing, require nothing, preach nothing, but what is according to the authority of God's Word, which is above the church, senates, general councils, or any authority whatsoever. These Ambassadors must act and do exactly according to their commission, &c.

Metaphor[118]	Parallel
X. An Ambassador must not only act according to his commission, as to matter, but must deliver his message also with much zeal, and with all due respect had to his master or prince that sent him. He must not prosecute his business coldly; or after he hath had audience, give himself to the pleasures of the court where he is resident, and mind his affairs no more, or not regard how his master's business succeeds. What answer will he be able to return? Surely, if he should do thus he could not say, he had done the work of a faithful Ambassador, &c.	X. So Ministers must be fitted with zeal, and act diligently in their places, or prosecute their business vigorously; their hearts must be deeply engaged in their spiritual embassy. They are to preach with all fervency, as having the sense of Christ's honour, and the worth of immortal souls upon their hearts; and not only say, Thus and thus saith the Lord, and be satisfied to see people willing to give them the hearing. Though they may thank them for that civility, yet they must not quit them, unless they see they accept of the terms of peace and reconciliation, offered to them in Christ's name through the Gospel. They must show them the profit that will accrue to them, if they do comply; and the danger, on the other hand, if they do refuse; and that it will be more intolerable for Sodom and Gomorrah in the day of judgment, than for them.
XI. It behooved an Ambassador to be faithful in all things to his master's interest, and not to become a pensioner to a foreign prince: for such an one is utterly unworthy of such an honorable employment.	XI. So Ministers must not comply with Christ's enemies, or seek for reward from them, such as would betray his interest, whatever is offered them, "But as we are allowed of God to be put in trust with the Gospel, even so we speak, not as pleasing men, but God which trieth our hearts. For neither at any time used we flattering words, as ye know, nor a cloak of covetousness, God is witness," 1 Thess. 2:4, 5.
XII. An Ambassador ought to seek the interest of his fellow-subjects, and show much love, care, and tenderness to them, so far as the interest of his prince will bear; and not to do any thing to the spoiling of their trade, &c.	XII. So Ministers ought to seek the good and welfare of all the saints and church of God, and help them by their counsel and prayers at all times; and not to weaken, but strengthen their hands, and protect them from the scorn, reproach, and oppression of the enemy, as much as lieth in them, &c.

Metaphor[118]	Parallel
XIII. When a prince finds his Ambassadors cannot succeed in their business, but that all terms of peace are rejected, he calls them home, and then bloody wars commonly follow.	XIII. So when God sees, that the messenger, and message he sends by his faithful Minister, is slighted, and that sinners remain obstinate, after long patience, he calls home his Ministers, perhaps takes them away by death, and resolves to treat with that people or state no more, but contrariwise, to let out his wrath upon them. And thus it fared with Israel of old. "The Lord God of their fathers sent to them by his messengers rising early, and sending them," &c. "But they mocked the messengers of God, and despised his Word, and misused his prophets, until the wrath of the Lord arose against his people, till there was no remedy," 2 Chron. 36:15, 16.

Based on the thirteen parallels, Keach interprets the ambassador metaphor by highlighting six inferences:

1. This shows what great dignity God hath conferred upon his faithful Ministers; and this title should procure an honorable esteem of them in the hearts of all persons to whom they are sent.

    Object. But some may say, If God will use Ambassadors to treat with sinners, why doth he not use angels? &c.

    Answ. 1. The Apostle answers this: "We have this treasure in our earthen vessels, that the excellency of the power may be of God, and not of us," 2 Cor. 4:7.

2. Ministers being men, have the advantage many ways above angels for this work. (1.) They are more concerned themselves in the message they bring, than angels are. What greater argument for a man's care than his own interest! (2.) They have a more deep sense arising in their hearts, upon the account of the temptations they are subject to, &c. (3.) The sufferings which ministers meet with for the Gospel's sake, are of great advantage to their brethren; had angels been the Ambassadors, they could not have sealed to the truth of their doctrine with their blood, they cannot die, &c. (4.) Besides the presence of angels might terrify and affrighted us, their glory is so great.

3. This shows, that Ministers have a special commission.
    Let poor sinners from hence be persuaded to hearken to them.

4. It shows the wonderful love of God, and the great care he hath of mens' souls.

5. It shows what an intolerable affront is offered to the Majesty of heaven by those that abuse or deride the ministers of the Gospel.

6. It shows the weight and importance of the preacher's message; it is not a slight or sleeveless errand they come about.[119]

Keach's work in *Tropologia* may at times stretch the implications of the images.[120] Nevertheless, the ambassadorial metaphor as reflected in Keach's theology of preaching, captures the dignity and duty of the minister. The metaphor expresses six particularities that can be defined as: (1) representative authority; (2) heavenly commission; (3) evangelistic persuasion; (4) divine care; (5) gospel affront; (6) eternal urgency. It is asserted that the concept of ambassador serves as the dominant metaphor that governs Keach's understanding of the minister's preaching. For Keach, the metaphor shaped ministerial identity, expressed eternal significance, and set forth the minister's primary charge.

Ambassador Metaphor in "The Gospel Minister's Maintenance Vindicated"

In *The Gospel Minister's Maintenance Vindicated* Keach grounds preaching in the ambassador metaphor.[121] While the document specifically argues for a minister's maintenance, Keach considers the duty of a preacher in the final section, "The Great and Weighty Work of a True Gospel Minister Opened." This is historically and theologically significant for two reasons. First, this represents a consensus view among early Particular Baptists on the function of the minister. Second, it provides particular insight into Keach's view of preaching.

The argument is divided into two parts. In the first part of the argument, the document begins with a claim concerning the preacher's office. Keach writes, "Tis a Holy and sublime Office; he is placed in a very high Sphere and Station, hence called the Ambassador of Christ."[122] The Ambassador metaphor is further explained: "They [ministers] are in

---

119. Keach, *Tropologia*, 854.

120. Keach seems to be aware of this possibility as he alludes to it in the preface of the work. See Keach, *Tropologia*, vi–viii.

121. Keach, *Gospel minister's maintenance vindicated*, 29.

122. Keach, *Gospel minister's maintenance vindicated*, 113.

Christ's stead employed in the great affairs of His spiritual kingdom; and have received authority from Him."[123] The first paragraph concludes, "Is it not a weighty thing to be made the Mouth of Christ?"[124] As shown in chapter 4, the ambassador metaphor serves as the dominant preaching motif in English Reformed preaching. It is central to Keach's own understanding of proclamation, for the preacher is representative of Christ in the preaching moment. The preacher "is the mouth of Christ." The representation element is tied to Christ's authority demonstrated in the preaching event.

In speaking directly to the task of preaching, Keach claims, "Our Preaching proves a Cause of Spiritual and Eternal Life."[125] He continues, "Your Preaching hath attendancy, either to save, or eternally to condemn the Souls of Men; and with what trembling then, ought this work to be undertaken and performed."[126] Keach makes clear that preaching holds eternal significance and must be taken seriously. Preachers must act as "watchmen" instructing men about "their Sins, and their Dangers, that so we (as instruments in God's Hand) may preserve their Souls."[127] This is part of the "Holy, High, and Peculiar Interest which Jesus Christ hath here below."[128] Likewise, preachers are "not only Stewards of the Mysteries of God" but also "Stewards of Christ's House."[129] What Keach means is explained in the statement, "For one chief End of Gospel Ministry is for the gathering together of the Saints; as well as for the Edifying the Body of Christ; therefore in every place where there is a Door opened for them, they must work hard whilst there are any Sinners to be called into the Vineyard."[130] Vital to the preacher's role are both evangelism and discipleship.

The second part of the argument discusses the various ministerial metaphors. He lists shepherds, guides, watchmen, planters, builders, laborers, fathers, angels, ambassadors, stars and rulers.[131] These metaphors describe the different functions of a pastor. The work is not easy

---

123. Keach, *Gospel minister's maintenance vindicated*, 114.
124. Keach, *Gospel minister's maintenance vindicated*, 114.
125. Keach, *Gospel minister's maintenance vindicated*, 117–18.
126. Keach, *Gospel minister's maintenance vindicated*, 118.
127. Keach, *Gospel minister's maintenance vindicated*, 119–20.
128. Keach, *Gospel minister's maintenance vindicated*, 121.
129. Keach, *Gospel minister's maintenance vindicated*, 122.
130. Keach, *Gospel minister's maintenance vindicated*, 123.
131. Keach, *Gospel minister's maintenance vindicated*, 124.

because it is "a Mysterious Work."¹³² It is difficult because it requires "the greatest Care and Exactness."¹³³ The work demands "the greatest strength" in "grace and wisdom."¹³⁴ It necessitates the preacher's "time and diligence."¹³⁵ Last, the work of preaching is difficult because of the "grand obstructions" from the preacher's own heart, from sin, Satan, the world, and from persecutors.¹³⁶ Thus, the tract concludes, "Remember we serve a good Master: Besides, a necessity is laid upon us, we must Preach the Gospel."¹³⁷

Ambassador Metaphor in Sermons

Keach uses the metaphor throughout his sermons. He frequently identifies the close relationship between representation and authority. Keach claims, "The office of a minister, or pastor of a church, is an office of dignity . . . for they represent Christ's person, therefore they are called ambassadors.¹³⁸ Preaching ministers, "being Christ's stewards, and also his ambassadors," have "honor due to them, as they represent Christ's person."¹³⁹ Since the minister represents Christ in the preaching event, Keach claims that to reject the minister's words is to reject Christ's word. He declares, "Christ's ambassadors do offer peace to you in their great Master's name; what answer will you give them. . . . What, doth God and Jesus Christ entreat and beseech you to be reconciled, and dare you refuse?"¹⁴⁰ In *A Golden Mine Opened*, he says, "Little do Sinners think what they do when they sleep under the Word, disregard, slight and despise the Word of this Salvation in the Mouths of Christ's Ministers, Christ's Ambassadors."¹⁴¹ For Keach, there is an evangelistic function expressed through the metaphor. He claims, "Ministers are Christ's spokesmen to persuade sinners to receive and embrace the Lord Jesus, and espouse him. . . . A minister is Christ's ambassador, and when one sinner

---

132. Keach, *Gospel minister's maintenance vindicated*, 126–27.
133. Keach, *Gospel minister's maintenance vindicated*, 128.
134. Keach, *Gospel minister's maintenance vindicated*, 128.
135. Keach, *Gospel minister's maintenance vindicated*, 129.
136. Keach, *Gospel minister's maintenance vindicated*, 129–31.
137. Keach, *Gospel minister's maintenance vindicated*, 131–32.
138. Keach, *Exposition of the Parables*, 264.
139. Keach, *Exposition of the Parables*, 635.
140. Keach, *Exposition of the Parables*, 64.
141. Keach, *Golden Mine Opened*, 431–32.

is converted under his ministry, he succeeds in his embassy."[142] Also, "So are Christ's Ministers, they are to pray, to intreat, to beseech Sinners to be reconciled to God; We pray you in Christ's stead. . . . Faithful Ministers are willing to spend their Lives to win Souls to Christ, yea, to die upon the spot to save one poor Sinner."[143]

Summary of the Ambassador Metaphor

Keach claims, "An Ambassador is a Person of Eminency and Honor in his Prince's Sight, they represent their Prince's Person; so is Christ's true and faithful Minister; he is one that Christ confers great Dignity and Honor upon."[144] He is consistent in the way he articulates the image. Keach uses the title of minister to refer to the role while the ambassadorial metaphor describes the function of proclamation. For Keach, the ambassador metaphor conveys the minister's duty and dignity. This is nuanced, expressing the concept of representative authority. Thus, ambassadors "act and do in his Name."[145] Ambassadorial preaching assumes an evangelistic function as ministers "sow the seed of the gospel . . . in his name, in his stead, or by his authority."[146] Consequently, ambassadorial preaching carries spiritual gravitas as it possesses eternal significance. Therefore, he states, "Consider well, and remember that your Pastors are the Ministers; nay, the Ambassadors of Jesus Christ; such who represent his Sacred Majesty, and have his Commission, for what they act and do in his Name, and dispense the Mysteries of God to you, according to their Duty."[147]

The Divine Preacher

For Keach, the locus of God's communication is in the Son. If God has spoken "himself in" the Son,[148] then "Jesus Christ is the mouth of God."[149] As a result, he sees a unique relationship between the human and divine

142. Keach, *Exposition of the Parables*, 369.
143. Keach, *Display of Glorious Grace*, 141.
144. Keach, *Display of Glorious Grace*, 136–37.
145. Keach, *Gospel minister's maintenance vindicated*, 77.
146. Keach, *Exposition of the Parables*, 122.
147. Keach, *Gospel minister's maintenance vindicated*, 77.
148. Keach, *Golden Mine Opened*, 430.
149. Keach, *Tropologia*, 370.

word. Expanding upon the ambassador metaphor, Keach states, "Moreover, he [Christ] speaks still, he it is that speaks to you now, day by day, by us his poor ministers."[150] Christ speaks in the present through his representative ambassador. Keach calls this ambassadorial preaching, "the Word of this salvation in the mouths of Christ's ministers."[151] So, if Christ is communicating in the preaching event, then those who listen should not reject the minister's exposition. In the same context, Keach preaches,

> All this is because it is Christ's Word, and *Christ that speaks to you by his Servants*; the same Contempt that is showed to the Ambassadors of an earthly King, is showed to him; and he treats them as if it were done unto himself. Moreover, the Esteem and Honor that is showed to an Ambassador in receiving his Word, or in hearkening with awe and respect to what he says in his Master's Name, is shown to the King. Ministers are not to be esteemed or had in Honor for their own sakes, but for Christ's sake: But if you love Christ, honor Christ, you will love and respect his faithful Servants, and hearken to what they speak unto you in his Name and by his Authority.[152]

Keach argues that those who show disrespect to the ambassador of Christ show contempt for Christ himself. He explains, "Moreover, it may inform us why some who do hear God's word profit not; alas, they hear it not as it is truly the Word of God, nor attend upon it with diligence, with faith, and godly reverence: the voice of the minister of Christ is God's voice, or the voice of Jesus Christ; but this they believe not."[153] To the extent that Keach is grounding his theology of preaching in the Second Helvetic Confession is unknown; however, he does maintain that the preached word is truly the word of God.[154] It is "Christ, by the preaching of the gospel and operations of his Spirit" who works in the preaching event.[155]

In Keach's homiletical theology, Christ is communicating to the audience in the preaching event. Thus, "it's his Voice that creates us again."[156] On one hand, this requires diligence on the part of the ambas-

---

150. Keach, *Golden Mine Opened*, 431–32.
151. Keach, *Golden Mine Opened*, 431–32.
152. Keach, *Golden Mine Opened*, 431–32; emphasis added.
153. Keach, *Exposition of the Parables*, 857.
154. It is known that Keach read Bullinger. See Arnold, *Reformed Theology*, 42. We can infer that Keach is aware of the Second Helvetic Confession.
155. Keach, *Exposition of the Parables*, 546.
156. Keach, *Golden Mine Opened*, 83.

sador to preach Christ's message faithfully. On the other, it demands the hearer to have faith to hear the preached word. Therefore, those who hear the preaching of the word must, "Labor to hear the Voice of Christ's Spirit in and with the Word, or you are undone forever."[157] In order to hear this divine voice, believers must, "hear Christ's Voice *in the Ministry of his Word*, they attend upon the preaching of the Gospel, and look upon the Word delivered in Christ's Name, by his faithful Ministers, to be the Voice of Christ unto them."[158]

Preaching is an act of participation between human and divine. This happens as the preacher relies upon the written word and the Spirit of God, for Christ's voice cannot be separated from either.[159] In *The Gospel Minister's Maintenance Vindicated*, Keach highlights this cooperative element between the preacher and Christ. Though preachers function as "instruments, serving him as the principal agent, and efficient Cause" both the minister and Christ "work together" in the preaching moment.[160] This takes place as the Spirit works upon the souls of men through the "exhortations, motives, and arguments" of the minister.[161] Hence, the preacher must be faithful in his work so that "our Labors are a sweet savor in the Nostrils of God."[162] For Keach, the minister is the instrumental cause while Christ is the "principal agent, and efficient cause" in the preaching event. Thus, "The success and blessing of the word wholly depends upon Jesus Christ."[163] Additionally, through the proclamation of the gospel the glory of the triune God is revealed.[164] In the gospel, "we may learn to give equal honor to the Father, and to the Son, and to the Holy Ghost, they being all but one and the same God . . . one in essence."[165]

---

157. Keach, *Golden Mine Opened*, 86.
158. Keach, *Golden Mine Opened*, 80–81.
159. Keach, *Golden Mine Opened*, 80.
160. Keach, *Gospel minister's maintenance vindicated*, 115.
161. Keach, *Gospel minister's maintenance vindicated*, 115.
162. Keach, *Gospel minister's maintenance vindicated*, 116.
163. Keach, *Exposition of the Parables*, 479.
164. Keach, *Exposition of the Parables*, 33–34.
165. Keach, *Exposition of the Parables*, 34.

Summary

In the third question, the relationship between the human and divine preacher is highlighted. For Keach, preaching is a synergistic association between the ambassador and God. Keach's homiletical theology demonstrates a theological logic. The Father has spoken through the Son, and the revelation of the Son is codified by the Spirit in the written word. The minister preaches the word in the power of the Spirit. Consequently, Jesus, the mouth of God, speaks through his minister, the mouth of Christ, as the preacher faithfully expounds the word in the demonstration of the Spirit's power. The effectiveness of this is detailed in the subsequent section. Nevertheless, in this way, "preaching is the continuation of the living voice of God (the *viva vox Dei*), now fully formed by Scripture."[166] While Keach does not explicitly use the phrase "preaching the word of God is the word of God," it is evident that he advocates a homiletical theology similar to the Bullingerian-Helvetic tradition.[167] Keach's theology of preaching aligns with the broader mainstream Reformed preaching tradition. Therefore, the voice of Christ is operative in the ministry of the word, which must be received by faith. The minister, as an ambassador, is given representative authority from Christ. The audience is invited to hear him/Him. The minister's authority to minister the word is not derived from giftedness. Rather, it stems from the divine call to the task. Consequently, preaching is an experiential process.

QUESTION FOUR (MEANS): HOW IS PREACHING MADE EFFECTIVE?

The fourth question logically follows from the third theo-homiletical conviction. This question elucidates how preaching becomes effective for the hearers. Specifically, it examines the interplay between the Spirit and human rhetoric in the preaching event. For Keach, the Reformed theological logic of the outward and inward means influences this aspect of his homiletical theology. Keach also draws upon Perkins's insights regarding the use of human rhetoric in the pulpit. Given the focus of Keach's proclamation, he comprehends the efficacy of preaching as the work of the Spirit. The question further reveals the spiritual potency of Keach's

---

166. Ward, "Preaching and Revelation," 59.

167. This substantiates Halstead's plea for a Baptist acceptance of a "sermon as revelation" theology of preaching. See, Halstead, "*Verbum Dei*."

theology of preaching. As observed in question three, this question also demonstrates that Keach holds a profound pneumatic conviction in his theology of preaching.

The Effectual Operations of the Spirit in Preaching

As mentioned in chapter 4, the Reformed preaching tradition described preaching using the language of *outward* and *inward means*. Keach follows this terminology. He claims, "Christ must change the Sinners Heart by the infusing of his Spirit, and so unite the Soul to himself, by which means he brings the Sinner into the Bonds of the Covenant: *The outward means* is indeed the Preaching of the Gospel, but the *inward and effectual means*, is the efficacious Operations of the Holy Spirit."[168] It is through the outward means of the ministry of the word and the inward means of the Spirit that sinners are regenerated.[169] In the *Short Confession of Faith*, Article XII sets forth a statement concerning the ordinary means of grace. Keach writes,

> We believe that the outward and more ordinary means, whereby Christ communicates to us the Benefits of Redemption, are his Holy Ordinances, as Prayer, the Word of God, and Preaching, with Baptism, and the Lord's Supper, and yet notwithstanding it is the Spirit of God that makes Prayer, Reading, and specially the Preaching of the Word, effectual to the convincing, converting, building up, and comforting, through Faith, all the Elect of God unto Salvation. And that it is the Duty of all, that the Word may become effectual to their Salvation, to attend upon it with all Diligence, Preparation, and Prayer, that they may receive it with Faith and Love, and lay it up in their Hearts, and practice it in their Lives.[170]

It is in these ordinary means of grace that Christ "communicates to us the benefits of redemption" inwardly by the Spirit of God. The language in this article is adapted from the Westminster Larger Catechism:

> Q. 154. *What are the outward means whereby Christ communicates to us the benefits of his mediation?* A. The outward and ordinary means whereby Christ communicates to his church

---

168. Keach, *Display of Glorious Grace*, 55; emphasis added.
169. Keach, *Golden Mine Opened*, 151.
170. Keach, *Short confession of faith*, 19–20.

> the benefits of his mediation, are all his ordinances, especially the word, sacraments, and prayer; all which are made effectual to the elect for their salvation.
>
> Q. 155. *How is the word made effectual to salvation?* A. The Spirit of God maketh the reading, but especially the preaching of the word, an effectual means of enlightening, convincing, and humbling sinners; of driving them out of themselves, and drawing them unto Christ; of conforming them to his image, and subduing them to his will; of strengthening them against temptations and corruptions; of building them up in grace, and establishing their hearts in holiness and comfort through faith unto salvation.[171]

According to Keach, preaching is the very means by which sinners are drawn by the Spirit unto faith. In commenting on John 6:44, Keach says, "This is not the drawing of ministers... but of the sublime and irresistible influences of the holy God upon the heart, by which he inclines, bows, and subjects the stubborn and rebellious will to believe and receive the Lord Jesus Christ."[172] Specifically, Christ communicates the benefits of redemption by the ordinance of preaching, therefore, identifying the act of proclamation as a means of grace. The outward means of preaching becomes efficacious by means of the inward working of the Spirit. God "by the Arm of his Power" brings sinners to salvation "by the effectual Operation of his Word and Spirit."[173] Therefore, the gospel of God's grace is the "means by which God works grace" in the hearts of the elect.[174] As a result, Keach believes that the preached word is ineffective without the agency of the Spirit. "The voice of Christ's Word, without the Spirit, is not sufficient; the Word will not make sinners hear, though it be spoken a thousand times over, except the Spirit voice do accompany it."[175]

The "voice of Christ" is heard through the ministry of the gospel. His voice is efficacious to the hearer by means of the Spirit. "The Gospel is the instrumental means, through the Spirit's Operations," and is effective in bringing sinners to salvation.[176] For, the Spirit is "an awakening voice... a convincing voice... soul-quickening voice... soul-humbling

---

171. Westminster Assembly, "Larger Catechism," 333–35.
172. Keach, *Exposition of the Parables*, 356.
173. Keach, *Golden Mine Opened*, 123.
174. Keach, *Tropologia*, 532.
175. Keach, *Golden Mine Opened*, 81.
176. Keach, *Display of Glorious Grace*, 121.

and a self-abasing voice . . . soul-regenerating voice . . . sin-killing voice . . . soul-strengthening voice . . . a comforting voice."[177] He says to the congregation, "Rest not therefore upon the bare hearing of the Word of Christ; take heed that the Gospel comes not to you in Word only, but in power also."[178]

He goes further to show that the "voice of Christ in the ministry of his Word" is "Christ's Spirit" illuminating the truth of Scripture. He claims, "Bless God you have Christ's voice, Christ's Word sounding in your ears. . . . Labor to hear the voice of Christ's Spirit in and with the Word, or you are undone forever."[179] According to Keach, the voice of Christ is the voice of the Spirit in the ministry of the preached word. He explicitly states, "The Holy Spirit is sent to treat with Sinners in Christ's Name, it is hereby Christ himself speaks to them from Heaven."[180] The Spirit of God actualizes the voice of the risen Christ in the preaching of the word.

The manifestation of this occurs through the specific functions of the Holy Spirit. The Spirit's primary function is the conviction of sin.[181] Furthermore, the Spirit enhances and strengthens faith through the power of the word.[182] The Spirit illuminates the truth of Scripture. The Spirit generates "zeal and fervency."[183] He claims, "The Word by the Spirit, softens the hard and stony heart, and makes it a heart of flesh."[184] It is through the word and the Spirit that regeneration transpires. Specifically, Keach writes, "The Spirit of God causes the saints to grow in grace, and in the knowledge of our Lord Jesus Christ. The Spirit moves upon the affections, and every other faculty of the heart, and by that means causes the seed of grace to take the deeper root."[185] This illustrates the pneumatological aspect of his homiletic. His reliance on the Spirit's role in relation to the preached word further reveals how the voice of Christ becomes known during the preaching event. Consequently, without the Spirit, the outward preaching of the word does not yield its intended effect. This

177. Keach, *Golden Mine Opened*, 81–83.
178. Keach, *Golden Mine Opened*, 86.
179. Keach, *Golden Mine Opened*, 86.
180. Keach, *Golden Mine Opened*, 462.
181. Keach, *Exposition of the Parables*, 126.
182. Keach, *Golden Mine Opened*, 499.
183. Keach, *Tropologia*, 577.
184. Keach, *Tropologia*, 578.
185. Keach, *Tropologia*, 499.

effective component is crucial in comprehending Keach's perspective on human rhetoric.

Human Eloquence and Learning

Scholars have shown Keach's homiletical application of metaphors.[186] Holmes argues that Keach used metaphors homiletically in three ways: "illustration, theological explanation, and sermonic application."[187] Thus, the use of metaphor was a means of God's condescension.[188] In this sense, Keach's plain preaching did possess a rhetorical element. However, he does warn that reliance on human eloquence stands in contrast to preaching *in the demonstration of the Spirit*.[189] He claims, "Maybe you come to hear men, and not Christ, speak to you; or had too great an eye upon the instruments by whom the gospel is administered. . . . Sirs, the efficacy of the word lies not in the gifts, learning, eloquence, or abilities of ministers, but alone in the agency of the Holy Spirit."[190] Keach ties the "efficacy of the word" to the "agency of the Holy Spirit." He uses the apostle Paul as an illustration of this conviction. He declares,

> He [Paul] acted not the part of a philosopher or orator at Athens, but used plainness of speech, and disowned human eloquence, and checked all plausible affectations and artifice of words, which the orators of his time used; he was not for rhetorical flourishes, or persuasive oratory; not for the inductions of Plato, nor the syllogisms of Aristotle, nor the subtilties of Seneca, nor the smooth and elaborate blandishments of Cicero. No, no, he delivered the gospel freely, boldly, and plainly, without rhetorical persuasions, in the demonstration of the Spirit; and so ought all Christ's ministers.[191]

Keach's refusal to implore rhetorical eloquence was not primarily the result of his disdain for rhetoric itself. Rather, his conviction concerning the Spirit's role in preaching prompts him to reject "persuasive oratory" in favor of plain preaching. Persuasive oratory only affects "the

---

186. See Holmes, "Role of Metaphor," 106–31.
187. Holmes, "Role of Metaphor," 175.
188. Vaughn, "Public Worship Practical Theology," 97.
189. See Perkins, *Art of Prophesying*, 349–50.
190. Keach, *Exposition of the Parables*, 20.
191. Keach, *Exposition of the Parables*, 254–55.

Ear rather than to work upon the Heart of their Hearers."[192] The concept of *plain* is related directly to the simplicity of the gospel and the Spirit's power. As a result, "the voice of Christ [i.e., preaching in the demonstration of the Spirit's power] does not only cause the Ear to hear, but the Heart to hear also."[193] Likewise, "philosophical learning" is not sufficient to "bring men to the saving knowledge of God and Jesus Christ."[194] A preacher should preach nothing "but sound doctrine" and "not to feed the People with *airy and empty Notions*."[195] This is because those "who are weak in knowledge" cannot discern truth and error.[196] Keach's bibliology also leads him to be cautious with the use of human eloquence in preaching. Thus, "Consider the majesty and authoritativeness of the Spirit of God speaking in them [Scripture] . . . its simplicity is joined with majesty commanding the veneration of all serious men. Not like the writings of men, filled with elaborate blandishments, or human elegancy, that tickle the ear and fancy, and relish with the flesh."[197] Scripture does not need to be aided by human embellishments. Rather, "Ministers ought to speak Intelligibly, so as the People may understand."[198] Additionally, there is a pastoral apprehension toward human eloquence. Keach is concerned particularly that using the means of human knowledge might lead the hearers to mere *head knowledge*. He says, "There is a twofold knowledge of divine things: One notional, the other an effective and experimental knowledge. Now some men only hear the mysteries of the gospel, out of curiosity to fill their heads with knowledge."[199]

Additionally, he warns of the danger of "fruitless and insufficient" *speculative knowledge*.[200] True wisdom does not consist "in bare head or mere speculative knowledge" but "Christ crucified."[201] Keach does not reject the value of learning. He is, however, cautious as it relates to ministers

192. Keach, *Golden Mine Opened*, 120.

193. Keach, *Golden Mine Opened*, 82. For Keach, "the voice of Christ in the ministry of his Word" is "Christ's Spirit" illuminating the truth of Scripture.

194. Keach, *Exposition of the Parables*, 712.

195. Keach, *Golden Mine Opened*, 132.

196. Keach, *Golden Mine Opened*, 132.

197. Keach, *Exposition of the Parables*, 849.

198. Keach, *Golden Mine Opened*, 119–20. Keach is quoting Matthew Poole, who says, "We speak intelligibly, so as all the people may understand. . . . We speak gravely and decently." See Poole, *Annotations upon the Holy Bible*, 543.

199. Keach, *Exposition of the Parables*, 4.

200. Keach, *Exposition of the Parables*, 118.

201. Keach, *Exposition of the Parables*, 659.

and preaching. He claims, "Men cannot make ministers of Christ: many are ministers of man's making, not of Christ's making. Also, human learning or knowledge of the tongues will not do it, nor can bishops do it; no, it is Christ's work only; nor may any preach that think they are gifted; for unless they are regularly called by a true church to whom they belong, they are intruders if they take upon them to preach the gospel."[202] God is the one who gives "all ministerial gifts and grace."[203] Keach contrasts the "ministers of man's making only" and "Christ's ministers."[204] This distinction is between the highly educated ministers of the Church of England and those who have been called by a local church.[205] He states,

> Though I am no enemy to human learning but have often wished (if God saw it good, and it might tend to his glory) that all that are true ministers had the knowledge of the tongues, but perhaps God hath on purpose chose such who are base things, or men unlearned, to confound the wise and learned. Learning is good, if not abused; it is a good handmaid, but a bad mistress. It is indeed a shame to some that have lately rendered men, who have not the knowledge of the tongues, unfit to preach, as if they could not speak sense, or good English, nor understand the scripture; and what is this but to magnify such learning above the Spirit's teaching, and the gifts of men above those ministerial gifts given by Jesus Christ? Man ought not to preach, to whom Christ hath not given ministerial gifts unto, and capacitated to open the word of life. It is one thing to do it by art or by human learning, and another to do it by virtue of that gift God hath given to a man; and he cannot be a minister of Christ, whom Christ never gave gifts to, nor authorized to preach the gospel.[206]

The phrase, "learning is good, if not abused; it is a good handmaid, but a bad mistress," summarizes Keach's view of human study. What qualifies one to preach is Christ's ministerial gifts. Christ empowers his ministers with these gifts because they proclaim his gospel.[207] He will not allow his gospel to falter or fail on account of the preacher's inadequacies.

---

202. Keach, *Exposition of the Parables*, 254.
203. Keach, *Exposition of the Parables*, 265–66.
204. Keach, *Exposition of the Parables*, 806.
205. Keach identifies the "ministers of man's making" as "national ministers." See Keach, *Exposition of the Parables*, 806.
206. Keach, *Exposition of the Parables*, 636–37.
207. Keach, *Exposition of the Parables*, 815.

Therefore, preaching is ultimately something that God does and humans participate in this divine work.

Summary

Keach's theological perspective on preaching emphasizes the pivotal role of the Holy Spirit in the preaching process. He firmly believes that the Spirit empowers the preacher, enabling them to manifest Christ's voice effectively during sermons. It is through the Spirit that the word becomes impactful and meaningful to the audience. For Keach, human rhetoric can hinder the preacher's ability to demonstrate the Spirit's power in their preaching. This notion is similar to Perkins's articulation, as presented in chapter 4. Yet, Keach used metaphor to his advantage, sometimes venturing into allegory.

While Keach acknowledged the value of human learning, he cautioned against relying solely on education or personal giftedness. Instead, the communicator of God's word must rely on Christ to bless them with ministerial gifts that enable them to preach effectively. Consequently, a synergetic relationship emerges between the human and divine preacher in the realm of preaching. As the minister proclaims the sermon outwardly, the Spirit works inwardly, contributing to the profound mystery of preaching.

QUESTION FIVE (CONTEXT): WHERE IS PREACHING TAKING PLACE?

As question four has shown, there is a spiritual and mysterious aspect to Keach's theology of preaching. This aspect is reflected in the larger Reformed preaching tradition. Question five, *where is preaching taking place*, is explored. James Renihan asserts that in Particular Baptist worship, "the act of preaching was the high point of public worship."[208] The ecclesiological function of preaching must be set within the context of worship and in relationship to the ordinances of baptism and the Lord's Supper.[209] Matthew Ward argues, "The strongest proof of the centrality

---

208. Renihan, *Edification and Beauty*, 129.

209. Ward argues, "Seventeenth-century English Christians understood 'worship' as the administration of ordinances in a church's corporate services. They understood that the Puritan mark of a true church as the right administration of the ordinances had

of pure worship to the early Baptists was the relationship they drew between pure worship and the pure message of salvation in the gospel of Jesus Christ."[210] As it pertains to worship, Keach believes that only those authorized and called by a particular church can administer "the ordinances of the gospel."[211] Therefore, seeing preaching as it relates to the ordinances demonstrates the nuances of how Keach understands the *sacramental* aspect of his homiletical theology.[212] As Vaughn comments on Keach's preaching, "There is a legitimate sense in which such spirituality can be called 'sacramental.'"[213]

Ecclesiology and Worship

Ward again writes, "In their worship, the Baptists wanted to celebrate the purity of the gospel, and they were willing to reevaluate much about their churches in the process."[214] This desire for gospel purity prompted the seventeenth-century Particular Baptists to consider the various implications of the gospel in relation to their worship practices. As a result, they cultivated what Ward calls the "gospel as a liturgical hermeneutic." He claims, "To call the gospel a liturgical hermeneutic simply means that Baptists considered and intended their worship to communicate and embody the gospel of Jesus Christ."[215] Therefore, the basis of worship for the early English Particular Baptists was the reality of the gospel. This provided them with the paradigm for their ecclesiology and liturgy. Keach is a primary figure in this liturgical reorientation. He codifies much of the early Particular Baptist views on the church in *The Glory of a True Church*. In the work, he provides the definition of a church:

---

to do with the church's worship, not simply the proper age for baptism. Early Particular Baptists absorbed that centrality of worship, taking it to new conclusions. Pure worship was their 'distinctive' not in the sense of 'only' concern but primary or overarching concern." Ward, *Pure Worship*, 217. For a contemporary discussion on the ordinances from a Baptist perspective, see Schreiner and Crawford, *Lord's Supper*, and Schreiner and Wright, *Believer's Baptism*.

210. Ward, *Pure Worship*, 219.
211. Keach, *Exposition of the Parables*, 266.
212. See Beach, "Real Presence of Christ," 92.
213. Vaughn, "Public Worship Practical Theology," 123.
214. Ward, *Pure Worship*, 150.
215. Ward, *Pure Worship*, 145.

> A Church of Christ, according to the Gospel-Institution, is a Congregation of Godly Christians, who as a Stated-Assembly (being first baptized upon the Profession of Faith) do by mutual agreement and consent give themselves up to the Lord, and one to another, according to the Will of God; and do ordinarily meet together in one Place, for the Public Service and Worship of God; among whom the Word of God and Sacraments are duly administered, according to Christ's Institution.[216]

A local congregation consists of "all converted persons" who "solemnly enter into a Covenant" with each other.[217] With reference to worship, Keach says, "The public worship of God ought to be preferred before private. This supposes there must be a visible church; and that they frequently meet together to worship God; they have an orderly ministry and one ordained elder."[218] As a result, individuals in public worship experience "more of His intimate presence" and see the "clearest manifestations of God's beauty."[219] The public worship of the church is "the nearest resemblance of heaven" on earth.[220] For him, "the word of God is the only rule for worship."[221] The intimacy of God's presence is directly related to the ordinary means of grace.

Specifically, regarding the ordinary means of grace, Keach writes, "We believe that the outward and more ordinary means, whereby Christ communicates to us the Benefits of Redemption, are his Holy Ordinances, as Prayer, the Word of God, and Preaching, with Baptism, and the Lord's Supper."[222] Consequently, only those who are regenerated can partake of their benefits.[223] Keach did hold a positive view of the means.[224] However, he did maintain that the means of grace were not salvific. For even if the sinner "reads, prays, is baptized, breaks bread with God's people . . .

---

216. Keach, *Glory of a true church*, 5–6.
217. Keach, *Glory of a true church*, 6–7.
218. Keach, *Glory of a true church*, 63–64.
219. Keach, *Glory of a true church*, 65–66.
220. Keach, *Glory of a true church*, 67.
221. Keach, *Exposition of the Parables*, 13.
222. Keach, *Short confession of faith*, 19–20.
223. Keach, *Exposition of the Parables*, 808.
224. Keach, *Exposition of the Parables*, 712. Keach says, "The outward means ought to be improved; God having appointed it in order to our obtaining grace . . . it is only to them the gospel comes in power unto, (by the mighty working of the Spirit) that grace is wrought in the hearts of some."

perish he must for all this, if he is not born again."[225] The means of grace, therefore, must lead to Christ alone for salvation. He affirms that all external religious practices or preparations cannot redeem sinners:

> Because salvation is only in Jesus Christ; all that seek justification and eternal life, and do not seek Jesus Christ, shall certainly perish.... No other name, or thing, not by repenting, nor mourning for sin, no, not by leaving off sin, or reformation of life, not by good works, nor by inherent righteousness, not by being baptized, nor by receiving the Lord's Supper, no, nor by giving to the poor, nor by suffering for Christ or religion; for there is no salvation to be had but by Christ alone. In the way of duty and of ordinances you ought to seek him, and may meet with him; but if any rest on their duties, works, or righteousness, nay, on faith itself as the matter by which they hope to be justified and saved, they will certainly perish. It is not faith itself, but Christ that faith receives, or the object faith relies upon, that saves us.[226]

For Keach, there is a close relationship between baptism, the Supper, and preaching. He argues that the two ordinances demonstrate before the eyes what the preached word announces to the ear.[227] For Keach, the ordinances possess no meaning apart from the preached word and faith.[228] Nevertheless, the ordinances and preaching work together to communicate Christ and edify those in the congregation. However, preaching has a distinct function. Proclamation, therefore, takes a primary role within Particular Baptist worship.[229] Keach claims preaching is the "great ordinance" given by Christ to redeem sinners.[230]

The Ordinances of Baptism and the Lord's Supper

Keach argues that baptism and the Supper are instituted by Christ to "hold forth . . . to the very sight of our visible eyes . . . .the glorious doctrine of his death, burial, and resurrection, which in the ministration of

---

225. Keach, *Exposition of the Parables*, 118.
226. Keach, *Exposition of the Parables*, 200–201.
227. Keach, *Gold Refin'd*, 43.
228. For a Puritan theology of the sacraments see Holifield, *Covenant Sealed*.
229. Ward, *Pure Worship*, 142.
230. Keach, *Golden Mine Opened*, 309.

the Word, is preached or held forth to the hearing of our ears."[231] Christ "ordained and appointed" the ordinances "to signify" realities of the gospel.[232] Keach uses the word *ordinance* to refer to specific elements of worship ordained by Christ (i.e., the reading of Scripture, preaching, prayer, singing, baptism, and Lord's Supper) and applies *sacrament* to baptism and the Lord's Supper.

Keach's theology of baptism is concerned with a "properly constituted, visible church."[233] For him, baptism has three primary components—"that is, into the profession of his faith, confession of his name, and communion with his Church."[234] Specifically, the ordinance is "a lively symbol of his death, burial, and resurrection . . . a pledge of the remission of all your sins."[235] Keach writes, "The sacramental dipping in water, baptism, represents his death and burial; and the coming from under the water, his resurrection."[236] Keach sees a spiritual aspect to the ordinance.[237] He claims, "We have Fellowship with Christ in his Death in Baptism, or the Efficacy of his Death evidenced to us, as the outward symbol of it is held forth in the external Administration of it."[238] Keach sees a connection between the sign and the thing signified: "There is a plain Representation of the Mystery and inward Grace, we are said to be buried and risen both in Signification and also in lively Representation of the inward and spiritual Burial and Resurrection with Christ. . . . Here is mention made of the Sign, and of the Thing signified."[239] Specifically,

> Baptism is a means of conveying this Grace, when the Spirit is pleased to operate with it; but it doth not work as a physical Cause upon the Soul as a Purge doth upon the Humours of the Body. . . . As a Man cannot be said to be nourished without Faith, so he cannot be said to be a new Creature without Faith . . . Faith

---

231. Keach, *Gold Refin'd*, 43.

232. Keach, *Gold Refin'd*, 42.

233. Riker, *Catholic Reformed Theologian*, 111. This section cannot show the specific aspects of Keach's baptism theology. However, see Riker's entire section in *Catholic Reformed Theologian*, 111–221.

234. Keach, *Tropologia*, 629.

235. Keach, *Exposition of the Parables*, 603.

236. Keach, *Tropologia*, 631.

237. Keach practiced the "laying on of hands" following baptism. This further indicates a spiritual aspect to the ordinances. This particular ordinance was known to be a General Baptist practice. See Keach, *Short confession of faith*, 23–24.

238. Keach, *Golden Mine Opened*, 133.

239. Keach, *Gold Refin'd*, 79.

only is the Principle of spiritual Life, and the Principle which draws Nourishment from the Means of God's Appointment.[240]

As it relates to the Supper, Keach proclaims, "A Crucified Christ is the Bread of Life, and by Faith in this Ordinance we feed on this Bread; it feeds and strengthens our Faith, and also our Love to the Lord Jesus.... When you take this Bread, and this Cup, you declare you take and accept of Christ as the only Food of your Souls."[241] He further states,

> By this Ordinance we learn, and clearly see, (1.) the horrible Evil of Sin, the cursed Nature of Sin, in that nothing could atone for it, nor satisfy the Law and Justice of God, but the precious Blood of the Son of God himself. (2.) Here likewise we see that infinite Love of the Father, in giving of Christ to die for us.... (3) Here also we perceive the wonderful Love of Jesus Christ, who willingly laid down his Life for us. (4.) Moreover, here we see how we come to be saved, or the Way of Life; and that it is only by a Sacrifice, and that by the Sacrifice of Christ himself alone. (5.) Here we see our near Union with Christ, and blessed Union one with another, as the Bread and Wine is turned into Nourishment.[242]

Likewise, "as a Sign and Token of this Confirmation of the New Covenant," the Lord's Supper demonstrates that Christ procured "justification, reconciliation, pardon of sin, and eternal life" for those who partake.[243] There is also "a mystical conveyance or communication of all Christ's blessed merits to our souls through faith held forth."[244] It is a "soul-reviving cordial."[245]

The ordinances of baptism and the Lord's Supper are indeed signs representing spiritual realities. In one sense, Keach maintains a memorialism akin to Zwingli's theological formulation.[246] Indeed, for Keach, baptism is a *living figure* while the Supper is considered a *sign/token*.[247] In

---

240. Keach, *Gold Refin'd*, 128–29.
241. Keach, *Golden Mine Opened*, 133–34.
242. Keach, *Golden Mine Opened*, 133–34.
243. Keach, *Golden Mine Opened*, 209.
244. Keach, *Tropologia*, 639.
245. Keach, *Tropologia*, 621. See Haykin, *Amidst Us Our Beloved*, 37.
246. See Grace, "Early English Baptists' View." For a recent discussion on Zwingli's view of the Supper, see Yeung, *Received by Christ*.
247. Keach, *Counter-antidote*, 9. Keach says, "Let all Men consider in the fear of God, and take notice of the gracious design, and condescension of our blessed Savior

another way, these ordinances possessed a spirituality that can be rightly described as sacramental in the Reformed sense.[248] Contrary to Rome, this spirituality did not have sacerdotal implications.[249] The benefits of the ordinances were not communicated ex opere operato.[250] Keach says of the Supper, "Jesus Christ is eaten spiritually, not as the papists do imagine."[251] Some scholars suggest that Keach was "surprisingly inconsistent" regarding his views of the ordinances.[252] However, Keach maintains that baptism and the Supper (signs) are the means the Spirit uses to communicate grace to faithful recipients. For example, in *Instructions for Children* the question is posed: "What does the eating of bread signify?" The answer: "It holds forth that we do spiritually feed, and live by faith on Jesus Christ." Additionally, "What further use is the ordinance of the Lord's supper to us?" The answer: "It strengthens our faith in Christ, and increases our love to Christ, and gloriously refreshes our souls, *by*

---

in his instituting of the two great ordinances of the Gospel, *viz. the Lords Supper* and *Baptism*; for as that of the Lords Supper doth in a lively Figure represent the breaking of his Body, and the pouring forth of his Blood, so the ordinance of Baptism doth as clearly (if rightly Administer) represent or hold forth the Death, Burial, and resurrection of the same Lord Jesus."

248. For more on sacramentality in the Baptist tradition, see Haykin, *Amidst Us Our Beloved*. For the divergent views of the Supper in the Reformed tradition see Gerrish, "Lord's Supper."

249. Keach, *Tropologia*, 632.

250. Owen says of the Supper, "We receive him *sacramentally*, by obedience in church-order; and, We receive him *spiritually* and really by faith, or believing in him. (1.) We receive him *sacramentally*. This consists in the due and orderly performance of what he has appointed in his word for this end and purpose, that therein and thereby he may exhibit himself to our souls. It doth not consist (as some have thought) *in partaking of the elements*; that is but one part of it, and but one small part. Our sacramental reception consists in the due observation of the whole order of the institution according to the mind of Christ. (2.) We receive him by faith *spiritually*; and if we could rightly understand that special *act of faith* which we are to exercise in the reception of Christ, when he does thus exhibit himself to us, then should we glorify God, then should we bring in advantage to our own souls." See Owen, *Works*, 9:591.

251. Keach, *Tropologia*, 418.

252. Arnold, *Reformed Theology*, 102. Arnold argues that Keach used anti-sacramental language to discuss the ordinances. In particular, he references Keach's statement, "Seeing then, my Son, that Faith alone, by the Operations of the holy Ghost, makes us Partakers of the Benefits and glorious Redemption, purchased by Jesus Christ, and so unites us to him; What are those Gospel Ordinances or Sacraments, which tend to confirm us in this Faith?" See Keach, *Instructions for Children*, 83. Arnold maintains that this "clearly" implies "that the ordinances themselves did not play an instrumental role in the process."

communion with him in all the graces & comforts of the Holy Spirit."[253] Baptism and the Supper represent a spiritual reality that confirms the recipient's union with Christ. Likewise, the sacraments are used by the Spirit to renew the faithful spiritually. This is consistent with the Second London Confession:

> Worthy receivers, outwardly partaking of the visible elements in this ordinance, do then also inwardly by faith, really and indeed, yet not carnally and corporally, but spiritually receive, and feed upon Christ crucified, and all the benefits of His death; the body and blood of Christ being then not corporally or carnally, but spiritually present to the faith of believers in that ordinance, as the elements themselves are to their outward senses.[254]

The ordinances themselves do not accomplish this function. Rather, in the same way as he does in preaching, the Spirit inwardly works as the faith of the individual is appropriated. This is why Keach says, "By the operations of the holy Ghost, [he] makes us Partakers of the Benefits and glorious Redemption, purchased by Jesus Christ, and so unites us to him."[255] The ordinances are not the principal cause of salvation but rather the seal of what already has been affected by faith alone in Christ. The Spirit sustains and strengthens the believer's union with Christ through the ordinances. As a result, seen in relation to preaching, Keach develops a robust real presence theology of the ordinances. "The Spirit hath its proper bounds, and always runs in its spiritual channel, viz., the word and ordinances."[256]

The Presence of Christ in the Word and Ordinances

Keach possesses an ecclesiological homiletic.[257] He viewed preaching as the central aspect of public worship and the primary means of shaping

---

253. Keach, *Instructions for Children*, 98; emphasis added.

254. *Confession of Faith Put Forth*, 102. Also, see Renihan's discussion concerning this article. Renihan, *To the Judicious and Impartial Reader*, 562–66.

255. Keach, *Instructions for Children*, 83.

256. Keach, *Tropologia*, 512.

257. The phrase, "ecclesiological homiletic" is adopted from Collier, "Preaching for the Church," 174. Collier defines an ecclesiological homiletic as "an approach to evangelistic, expositional preaching that understands the role of preaching in the life of the church and intentionally uses preaching to shape a church's ecclesiology and its members' understanding of the corporate nature of the Christian life."

congregational life. Thus, he calls preaching the *great ordinance*: "God hath ordained the preaching of the Gospel as the great Ordinance, to call in his Elect, and to beget Faith in them."[258] He says of this great ordinance, "The Ordinance of Preaching, or Administration of the Gospel, is a rich Pasture, especially when it is preached powerfully by the Influence and Demonstration of the Spirit; the opening and explaining the Word of the Gospel, is like the opening the Pasture-Gate, and so letting the Sheep into it."[259]

Likewise, Keach calls preaching a means of grace, stating, "Will you consider what *Means of Grace* God is pleased to afford you for the good of your Souls, and know it is by the *preaching of the Gospel* that God commonly saves the Souls of Men."[260] The parallelism identifies the dual nature of preaching. Preaching (i.e., means of grace) is good for souls and the preaching of the gospel saves the souls of men. For Keach, the proclamation of "the gospel is the symbol of God's presence."[261] So where "the gospel goes, God goes."[262] As an ordinance, Keach sees the real presence of Christ in the preaching event. He argues, "The word and ordinances are but dry bread if we do not meet with Christ in them."[263] God "draws near to poor sinners by his word and ordinances" and "by the influences and most gracious operations upon their hearts" the Spirit prompts individuals to seek him.[264] Also, "The Word of God, without the God of the Word, will not satisfy these Men's Souls; 'tis not a bare Ordinance, no, no, but they must have God in and with the Ordinance."[265]

He also claims, "I prize the word of God, and the ministry thereof. . . . I prize the Holy Supper of the Lord, for I have met with God and with Christ in these ordinances, I have had sweet fellowship with him in them."[266] Last, "Does nothing satisfy your souls short of God and Jesus Christ? . . . Will not the Word and Ordinances quiet you, unless you *meet with Christ in them*?"[267] For Keach, the ordinances along with the word and prayer are the means for an individual's experience with Christ's

---

258. Keach, *Golden Mine Opened*, 309.
259. Keach, *Golden Mine Opened*, 131.
260. Keach, *Golden Mine Opened*, 411; emphasis added.
261. Keach, *Exposition of the Parables*, 498.
262. Keach, *Exposition of the Parables*, 498.
263. Keach, *Exposition of the Parables*, 270–71.
264. Keach, *Exposition of the Parables*, 197–98.
265. Keach, *Golden Mine Opened*, 341.
266. Keach, *Exposition of the Parables*, 427.
267. Keach, *Golden Mine Opened*, 343; emphasis added.

presence.[268] The believer's union and communion with Christ are renewed in these ecclesiological elements. This is why he exhorts his hearers, "Attend diligently upon the word of God, and upon all the means of grace; it is good to be there where God usually works upon men's hearts."[269] The Spirit uses the ordinary means of the preached word and ordinances to communicate the presence of Christ to believers in the context of public worship.

Summary

Question five shows the relationship between the ordinances and the work of preaching. For Keach, there is a *real presence* aspect in his understanding of proclamation.[270] In relation to the ordinances, preaching is the "great ordinance." In this sense, therefore, it is argued that there is a unique *sacramental* aspect of his homiletical theology. Christ is uniquely present in the proclamation of the word. While the ordinary means of grace are not salvific, they do encourage individuals to experience Christ in them. This is uniquely true about preaching. The risen Christ is present to the hearers in the preaching event. Therefore, for Keach, there is a spiritual, sacramental, and experiential characteristic to his theology of preaching. This is grounded in his ecclesial and doxological homiletic.

QUESTION SIX (GOAL): WHAT IS THE PURPOSE OF PREACHING?

The aim of this entire chapter has attempted to examine Keach's theology of preaching by exploring the basis, object, subject, means, and context. This last question explores the purpose of preaching for the Christian and non-Christian. Quite simply, the intended goal of preaching is: (1) to edify the saints; (2) to exhort sinners to believe in Christ. Ward claims, "But whereas the [Westminster] Directory gave edification and not salvation as an application of the sermon, the Baptists sought both. . . . Particular Baptists consistently made the presentation of salvation one of the 'uses'

---

268. Keach, *Exposition of the Parables*, 438.
269. Keach, *Exposition of the Parables*, 799.
270. See Ward, "Preaching and Revelation," for a discussion on the presence of Christ in preaching within the Reformed tradition.

in their sermons."[271] Indeed, this is the case in Keach's theology of preaching. It also indicates a unique element to Particular Baptist preaching that differentiated them from their Reformed counterparts. Thus, this section will dedicate space to Keach's free-offer gospel. His theology of preaching possesses a full-throated and warm-hearted evangelical impulse.

Preaching to the Christian

Many of the sermonic goals for believers have been addressed already in this chapter. However, a few are noteworthy. These sermonic aims can be summarized under the theme of godliness, for "Godliness is the occupation of every true Christian."[272] Preaching strengthens Christians. Keach states, "The word is the food of the soul, it is that which tends to strengthen our hearts: I mean, God thereby does in a gracious manner [through preaching] strengthen us."[273] Preaching is food to Christians, which results in inward strength. The Spirit uses the preaching of the word to grow people's faith.[274] Preaching is essential in building up the church. He claims, "So ministers do not only preach for conviction and conversion, but also for consolation, and building up, that believers may grow in grace, and in the knowledge of Jesus Christ."[275]

Likewise, Keach says, "The word is said to heal us here . . . it makes known the only way of our cure, and in its promises gives us encouragement to believe."[276] Preaching directed at Christians, he explicitly argues, "For one chief End of Gospel Ministry is for the gathering together of the Saints; as well as for the Edifying the Body of Christ; therefore in every place where there is a Door opened for them, they must work hard whilst there are any Sinners to be called into the Vineyard."[277] The dual purposes of gathering and edifying are grounded in Keach's view of the church.

---

271. Ward, *Pure Worship*, 166–67. Coxe writes, "The preaching of the Gospel, [is] both for the conversion of sinners, and the edifying of those that are converted." See Coxe, *Appendix*, 10.

272. Keach, *Tropologia*, 931. See Deane's insightful discussion on Keach's view of godliness: Deane, "Golden Mine Opened," 42–49.

273. Keach, *Exposition of the Parables*, 150.

274. Keach, *Exposition of the Parables*, 245–46.

275. Keach, *Exposition of the Parables*, 807.

276. Keach, *Exposition of the Parables*, 319.

277. Keach, *Gospel minister's maintenance vindicated*, 123.

Furthermore, as claimed in the previous section, edification must be seen in relationship to the ordinances.

Keach provides instructions to his hearers on how they should receive the preached word.[278] The spoken word must be heard as the word of God in order for it to be profitable. To do this, the hearer should "join prayer with hearing."[279] Diligence and reverence are required. Additionally, tender love and affection for the word brings about the preached word intended result. The hearer should apply their whole hearts to receive the word. Last, "If we do not mix faith with the Word it will not profit us, we must feed upon the Word."[280]

Preaching to the Non-Christian

Keach stands in the Reformed preaching tradition. Particularly, he embraces an explicit evangelical Calvinism.[281] He writes, "A true Minister's design in preaching, is to lead men to Christ."[282] It is evident from Keach's preaching that he proclaimed and offered the gospel to all. He speaks directly to the free and open invitation of the gospel in a sermon on the parable of the marriage feast.[283] For the offer of the gospel is "an invitation of the greatest and highest pity." The invitation is "full of love" from God. It is a "repeated offer and invitation." Last, it is a "free offer." Keach makes specific appeals to non-Christians to believe in Christ.[284] There is sufficient evidence for this throughout his sermons. However, here are five pieces of evidence in their entirety:

278. Keach, *Exposition of the Parables*, 856.

279. Keach, *Exposition of the Parables*, 856.

280. Keach, *Exposition of the Parables*, 856.

281. Deane claims that Keach used two methods for preaching Christ, "the Tropologia method" and the "sin-salvation method." He writes, "Keach's Tropologia method was twofold. Keach used typology when he highlighted persons, events, or institutions that foreshadowed Christ. Then, Keach used metaphors that conveyed parallels and/or disparities between the metaphor and Christ. Keach's sin-salvation method encompassed his sermon by revealing man's sin and the solution found in Christ's salvation. Keach achieved this by preaching about the covenant of works and the covenant of grace, or the imputation of sin through Adam and the imputation of Christ's righteousness." See Deane, "Golden Mine Opened," 237–38.

282. Keach, *Tropologia*, 830.

283. Keach, *Exposition of the Parables*, 611.

284. Brown writes, "With all his emphasis on election, particular redemption, human impotence and the divine initiative, preachers like Keach could still appeal [evangelistically] and did so." Brown, "Baptist Preaching," 15.

1. Here is comfort and encouragement for the worst of sinners. Are you such who are and have been great sinners? Well, let it be so, yet be not cast down into utter despair, for here is a great Savior . . . *receive this Savior, believe in him*, and you shall be saved whoever you are: it is not the greatness of your sins that can hinder or obstruct him from saving your souls; though your sins be as red as scarlet . . . he will wash them all away and make you as white as wool, as white as snow.[285]

2. Such indeed who are conceited of their own righteousness, or swelled with a good opinion of their own good works, good deeds, and good duties, will not come to Christ, such think they need no such physician as Christ is: but you that see you have no righteousness of your own, but that all your righteousness as dung, *O look to Christ, come to Christ*, hear what he says to such that are lost, that are under the burdens of their sins, and wounded ones, come to me all ye that are labor and are heavy laden, and I will give you rest.[286]

3. Will you not open the door, nor cry to him to help you to open to him, to enable you to believe in him? What do you say, shall the Son of God stand at your doors, and you not so much as ask, who is there? Who is at my door? *Shall Christ be kept out of your hearts and stand at your doors . . . he comes through a sea of blood to offer his love to you . . . this great Savior is offered to you.* The Lord help every one of you to consider of this, and to lay it to heart.[287]

4. But, Sinner, know thou must come to Christ to be washed, come as one that sees what need thou hast to be put into the Fountain, which is set open for Sin and Uncleanness; and come as one naked, that Christ may clothe thee. Christ calls Sinners to him; maybe you will say, *What is it to come to Christ? Why, to believe in him, to lay hold by Faith upon him: And if thou dost thus, though thou art never so great a Sinner, thou shalt be saved.*[288]

5. Ministers ask sinners will you come to Christ, cleave to Christ, go with him, follow your Shepherd whithersoever he leads you? Will you venture your souls upon him, deny yourselves, and take up your cross and follow him? But alas! how few say (and resolve in their hearts) to do this? *What do you say, sirs, that hear me this day? Will you receive the Lord Jesus, hear his voice?*

285. Keach, *Golden Mine Opened*, 385; emphasis added.
286. Keach, *Golden Mine Opened*, 386; emphasis added.
287. Keach, *Golden Mine Opened*, 386–87; emphasis added.
288. Keach, *Golden Mine Opened*, 447–48; emphasis added.

> Is it in your hearts to cleave unto him? Or will you remain in the jaws of devils, polluted in your sins, condemned creatures, and under wrath, and the curse, and so perish forever?[289]

The common objections posed concern the perceived inconsistencies between the belief of election, particular redemption, and the free offer. Keach anticipates these objections in a sermon:

> Well, say some, say what you will, if this Doctrine of Election and Final Perseverance be true, we see not to what purpose we should preach the Gospel to Sinners anymore. . . . I am weary of these impertinent Objections: God hath ordained the preaching of the Gospel as the great Ordinance, to call in his Elect, and to beget Faith in them. . . . These Men dream of an Election without the Means and of a Salvation without Faith and Regeneration.[290]

He did not see any theological inconsistency between election and preaching. Rather, there is a theo-homiletical logic. If God has elected, he has also ordained the means. Thus, preaching is the means through which salvation is offered. The Spirit works effectually through the preached word to draw sinners to salvation. Regeneration occurs as the Spirit gives new life, resulting in the human response of faith and repentance. Based on this reading of Keach, he did not hold a hyper-Calvinist view of salvation.[291] Additionally, Keach asks the question: "If Christ died not for all, what ground have I to believe he died for me?" He then lists nine answers:

> 1. What does it signify to believe Christ died for all, unless you find the Effects of his Death in you? Many thousands shall perish, notwithstanding Christ died for them in their Judgment that make this Objection, yea the generality of them for whom

---

289. Keach, *Exposition of the Parables*, 347; emphasis added.
290. Keach, *Golden Mine Opened*, 309.
291. Though Vaughn does not directly call Keach a hyper-Calvinist, he writes, "It is likely that Keach's high Calvinist soteriology did contribute to the development of hyper-Calvinism in the succeeding generation." He maintains that Keach's attitude was the same as the hyper-Calvinists of the eighteenth century. See, Vaughn, "Benjamin Keach," 52. However, this cannot be sustained. Keach spoke about the necessity of the gospel going to the nations. Keach says, "Peace and glad Tidings is to be preached or proclaimed to all the World; Go ye therefore into all the World and Preach the Gospel to every Creature." See Keach, *Display of Glorious Grace*, 155. Keach does claim that it is God's sovereignty that has resulted in the darkness of the nations. See, Keach, *Exposition of the Parables*, 558. Yet, Keach explicitly says, "The heathen or Pagan nations and Mahometans, *must have the gospel preached to them* before the coming of our Lord, and so shall the Antichristian nations also." See, Keach, *Exposition of the Parables*, 694.

he died; therefore unless all were saved, what Encouragement is there to believe from hence?

2. He that believes, shall be saved: If thou therefore dost believe, thou shalt be saved. Is not this a better Ground of Faith, than that of Christ's dying for all?

3. A bare believing that Christ died for all, I have proved is no Ground of thy Interest in his Death, for that may be without any Fruits or gracious Effects.

4. Thou hast the same Ground to believe as any have, or as such had who do now believe before they did believe; or as they had once, who now are in Heaven.

5. Christ died for the chiefest of Sinners; and the Promises of Mercy upon believing, are made to the vilest Sinners on Earth.

6. Great and black Sinners have found Mercy, and are now in Heaven, even some of them that put Christ to Death; And is here not Ground of Faith and Hope for thee?

7. Remember, that if you believe not, but do continue in your Sin and Rebellion against God, you shall be certainly damned, your rejecting of Christ will have that Effect at last upon all Unbelievers.

8. Moreover, Christ calls to stout-hearted Sinners, such that are far from Righteousness; He brings his Salvation near to them: He calls upon a People not called by his Name: He hath received Gifts for the Rebellious also, that God might dwell among them. And is not here a good Ground to venture your Soul upon Jesus Christ.

9. No Person is excluded by the Lord that we know of: Can any Man say there is no Mercy for him, unless he has sinned against the Holy Ghost, which may be not one in an Age is guilty of? The Nature of which Sin I purpose to open, after I have closed with this Text. Your Condemnation, O Sinner, will be of yourself: God will judge the World in Righteousness: this we are all agreed in, and set down as an undeniable Article of our Faith. None shall have this to plead at the last Day, I was not Elected.[292]

---

292. Keach, *Golden Mine Opened*, 301–2.

Summary

Keach believes his answers are sufficient to counteract the objections.[293] He did not see his Reformed convictions as a hinderance to a free offer of the gospel. Rather, he shows that preaching is absolutely essential, for it is the means by which God saves sinners. Indeed, God saves. He saves through the preaching of the gospel. Additionally, Keach states that one's condemnation is not the result of God's decree. It is because of the individual's own rejection of the gospel.

Keach believes that preaching is the primary means of edification and evangelism. He provides answers to the common objections posed to the Reformed preaching tradition. What can be said is that Keach explicitly practiced pulpit evangelism. His free-offer proclamation is personal (e.g., *you*), warm-hearted (e.g., *offer his love to you*), imperatival (e.g., *come to Christ*), instructive (e.g., *believe in him*), redemptive (e.g., *thou shalt be saved*), and immediate (e.g., *hear me this day*).

SUMMARY OF BENJAMIN KEACH'S THEOLOGY OF PREACHING

It is demonstrated that Benjamin Keach's sermons and writings reflect a mature theology of preaching that is grounded biblically and informed theologically. It is argued that, for Keach, preaching was the means by which the risen Christ spoke spiritually through the written word to the congregation in order to offer himself to sinners and to sanctify the saints.

The basis of preaching explores God's revelation and the Bible: Keach's theology of preaching rests on the authority, efficacy, sufficiency, and necessity of the written word. He honored the word and sought to expound its teaching to his congregation. God reveals himself in creation, in Christ, and in the Scriptures. His preaching was epiphanical, grounded in God's divine revelation of himself in the Bible.

The object of preaching explores the gospel and its nuances: Keach was Christ centered in his proclamation. Central to his theology of preaching is the covenant of peace, particularly the doctrine of justification by faith alone. He expounded the classical Reformed doctrines from the Bible.

The subject investigates the role of the human preacher and the divine preacher: The act of preaching is a synergistic relationship between

---

293. For a non-Calvinist objection see Allen, *Extent of the Atonement*, 785–90.

the human ambassador and the Spirit. The Father has spoken in the Son through the Spirit and word. The minister, therefore, speaks the word by the power of the Spirit. Thus, the voice of Christ is operative in the ministry of the word, which must be received by faith. The minister, as ambassador, is given representative authority from Christ. In his preaching, there is an experiential aspect.

The means aims at understanding the role of the Spirit and rhetoric in preaching: Keach is convinced that the Spirit empowers the preacher and actualizes Christ's voice in the preaching event. An emphasis on human eloquence hinders the preacher's ability to preach in the demonstration of the Spirit's power. The communicator of God's word must depend on Christ to bless him with ministerial gifts to preach effectively. As the minister proclaims the sermon outwardly, the Spirit works inwardly. In his preaching, there is an effectual component.

The context details the ecclesiological setting of preaching with other liturgical elements, particularly baptism and the Lord's Supper: There is indeed a real presence aspect in Keach's understanding of preaching. The presence of the risen Christ is made real in the preaching event. This occurs in relationship to the ordinances in public worship. Preaching is the "great ordinance" of the church. In this sense, there is a unique sacramental aspect of his homiletical theology. Preaching is an invitation to meet Christ as he is among his people. In Keach's preaching, there is an ecclesiological element.

The goal examines the intended purpose of proclamation for Christians and non-Christians: Keach believes that preaching is the primary means for edification and evangelism. His free-offer proclamation is personal, warm-hearted, imperatival, instructive, redemptive, and immediate. In his preaching, there is an evangelical impulse. Based on the six questions for evaluating a theology of preaching, it is therefore claimed that Benjamin Keach's theology of preaching can be defined: it is *epiphanical, expositional, experiential, effectual, ecclesial, and evangelical.*

CHAPTER 6

Conclusion

TIMOTHY GEORGE POSITS FIVE fundamental principles for comprehending Baptist theological identity: orthodox convictions, evangelical lineage, Reformed perspective, Baptist distinctive features, and confessional context.[1] I concur that these principles encapsulate the broader Baptist heritage and should be reclaimed as Baptists continue to affirm our identity in the present. Furthermore, I contend that this holds true in the realm of preaching. As we have discussed, these principles are embodied in Benjamin Keach's theology of preaching. In our contemporary context, particularly as Southern Baptist preaching enters a post-Christian era, the "task of truth-telling is stranger than it used to be."[2] Only a robust foundation can support the weight of preaching in this strange new world.

THE CONTEXT OF SOUTHERN BAPTIST PREACHING AND CONTEMPORARY IMPLICATIONS

Scholars of the past have advanced that the Southern Baptist denomination emerged from the synthesis of the Charleston and Sandy Creek traditions. This distinction is usually discernible within their respective ecclesiological streams: the Charleston tradition is characterized by Reformed theology, while the Sandy Creek tradition is rooted in revivalist practices. Thus, "Southern Baptists are still trying to maintain balance

---

1. George, "Future of Baptist Theology."
2. Mohler, *He Is Not Silent*, 115.

between two streams of their heritage, the order of Charleston and the ardor of Sandy Creek."[3] However, this older reading of Baptist history may not actually reflect the relationships and nuances within these early expressions of the Baptist faith. Despite these distinctions, these traditions are still employed to describe two prominent Southern Baptist preaching traditions. However, I am not entirely convinced that this perspective is particularly instructive when examining contemporary Southern Baptist preaching. The differences may lie in the varying degrees to which each stream endeavored to articulate their convictions in distinct ways, rather than interpreting the distinction solely as theological. I believe this approach can be applied to homiletical theology. Southern Baptists can share similar theo-homiletical convictions and express them in diverse ways. Regardless of whether one is Reformed or revivalistic, the convictions presented in this work transcend those nuances.

In their work *The Baptist Vision*, Matthew Emerson and Lucas Stamps argue, "If the Baptist vision is to remain a vibrant part of the church in the twenty-first century and beyond, it must focus its lenses unswervingly on the only word that can redeem and reconcile sinners to God: 'Jesus Christ and him crucified.' God grant us grace to remain faithful to our Lord's Commission."[4] Preaching is essential for a revitalized Baptist vision, as it forms the bedrock of the Lord's Commission. This book aims to establish a solid foundation for proclamation. While pragmatic homiletics pose inherent risks, we have endeavored to reclaim a historically rooted Baptist theology of preaching. The following sections delineate specific implications for both preachers and homiletics educators within a Southern Baptist milieu. Consequently, as Southern Baptist preachers, we can share common theo-homiletical convictions and articulate them in diverse ways.

Epiphanical

Bush and Nettles write, "Baptists have built their theology from a solid foundation. Holy Scripture was taken to be God's infallible revelation in words. What God said, Baptists believed."[5] In a Southern Baptist context,

---

3. McBeth, *Baptist Heritage*, 234.
4. Emerson and Stamps, *Baptist Vision*, 162.
5. Bush and Nettles, *Baptists and the Bible*, 396.

the fight for biblical inerrancy took center stage from 1979 to 2000.⁶ As a grandson of these events, I am grateful for the recovery of orthodox views on Scripture. I have personally benefited from Southern Baptist education post–Conservative Resurgence. Now I believe there needs to be a recovery of revelatory preaching. "Revelation, in the distinctive Christian sense, is not merely God's making available information about himself but the personal unveiling of God that transforms and reconciles the believing recipient of the revelation."⁷ When I speak of epiphanical preaching, I mean that the task of proclamation is God revealing himself to humanity. God has revealed himself in the Bible and preaching seeks to amplify this revelation. Thus, "preaching/proclamation can be understood as a form of revelation with a specific oral nature, informative purpose, and relational (or covenantal) context."⁸ God is indeed doing something in the proclamation of his word. As Mounce claims,

> Thus, preaching is that timeless link between God's great redemptive act and man's apprehension of it. It is the medium through which God contemporizes His historic Self-disclosure and offers man the opportunity to respond in faith. Without response, revelation is incomplete. Without preaching, God's mighty act remains an event in the past. What man desperately needs is a redemptive encounter in the ever present Now. Preaching answers to this need by contemporizing the past and moving the individual to respond in faith. The contemporaneity of what took place long ago is an ultimate and inescapable miracle of Christianity. It defies explanation. Yet without this miracle, preaching is not really preaching.⁹

Preaching transcends mere information transmission; it constitutes revelation. This notion aligns with the New Testament's perspective and the earliest Baptist preaching tradition, as exemplified by Benjamin Keach. It is imperative to recognize that preaching the word of God is, in fact, the word of God. Our preaching methods and homiletical instruction should emphasize this extraordinary reality. As heralds, we proclaim the sermonic word to the assembled congregation, transforming that moment into a redemptive event. It is within the pulpit that the crucified

---

6. This was known as the Conservative Resurgence. For a conservative retelling of the events see Sutton, *Baptist Reformation*.
7. Garrett, *Systematic Theology*, 51.
8. Halstead, "*Verbum Dei*," 212.
9. Mounce, *Essential Nature*, 153.

and risen Christ addresses his people through the inspired word. Hence, "preaching is the effective communication of the divine truth of the Christian Scriptures, by a person called of God to witness for Him to a redemptive deed for the purpose of giving eternal life through Jesus Christ."[10]

Expositional

In terms of the six theological convictions, contemporary Southern Baptist preachers seek to maximize the exposition of Scripture. Again, Bush and Nettles note, "The word and the message of Scripture is the word and the message of God."[11] As a result of this theological truth, expository preaching is the natural outflow of one's view of Scripture.[12] Consider the words of John Broadus when he writes, "For one, I am quite sure that expository preaching will become increasingly popular in our country throughout the next generation of ministerial life."[13] A few decades following Broadus's comments, the first preaching professor at Southwestern Baptist Theological Seminary, Jeff Ray, argues, "In preaching, exposition is the detailed interpretation, logical amplification, and practical application of a passage of Scripture."[14] The commitment to biblical inerrancy in the Southern Baptist Convention places a profound emphasis on expository preaching.

Yet, the expository tradition did not originate with Broadus or Ray. It can be traced back to our Baptist forebears. While individuals like Keach did not exposit the Scriptures within contemporary expository preaching models, he did endeavor to expound the biblical text in his sermons. He genuinely believed that he was fulfilling the role of biblical exposition. In the twenty-first century, many Southern Baptist pastors continue to practice expository preaching in various forms. Debates regarding the most faithful method of expository preaching are appropriate within homiletical discourse. However, Baptist preachers must exercise caution to avoid prioritizing sermonic method over the sermon's message. Sermonic method serves the broader objective of proclamation,

10. Brown et al., *Steps to the Sermon* (rev. ed.), 8–9.
11. Bush and Nettles, *Baptists and the Bible*, 396.
12. Pace, *Preaching by the Book*, 8.
13. Broadus, "On Expository Preaching," 216.
14. Ray, *Expository Preaching*, 71.

acting as a guide to the destination of the sermon. It is crucial to avoid the modern trap of being subservient to method and overlooking the primary purpose of preaching. This should naturally raise questions, such as Is preaching truly expository if it is not explicitly Christ centered?[15] Does the redemptive-historical approach divert from a text-driven preaching method? These are not merely questions reserved for the academy. Preachers must do rigorous theo-homiletical work to answer them.[16] Thus, we should value expository preaching because it elevates the Bible, which in turn elevates Christ.

Additionally, taking a cue from Keach, Christ-centered preaching should aim at articulating orthodox Christology. Preachers are not mere motivators or life coaches. Rather, preachers must be theologians doing the work of theology in the midst of a congregation. This means communicating the faith once for all delivered to the saints. In recent decades, the Trinity debate brought this to the forefront of Baptist theological conversations.[17] Questions concerning the eternal functional subordination of the Son, which took place on the internet and in print, shaped proclamation in local churches.[18] Practitioners of the word must be equipped to engage in this theological work as it is central to proclamation, as evident in Keach.

Experiential

The experiential nature of preaching is often related to the preacher's ethos, focusing on the individual's relationship with God and his doctrinal fidelity.[19] To preach Christ, preachers must know Christ. A renewed emphasis on biblical spirituality in seminary classrooms should transition into the preaching lab. Additionally, the warm heart cultivated in the study should burn in the pulpit. The experiential aspect of the Christian faith gives credence to the message proclaimed. In a real sense, one cannot divorce the message and messenger. Phillip Brooks is right when he

---

15. Christ-centered preaching is an ongoing homiletical debate: Clowney, *Preaching and Biblical Theology*; Chapell, *Christ-Centered Preaching*; Kuruvilla, *Privilege the Text*.

16. Adegoke's recent dissertation addresses a theological question relating to the exaltation of Christ and Christ-centered preaching. This is an example of thoughtful theo-homiletical reflection by a Baptist. See Adegoke, "Examination of the Exaltation."

17. See Smith, "Trinity Debate."

18. Barrett et al., *Proclaiming the Triune God*.

19. Mathews, "Disciplines of a Text-Driven Preacher."

states, "Truth through personality is our description of real preaching. The truth must come really through the person, not merely over his lips, not merely into his understanding and out through his pen. It must come through his character, his affections, his whole intellectual and moral being."[20]

Similarly, the act of preaching is a synergistic relationship between the human minister and the Holy Spirit. The Father has communicated through the Son, the Spirit, and the word. The minister delivers the word by the power of the Spirit. Consequently, the voice of Christ is operative in the ministry of the word, which requires faith for reception. Indeed, the minister serves as an expositor. However, the preacher also assumes the role of an ambassador, pleading on Christ's behalf to the congregation. This aspect is transformative and impactful. However, popular homiletical textbooks used in seminary classrooms have little to say about the ambassador role.[21]

The metaphor, as has been argued, is central to the Reformation tradition of preaching. The ambassador metaphor provides clarity for both the preacher and his assignment in proclamation. Listen to the words of Keach when he writes, "Consider well, and remember that your Pastors are the Ministers; nay, the Ambassadors of Jesus Christ; such who represent his Sacred Majesty, and have his Commission, for what they act and do in his Name, and dispense the Mysteries of God to you, according to their Duty."[22] Calling, therefore, is linked to this ambassadorial commission. Preaching becomes a part of the dynamic event where the living God reproduces his redemptive act to men and women.[23] In the sermon, the real Preacher speaking is not the man behind the pulpit. It is the One enthroned in heaven. This is why Keach can say, "Know Christ's faithful Ministers personate him, they are his ambassadors, they

---

20. Brooks, *Lectures on Preaching*, 8.

21. Pace has one reference to the ambassador metaphor. See Pace, *Preaching by the Book*, 14. Haddon Robinson's popular book *Biblical Preaching* has zero references. *Text-Driven Preaching* by Akin et al. contains zero references to the ambassador. Additionally, Vines and Shaddix's *Power in the Pulpit* has zero direct references to the metaphor related to preaching. I am not suggesting that these works are not beneficial. On the contrary, I find them to be extremely helpful in teaching homiletical method. The point is simply to say that the central identifying mark of the Reformational preaching tradition (ambassador) is often neglected in contemporary homiletical instruction.

22. Keach, *Gospel minister's maintenance vindicated*, 77.

23. Miller, *Fire in Thy Mouth*, 17.

represent the very Person of Christ."[24] The minister is preaching "in the stead of Christ."[25] The risen Christ, who is ascended in the heavens, is presently working by means of the minister.

In Keach's theology of preaching, the ambassador metaphor is related to the twofold work of preaching. The ambassador is an instrument. Christ by means of the Spirit is the One communicating through the human ambassador as he faithfully expounds the Scriptures. The efficacy of gospel proclamation is grounded in the Father who, by means of the outward preaching of the gospel and inward working of the Spirit, affectionally opens the eyes of lost sinners to the glory of Christ. If faith comes by hearing, the presence of an ambassador reveals God's kindness to sinners. God desires to speak to his people and does so through an ambassador expounding the word. Yet, since the ambassador bears the mark of Christ's authority, to reject the word of the minister is to reject the word of Christ. Christ has identified himself with his faithful minister in such a way that when the minister preaches, it is Christ preaching. In this sense, the minister is the mouth of Christ. This should prompt greater faithfulness to sound exposition. To preach the word of Christ is to hear the voice of Christ. I am convinced that this aspect must be recovered in contemporary Baptist pulpits.

Effectual

If the larger Reformation preaching tradition declares that "preaching the word of God is the word of God," then how? This is related to the effectual conviction. While Baptists have written on the role of the Spirit in preaching, more work could be done as it relates to the participatory aspect of proclamation.[26] Above all, preaching is a spiritual event. A retrieval of a profoundly spiritual homiletic is crucial in Southern Baptist preaching classrooms and pulpits. In the Baptist preaching tradition, as expounded by Keach, the Spirit actualizes the voice of Christ as the human ambassador expounds the word. This is a profound theological reality. The event of redemption, situated in the past, is brought into the present as Christ communicates with the congregation.

---

24. Keach, *Golden Mine Opened*, 431.
25. Keach, *Tropologia*, 851.
26. See Heisler, *Spirit-Led Preaching*.

Keach was Reformed. His Calvinistic framework governed much of his homiletical thought. However, one does not need to be a Calvinist to adopt his homiletical theology. All non-Calvinists and Calvinists agree that the Spirit is the one who makes the preached word effectual for salvation. Whether faith precedes regeneration or vice versa is not of concern at this point. The effectual conviction testifies to the mysterious working of the Spirit to accomplish the intended goal of proclamation.

The preaching of the Reformed tradition was cautious in the usage of human rhetoric. However, Keach serves as an individual who judiciously used rhetoric in proclamation. In particular, his use of metaphor throughout his sermons demonstrates how language can be crafted to communicate biblical truth. Though at times Keach may have stretched metaphorical ideas beyond their intended meaning, he nevertheless saw a role for rhetoric. But it was never at the expense of preaching in the demonstration of the Spirit's power.

Ecclesial

Contemporary Baptist preachers should reexamine preaching and its role in the context of public worship. At this point questions abound. How is preaching doxological? How does preaching shape the worship of the local church? How does preaching cultivate congregational catechesis? The perspective presented in this project agrees with Dockery's sentiment: "The first step in rediscovering the missing jewel of worship is simply to help the redeemed community recognize the worship of God as a primary function of the church."[27] Some scholars have critiqued contemporary Baptist worship practices with the early English Baptist tradition. For example, Haykin argues that the richness of the ordinances has been replaced by the "altar call."[28] It is possible that in many contemporary Baptist pulpits the ecclesial nature of proclamation is eclipsed by the evangelistic element. Preaching should without a doubt possess an evangelical aspect, but proclamation has a significant role in edification and worship. The ecclesiological nature of preaching should not be overlooked by Baptists since it was the ecclesiological reorientation that shaped early Baptist preaching in the first place. Collier writes, "A robust

---

27. Dockery, *Southern Baptist Consensus*, 125. See Dockery, "Lord's Supper."
28. Haykin, *Amidst Us Our Beloved*, 124.

theology of preaching and a healthy ecclesiology are imperative; one must always inform the other."[29]

Additionally, Baptists should give greater attention to preaching and its relationship to the ordinances within the setting of worship.[30] In what ways do they relate? Is Christ present in them? These are theological questions that preachers must ask and attempt to answer. Wymer notes, "The writings of many Baptist theologians have recognized the human matter of the preaching event as the primary means through which God is active and present in the church and the world, whether or not it has been explicitly named. Most do not thoroughly grapple with the technical aspects of exactly how matter symbolizes and enacts God's presence and action in preaching."[31] Keach's sacramental language applied to preaching should cause contemporary Baptists to pause and reflect. It should cause some discomfort. Those who hold to a strict memorialist view of the ordinances should give honest homiletical reflection concerning the presence of Christ in preaching. As Haymes writes in *Baptist Sacramentalism*, "A theology that is sacramental produces a strong theology of preaching related to the world in which we live."[32] Thus, based on the work of this book, "Preaching, we should not hesitate to say, has a sacramental character."[33] In the words of P. T. Forsyth, "The real presence of Christ crucified is what makes preaching. It is what makes of a speech a sermon, and of a sermon Gospel. . . . It is a sacramental act, done together with the community in the name and power of Christ's redeeming act and our common faith."[34] Though Baptists may be hesitant to speak about sacramentalism, Keach's preaching shows that it is indeed part of the Baptist preaching tradition. How one conceives of the ordinances and public worship will influence proclamation. Thus, "The early Baptists believed that the ordinary way that sinners receive the benefits of Christ's redemptive work are his ordinances, that is, the practices he put in order so that

---

29. Collier, "Preaching for the Church," 221.

30. Billings provides a discussion on this relationship from a Reformed perspective. See Billings, "Sacraments," 340.

31. Wymer, "Word of God," 439.

32. Haymes, "Towards a Sacramental Understanding," 264.

33. Olford writes, "On the other hand, the sermon is indeed the visible and audible sign of the grace that is given when, to borrow the language of the Epistle to the Hebrews, 'the word preached' is 'mixed with faith' on the part of those who hear. The pulpit should be seen as a sign of the grace of God standing within the divinely created community of faith the Church." Olford, "Restoring the Scriptures," 26–27.

34. Forsyth, *Positive Preaching*, 82–83.

we might be united to him: the preaching of the Word, the celebration of baptism and of the Lord's Supper, and prayer."[35]

Evangelical

The evangelical compulsion is usually expressed in Baptist circles through conversations on the usefulness of the *public invitation*.[36] While some concerns regarding the method are valid (in my opinion), those of the Reformed persuasion should consider the history of the free offer of the gospel in the Reformed preaching tradition.[37] Pulpit evangelism is compatible with the Reformed tradition. It is grounded theologically in the conviction that, through the powerful word of the gospel, dead sinners can be saved by the definitive act of the Lord Jesus. It is not that sinners *might come*, but rather, sinners *will come*.

It is quite possible that Reformed theology provides a robust theological basis for offering a full-throated public invitation that is genuinely effectual.[38] Pastoral prudence and discernment are key in this homiletical aspect. However, "I would argue, then, that pleading and using appropriate persuasion in presenting the gospel and extending the invitation is needful for our gospel witness."[39] The present research includes a humble attempt to correct some of the mischaracterizations of Reformed preaching by appealing to a Reformed evangelical Baptist witness.[40] But

---

35. Emerson and Stamps, *Baptist Vision*, 160.

36. See Fish, *Giving a Good Invitation*; Streett, *Effective Invitation*; Hawkins and Queen, *Gospel Invitation*.

37. Lloyd-Jones, *Preaching and Preachers*, 265–82. Lloyd-Jones writes, "As you preach your sermon you should be applying it all the time, and especially, of course, at the end, when you come to the final application and to the climax. But the appeal is a part of the message; it should be so inevitably. The sermon should lead men to see that this is the only thing to do."

38. See MacLeod, *Compel Them to Come*. While this work does not necessarily aim to address the public invitation, it does show that the free offer of the gospel and Calvinism do not contradict.

39. Tolbert, "Public Invitation," 473. Tolbert's chapter is a thoughtful and fair appeal for using the method of the public invitation.

40. Trevin Wax notes, "Non-Calvinists sometimes assume that certain methods of ministry are so tightly connected to the experience of evangelism that any deviation calls into question one's commitment to the gospel or evangelism. For example, the lack of a public invitation, usually expressed through an 'altar call' or through repeating the 'sinner's prayer,' is assumed to indicate theological and methodological compromise. Over the years, I've seen gospel-preaching, gospel-sharing pastors on the Calvinist side of the spectrum unfairly castigated due to caricatures that were dishonest." Wax,

it also encourages those who identify with a Reformed understanding to consider the "normative" aspect of seventeenth-century Particular Baptist free-offer proclamation.[41]

MOVING FORWARD

Timothy Ward states, "Preaching is therefore an instrument by which Christ, in the power of the Spirit, teaches and works. Within this Christological understanding of the nature of pastoral ministry, human proclamation is rightly called God's word because in and through it, Christ is at work, as head of the church, applying the salvation that he has accomplished."[42] Preaching, the assignment of the church of the Lord Jesus, is a theological task. Proclamation is not just theological in its content, but also in its basis. Preaching is something God does. Preaching is, in the words of Keach, "the Word of this salvation in the mouths of Christ's ministers."[43]

As Southern Baptist preaching ventures into the uncharted territory of a postmodern and post-Christian cultural milieu, a robust and consistent homiletical theology emerges as the indispensable foundation for effective proclamation. Consequently, a theology of preaching

---

"Epilogue," 487. Some examples of these caricatures are Streett's comments in *Effective Invitation* and Adrian Rogers's discussion on Reformed Theology. Streett writes, "Most preachers holding to Reformed theology prefer to conclude their gospel sermons without such an appeal." The "appeal" is referring to the altar call. He also says, "If Calvinist preachers . . . would start calling their hearers to a public profession of faith, I believe the Holy Spirit would draw many more people to Christ under their ministry." For Streett, the "public profession of faith" is the altar call. However, this is problematic. Calvinists, like Keach, called his hearers to believe in Christ. To equate the altar call (mechanism) with the invitation to believe (free offer) is a false equivalent. See Streett, *Effective Invitation*, 238, 244. Non-Calvinists have mistakenly conflated high Calvinism with hyper-Calvinism. Adrian Rogers says, "Now, there are five points in historic, extreme Calvinism. Some call it 'hyper-Calvinism.'" Rogers quoted in Spradlin, "Reformed Theology," para. 7. The conflation of "high Calvinism" and "hyper-Calvinism" is historically inaccurate. While not necessarily a caricature, Allen argues, "From the standpoint of preaching, the free and well-meant offer of the gospel for all people necessarily presupposes that Christ died for the sins of all people." See Allen, *Extent of the Atonement*, 789. Keach addresses this issue. He concludes that God ordained preaching to be the means by which salvation is wrought. For Keach, the free offer is not grounded in Christ dying for all. Rather, the free offer is grounded in the means God uses to accomplish his redemptive purposes.

41. Haykin, *Amidst Us Our Beloved*, 124–25.
42. Ward, "Preaching and Revelation," 60–61.
43. Keach, *Golden Mine Opened*, 431–32.

that encompasses epiphanical (basis), expositional (object), experiential (subject), effectual (means), ecclesial (context), and evangelical (goal) elements provides contemporary Baptist preachers with a comprehensive framework and structure for their preaching endeavors. The present research aims to assist Baptist preachers by preserving the homiletical continuity of their own ecclesial tradition. While Baptists may disagree with certain nuances of Keach's theology, the six theo-homiletical convictions presented offer a robust framework for comprehending the multifaceted nature of preaching. By reclaiming a historically Baptist theology of proclamation, perhaps contemporary Baptist preaching can be revitalized and renewed.

> *O Praise the Lord, and look to him,*
> *sing Praise unto his Name;*
> *O all ye Saints of Heaven and Earth*
> *set forth his glorious Fame:*
> *For sending his bless'd Word to us,*
> *and Ministers to raise,*
> *To Preach the Gospel of his Son;*
> *sing forth his glorious Praise!*[44]

---

44. Keach, *Spiritual Songs*, 74.

Bibliography

Adam, Peter. *Speaking God's Words: A Practical Theology of Preaching*. Vancouver, Can.: Regent College, 2004.
Adegoke, Abiodun Oluwasogo. "An Examination of the Exaltation of Christ and Its Implications for Christian Preaching." PhD diss., Southwestern Baptist Theological Seminary, 2023.
Ainslie, James L. *The Doctrines of Ministerial Order in the Reformed Churches of the 16th and 17th Centuries*. Edinburgh: T&T Clark, 1940.
Akin, Daniel L., et al. *Engaging Exposition: A 3-D Approach to Preaching*. Nashville: B&H Academic, 2011.
Akin, Daniel L., et al., eds. *Text-Driven Preaching: God's Word at the Heart of Every Sermon*. Nashville: B&H Academic, 2010.
Alan of Lille. *Summa de arte praedicatoria*. Patrologia Latina 210. Edited by Jacques-Paul Migne. Paris: 1855.
Allen, David L. *The Extent of the Atonement: A Historical and Critical Review*. Nashville: B&H Academic, 2016.
———. Introduction to *Text-Driven Preaching: God's Word at the Heart of Every Sermon*, edited by Daniel L. Akin et al., 1–12. Nashville: B&H Academic, 2010.
———. "A Tale of Two Roads: Homiletics and Biblical Authority." *Journal of the Evangelical Theological Society* 43 (2000) 489–515.
Allen, Michael, and Scott R. Swain, eds. *Christian Dogmatics: Reformed Theology for the Church Catholic*. Grand Rapids: Baker Academic, 2016.
Allen, O. Wesley, Jr. *The Renewed Homiletic*. Minneapolis: Fortress, 2010.
Appleby, David. *Black Bartholomew's Day: Preaching, Polemic and Restoration Nonconformity*. Manchester: Manchester University Press, 2007.
Arnold, Jonathan W. "Radical, Baptist Eschatology: The Eschatological Vision of Vavasor Powell, Hanserd Knollys, and Benjamin Keach." *Perichoresis* 17 (2019) 75–93.
———. "The Reformed Theology of Benjamin Keach (1640–1704)." DPhil diss., University of Oxford, 2010.
———. *The Reformed Theology of Benjamin Keach 1640–1704*. Oxford: Regent's Park College, 2019.
———. "The Universal Tradition and the Clear Meaning of Scripture: Benjamin Keach's Understanding of the Trinity." *Perichoresis* 20 (2022) 23–34.
Augustine. *Teaching Christianity (De Doctrina Christiana)*. Vol. I/11 of *The Works of Saint Augustine: A Translation for the 21st Century*, edited by John E. Rotelle, translated by Edmund Hill. Hyde Park, NY: New City, 1996.

Autrey, Denny. "Factors Influencing the Sermonic Structure of Jean Claude and His Influence on Homiletics." PhD diss., Southwestern Baptist Theological Seminary, 2013.

Ballitch, Andrew S. *The Gloss & the Text: William Perkins on Interpreting Scripture with Scripture*. Studies in Historical and Systematic Theology. Bellingham: Lexham, 2020.

Barlow, William. *The summe and substance of the conference, which it pleased His Excellent Majestie to have with the lords bishops, and others of his clergie (at which the most of the lords of the councill were present) in His Majesties privie-chamber, at Hampton Court, Jan. 14. 1603*. London: 1804.

Barrett, Matthew, et al. *Proclaiming the Triune God: The Doctrine of the Trinity in the Life of the Church*. Nashville: B&H, 2024.

Barth, Karl. *Church Dogmatics: The Doctrine of the Word of God*. Edited by Geoffrey William Bromiley and Thomas F. Torrance. Pt. 1., vol. 1. New York: T&T Clark, 2004.

———. *Homiletics*. Translated by Geoffrey W. Bromiley and Donald E. Daniels. Louisville: Westminster John Knox, 1991.

Bartow, Charles L. *God's Human Speech: A Practical Theology of Proclamation*. Grand Rapids: Eerdmans, 1997.

Baxter, Richard. *The Reformed Pastor*. In *The Practical Works of the Rev. Richard Baxter, with a Life of the Author, and a Critical Examination of His Writings*, edited by William Orme, 3–400. Vol. 14. London: James Duncan, 1830.

Beach, J. Mark. "The Real Presence of Christ in the Preaching of the Gospel: Luther and Calvin on the Nature of Preaching." *Mid-America Journal of Theology* 10 (1999) 77–134.

Bebbington, David W. *Baptists Through the Centuries: A History of a Global People*. 2nd ed. Waco: Baylor University Press, 2018.

———. *Evangelicalism in Modern Britain: A History from the 1730s to the 1980s*. New York: Routledge, 1989.

———. "The Nature of Evangelical Religion." In *Evangelicals: Who They Have Been, Are Now, and Could Be*, 3–18. Grand Rapids: Eerdmans, 2019.

———. *Patterns in History: A Christian View*. Downers Grove, IL: InterVarsity, 1979.

Beeke, Joel R. *Living for God's Glory: An Introduction to Calvinism*. Sanford, FL: Reformation Trust, 2008.

———. *Reformed Preaching: Proclaiming God's Word from the Heart of the Preacher to the Heart of the People*. Wheaton, IL: Crossway, 2018.

Beeke, Joel R., and Mark Jones. *A Puritan Theology: Doctrine for Life*. Grand Rapids: Reformation Heritage, 2012.

Beeke, Joel R., and Paul Smalley. *Prepared by Grace, for Grace: The Puritans on God's Ordinary Way of Leading Sinners to Christ*. Grand Rapids: Reformation Heritage, 2013.

Bennett, Bill. "The Secret of Preaching with Power." In *Text-Driven Preaching: God's Word at the Heart of Every Sermon*, edited by Daniel L. Akin et al., 233–48. Nashville: B&H Academic, 2010.

Bernard, Richard. *Faithfull Shepheard: Shepheards Practice; or, His Manner of Feeding His Flocke*. London: Eliot's Court, 1621.

Bickel, R. Bruce. *Light and Heat: The Puritan View of the Pulpit and the Focus of the Gospel in Puritan Preaching*. Morgan: Soli Deo Gloria, 1999.

Billings, Todd. "Sacraments." In *Christian Dogmatics: Reformed Theology for the Church Catholic*, edited by Michael Allen and Scott R. Swain, 339–62. Grand Rapids: Baker Academic, 2016.

Bingham, Matthew C. *Orthodox Radicals: Baptist Identity in the English Revolution*. Oxford: Oxford University Press, 2019.

Birch, Ian. *To Follow the Lambe Wheresoever He Goeth: The Ecclesial Polity of the English Calvinistic Baptists 1640–1660*. Eugene, OR: Pickwick, 2017.

Blench, J. W. *Preaching in England in the Late Fifteenth and Sixteenth Centuries: A Study of English Sermons 1450–1600*. Oxford: Blackwell, 1964.

Blythe, Stuart. "Teaching Preaching: As Practical Theology." *Journal of European Baptist Studies* 21 (2021) 45–65.

Bremer, Francis J. *Lay Empowerment and the Development of Puritanism*. New York: Palgrave Macmillan, 2015.

———. *Puritanism: A Very Short Introduction*. Very Short Introductions. New York: Oxford University Press, 2009.

Broadus, John. *Lectures on the History of Preaching*. New York: Sheldon, 1876.

———. "On Expository Preaching." *The Old and New Testament Student* 1 (1890) 213–16.

———. *Sermons and Addresses*. 2nd ed. Baltimore: Wharton, 1887.

———. *A Treatise on the Preparation and Delivery of Sermons*. New York: Sheldon, 1870.

Brooks, Phillips. *Lectures on Preaching: Delivered Before the Divinity School of Yale College in January and February, 1877*. New York: Dutton, 1878.

Brooks, Thomas. *The Complete Works of Thomas Brooks*. Edited by Alexander Balloch Grosart. Vol. 3. Edinburgh: Nisbet, 1866.

Brown, H. C., Jr., et al. *Steps to the Sermon: An Eight-Step Plan for Preaching with Confidence*. Rev. ed. Nashville: Broadman & Holman, 1996.

Brown, H. C., Jr., et al. *Steps to the Sermon: A Plan for Sermon Preparation*. Nashville: Broadman, 1963.

Brown, John. *Puritan Preaching in England: A Study of Past and Present*. New York: Scribner's Sons, 1900.

Brown, Raymond. "Baptist Preaching in Early 18th Century England." *The Baptist Quarterly* 31 (1985) 15–17.

Browne, Robert. *Treatise of Reformation Without Tarying for Anie*. London: Congregational Union of England and Wales, 1903.

Buckley, Theodore Alois. *The Canons and Decrees of the Council of Trent*. London: Routledge, 1851.

Bullinger, Heinrich. *The Decades of Henry Bullinger: The Fifth Decade*. Edited by Thomas Harding, translated by H. I. Cambridge: Cambridge University Press, 1852.

Bumpers, Jared. "'Worse than Idle' or 'Mysteries of the Gospel': John Albert Broadus and Benjamin Keach on Interpreting and Preaching the Parables of Jesus." *Journal for Baptist Theology & Ministry* 16 (2019) 57–73.

Burnett, Amy Nelson. "How to Preach a Protestant Sermon: A Comparison of Lutheran and Reformed Homiletics." *Theologische Zeitschrift* 63 (2007) 109–19.

Burrage, Champlin. *Illustrative Documents*. Vol. 2 of *The Early English Dissenters in the Light of Recent Research (1550–1641)*. Cambridge: Cambridge University Press, 1912.

Burroughs, Jeremiah. *Gospel Reconciliation, or, Christ's Trumpet of Peace to the World* [...] *to Which Is Added Two Sermons*. London: Cole, 1657.

Bush, L. Russ, and Tom J. Nettles. *Baptists and the Bible*. Rev. ed. Nashville: Broadman, 1999.

Bustin, Dennis C. *Paradox and Perseverance: Hanserd Knollys, Particular Baptist Pioneer in Seventeenth-Century England*. Studies in Baptist History and Thought 23. Milton Keynes, UK: Paternoster, 2006.

Bustin, Dennis C., and Barry Howson. *Zealous for the Lord: The Life and Thought of the Seventeenth-Century Baptist Hanserd Knollys*. Monographs in Baptist History. Eugene, OR: Pickwick, 2019.

Buttrick, David. *A Captive Voice: The Liberation of Preaching*. Louisville: Westminster John Knox, 1994.

Calvin, John. *Commentaries on the Epistles of Paul the Apostle to the Corinthians*. Edited and translated by John Pringle. 2 vols. Bellingham, WA: Logos, 2010.

———. "The Genevan Confession (1536)." In *Calvin: Theological Treatises*, translated by J. K. S. Reid, 25–33. Library of Christian Classics 22. Philadelphia: Westminster, 1954.

———. *Institutes of the Christian Religion*. Edited by John T. McNeill, translated by Ford Lewis Battles. Vol. 1. The Library of Christian Classics. Louisville: Westminster John Knox, 2011.

———. "Reply by John Calvin to Letter by Cardinal Sadolet." In *Tracts Relating to the Reformation*, translated by Henry Beveridge, 1:1–68. Edinburgh: Calvin Translation Society, 1844.

———. *A Short Treatise on the Supper of Our Lord*. In *Tracts Relating to the Reformation*, translated by Henry Beveridge, 2:163–98. Edinburgh: Calvin Translation Society, 1849.

———. "Summary of Doctrine Concerning the Ministry of the Word and Sacraments." In *Calvin: Theological Treatises*, translated by J. K. S. Reid, 167–75. Library of Christian Classics 22. Philadelphia: Westminster, 1954.

Campbell, Charles L. *Preaching Jesus: The New Directions for Homiletics in Hans Frei's Postliberal Theology*. Eugene, OR: Wipf and Stock, 2006.

Canlis, Julie. *Calvin's Ladder: A Spiritual Theory of Ascent and Ascension*. Grand Rapids: Eerdmans, 2010.

Carlson, Eric Josef. "The Boring of the Ear: Shaping the Pastoral Vision of Preaching in England, 1540–1640." In *Preachers and People in the Reformations and Early Modern Period*, edited by Larissa Taylor, 249–96. A New History of the Sermon 2. Leiden: Brill, 2001.

Carnes, James Patrick. "The Famous Mr. Keach: Benjamin Keach and His Influence on Congregational Singing in Seventeenth-Century England." MA thesis, North Texas State University, 1984.

Carrick, John. *The Imperative of Preaching: A Theology of Sacred Rhetoric*. London: Banner of Truth, 2016.

Carroll, Thomas K. *Preaching the Word: Message of the Fathers of the Church*. Wilmington, DE: Glazier, 1984.

Cary, Phillip. "The Inner Word Prior to Language: Augustine as Platonist Alternative to Gadamerian Hermeneutics." *Philosophy Today* 55 (2011) 192–98.

———. *Outward Signs: The Powerlessness of External Things in Augustine's Thought*. Oxford: Oxford University Press, 2008.

Chadwick, Owen. *The Reformation*. New York: Penguin, 1985.
Chan, Sam. *Preaching as the Word of God: Answering an Old Question with Speech Act Theory*. Eugene, OR: Pickwick, 2016.
Chandos, John. *In God's Name: Examples of Preaching in England from the Act of Supremacy to the Act of Uniformity, 1534–1662*. New York: Bobbs-Merrill, 1971.
Chapell, Bryan. *Christ-Centered Preaching: Redeeming the Expository Sermon*. 3rd ed. Grand Rapids: Baker Academics, 2018.
Chappell, William. *The Preacher, or the Art and Method of Preaching: Shewing the Most Ample Directions and Rules for Invention, Method, Expression, and Books Whereby a Minister May be Furnished with Such Helps as May Make Him a Useful Laborer in the Lord's Vineyard*. London: Farnham, 1656.
Charnock, Stephen. *Two Discourses: The First of Man's Enmity to God; The Second, of the Salvation of Sinners*. London: Veel, 1699.
Chun, Chris. *The Legacy of Jonathan Edwards in the Theology of Andrew Fuller*. Studies in the History of Christian Traditions 162. Boston: Brill, 2012.
Church of England. *The Second Tome of Homilees: Of Such Matters as Were Promised, and Intituled in the Former Part of Homilees*. London: Jugge and Cawood, 1571.
Chute, Anthony L., et al. *The Baptist Story: From English Sect to Global Movement*. Nashville: B&H Academic, 2015.
Clary, Ian Hugh. "The Centre of Christianity—The Doctrine of the Cross: Andrew Fuller as a Reformed Theologian." *Evangelical Quarterly* 90 (2019) 195–212.
Claude, Jean. *An Essay on the Composition of a Sermon*. Edited and translated by Robert Robinson. Vol. 1. London: Lepard, 1779.
Clowney, Edmund P. *Preaching and Biblical Theology*. Grand Rapids: Eerdmans, 1961.
Coffey, John. Introduction to *The Post-Reformation Era, 1559–1689*, edited by John Coffey, 1–20. Vol. 1 of *The Oxford History of Protestant Dissenting Traditions*. Oxford: Oxford University Press, 2020.
———. *Persecution and Toleration in Protestant England, 1558–1689*. Edinburgh Gate, UK: Pearson Education, 2000.
Coffey, John, and Paul C. H. Lim, eds. *The Cambridge Companion to Puritanism*. Cambridge: Cambridge University Press, 2008.
Coggan, Donald. *Preaching: The Sacrament of the Word*. New York: Crossroad, 1988.
Collier, Keith Allen. "Preaching for the Church: An Evaluation of Mark E. Dever's Ecclesiological Homiletic." PhD diss., Southwestern Baptist Theological Seminary, 2016.
Collins, Hercules. *The Temple Repair'd: or, An Essay to Revive the Long Neglected Ordinances, of Exercising the Spiritual Gift of Prophecy for the Edification of the Church, and of Ordaining Ministers Duly Qualified*. London: Marshal, 1702.
Collinson, Patrick. *The Birthpangs of Protestant England: Religious and Cultural Change in the Sixteenth and Seventeenth Centuries*. London: Macmillan, 1988.
———. *The Elizabethan Puritan Movement*. Oxford: Clarendon, 1990.
The Confession of Faith of those Churches which are Commonly, Though Falsly, Called Anabaptists Presented to the View of all that Feare God to Examine by the Touchstone of the Word of Truth, as Likewise for the Taking Off those Aspersions which are Frequently both in Pulpit and Print, although Unjustly, Cast upon them. London: 1644.

A Confession of Faith Put Forth by the Elders and Brethren of Many Congregations of Christians (Baptized upon Profession of their Faith) in London and the Country. London: 1677.

Cooper, Michael R., Jr. "Word of this Salvation in the Mouths of Christ's Ministers": Retrieving a Theology of Preaching as Reflected in the Sermons and Writings of Benjamin Keach (1640–1704)." PhD diss., Southwestern Baptist Theological Seminary, 2024.

Copeland, David A. *Benjamin Keach and the Development of Baptist Traditions in Seventeenth Century England*. Lewiston, NY: Mellen, 2001.

Coxe, Benjamin. *An Appendix, to a Confession of Faith, or, A More Full Declaration of the Faith and Judgement of Baptized Beleevers. Occasioned by the Inquiry of some Wel Affected and Godly Persons in the Country*. London: 1646.

Coxe, Nehemiah. *A discourse of the covenants that God made with men before the law wherein the covenant of circumcision is more largely handled, and the invalidity of the plea for pædobaptism taken from thence discovered*. London: Ponder and Alsop, 1681.

——— . *A Sermon Preached at the Ordination of an Elder and Deacons in a Baptized Congregation in London*. London: Fabian, 1681.

Craddock, Fred B. *As One Without Authority*. Nashville: Abingdon, 1971.

——— . *Preaching*. Nashville: Abingdon, 1985.

Cranmer, Thomas. *Certayne Sermons, or Homelies, appoynted by the kynges Maiestie, to be declared and redde, by all persones, Vicars, or Curates, every Sondaye in their churches, where they have Cure*. London: 1547.

Crosby, Thomas. *The History of the English Baptists*. 4 vols. Bellingham, WA: Logos, 2011.

Cross, Brenton. *Southern Baptist and Expository Preaching: Biblical Interpretation, Values, and Politics in Twentieth-Century America*. Eugene, OR: Wipf & Stock, 2021.

Cross, F. L., and Elizabeth A. Livingstone. *The Oxford Dictionary of the Christian Church*. Oxford: Oxford University Press, 2005.

Cunnington, Ralph. *Preaching with Spiritual Power: Calvin's Understanding of Word and Spirit in Preaching*. Scotland: Christian Focus, 2015.

Dagg, J. L. *A Treatise on Church Order*. Vol. 2 of *Manual of Theology*. Charleston: Southern Baptist Publication Society, 1859.

Dahlman, Jason E. "Opening a Box of Sweet Ointment: Homiletics Within the Church of England, 1592–1678." PhD diss., Trinity International University, 2012.

Dargan, Edwin Charles. *A History of Preaching*. 2 vols. New York: Hodder & Stoughton, 1912.

D'Aubigné, J. H. Merle. *History of the Reformation in the Sixteenth Century*. Translated by Henry Beveridge and H. White. Collin's Select Library 5. London: Groombridge & Sons, 1862.

Davies, Horton. *Like Angels from a Cloud: The English Metaphysical Preachers, 1588–1645*. San Marino, CA: Huntington Library, 1986.

——— . *Worship and Theology in England: From Cranmer to Baxter and Fox, 1534–1690*. Grand Rapids: Eerdmans, 1996.

——— . *The Worship of the English Puritans*. 2nd ed. Grand Rapids: Soli Deo Gloria, 1997.

Deane, Shane Jonathan. "A Golden Mine Opened": The Role of Christ-Centered Preaching in the Sermons of Benjamin Keach (1640–1704)." PhD diss., Southern Baptist Theological Seminary, 2024.

Denault, Pascal. *The Distinctiveness of Baptist Covenant Theology: A Comparison Between Seventeenth-Century Particular Baptist and Paedobaptist Federalism*. Port St. Lucie, FL: Solid Ground Christian, 2013.

Dennison, James T., Jr. "The Bern Synod (1532)." In *Reformed Confessions of the 16th and 17th Centuries in English Translation: 1523–1693*, 1:226–76. Grand Rapids: Reformation Heritage, 2008.

———. "The Bohemian Confession (1573)." In *Reformed Confessions of the 16th and 17th Centuries in English Translation: 1523–1693*, 3:323–91. Grand Rapids: Reformation Heritage, 2012.

———. "The Canons of Dort (1618)." In *Reformed Confessions of the 16th and 17th Centuries in English Translation: 1523–1693*, 4:120–53. Grand Rapids: Reformation Heritage, 2014.

———. "The Confession of the Heidelberg Theologians (1607)." In *Reformed Confessions of the 16th and 17th Centuries in English Translation: 1523–1693*, 4:27–40. Grand Rapids: Reformation Heritage, 2014.

———. "The Heidelberg Catechism (1563)." In *Reformed Confessions of the 16th and 17th Centuries in English Translation: 1523–1693*, 2:769–99. Grand Rapids: Reformation Heritage, 2010.

———. "The London Baptist Confession (1644)." In *Reformed Confessions of the 16th and 17th Centuries in English Translation: 1523–1693*, 4:513–36. Grand Rapids: Reformation Heritage, 2014.

———. "The Second Helvetic Confession (1566)." In *Reformed Confessions of the 16th and 17th Centuries in English Translation: 1523–1693*, 2:809–81. Grand Rapids: Reformation Heritage, 2010.

———. "Westminster Shorter Catechism (1647)." In *Reformed Confessions of the 16th and 17th Centuries in English Translation: 1523–1693*, 4:337–64. Grand Rapids: Reformation Heritage, 2014.

———. "Zwingli, Fidei Ratio (1530)." In *Reformed Confessions of the 16th and 17th Centuries in English Translation: 1523–1693*, 1:112–36. Grand Rapids: Reformation Heritage, 2008.

Dever, Mark, and Greg Gilbert. *Preach: Theology Meets Practice*. Nashville: B&H, 2012.

Dickens, A. G. *The English Reformation*. 2nd ed. University Park, PA: Pennsylvania State University Press, 2005.

Dockery, David S. "The Lord's Supper in the New Testament and in Baptist Worship." *Search* 19 (1988) 38–48.

———. *Southern Baptist Consensus and Renewal: A Biblical, Historical, and Theological Proposal*. Nashville: B&H Academics, 2008.

Doran, Susan, and Christopher Durston. *Princes, Pastors and People: The Church and Religion in England, 1500–1689*. Oxford: Taylor & Francis, 2002.

Dunn-Wilson, David. *A Mirror for the Church: Preaching in the First Five Centuries*. Grand Rapids: Eerdmans, 2005.

Dupont, Anthony, et al., eds. *Preaching in the Patristic Era: Sermons, Preachers, and Audiences in the Latin West*. A New History of the Sermon 6. Boston: Brill, 2018.

Durston, Christopher, and Jacqueline Eales, eds. *The Culture of English Puritanism: 1560–1700*. New York: St. Martin's, 1996.

Earls, Rod. *Spurgeon's Theology for Multiplying Disciples and Churches: The Story of How Spurgeon and the Metropolitan Tabernacle Followed Christ*. Eugene, OR: Wipf and Stock, 2022.

Early, Joe, Jr. *The Life and Writings of Thomas Helwys*. Early English Baptist Texts. Macon: Mercer University Press, 2009.

Earngey, Mark. "Soli Deo Gloria: The Reformation of Worship." In *Reformation Worship: Liturgies from the Past for the Present*, edited by Jonathan Gibson and Mark Earngey, 1–24. Greensboro: New Growth, 2018.

Edwards, Aaron P. *A Theology of Preaching and Dialectic: Scriptural Tension, Heraldic Proclamation and the Pneumatological Moment*. London: T&T Clark, 2018.

Edwards, O. C., Jr. *The History of Preaching*. Nashville: Abingdon, 2004.

Emerson, Matthew Y., and R. Lucas Stamps. *The Baptist Vision: Faith and Practice for a Believers' Church*. Brentwood: B&H Academics, 2025.

Emerson, Matthew Y., et al., eds. *Baptists and the Christian Tradition: Towards an Evangelical Baptist Catholicity*. Nashville: B&H Academic, 2020.

Fasol, Al. *With a Bible in Their Hands: Baptist Preaching in the South, 1679–1979*. Nashville: B&H, 1994.

Fesko, J. V. *The Theology of the Westminster Standards: Historical Context and Theological Insights*. Wheaton, IL: Crossway, 2014.

Fish, Roy J. *Giving a Good Invitation*. Nashville: Broadman, 1974.

Flavel, John. "The Character of a True Evangelical Pastor." In vol. 6 of *The Works of the Rev. Mr. John Flavel*, 564–85. London: Baynes and Son, 1820.

Ford, Coleman M., and Shawn J. Wilhite. *Ancient Wisdom for the Care of Souls: Learning the Art of Pastoral Ministry from the Church Fathers*. Wheaton, IL: Crossway, 2024.

Ford, James Thomas. "Preaching in the Reformed Tradition." In *Preachers and People in the Reformations and Early Modern Period*, edited by Larissa Taylor, 65–88. A New History of the Sermon 2. Boston: Brill, 2001.

Forde, Gerhard O. *Theology Is for Proclamation*. Minneapolis: Augsburg Fortress, 1990.

Forsyth, P. T. *Positive Preaching and Modern Mind*. New York: Armstrong & Son, 1907.

Franks, Ben. "Rightly Handling the Word of Truth: Puritan Interpretation of Scripture." *Puritan Reformed Journal* 11 (2019) 43–52.

Frei, Hans W. *The Eclipse of Biblical Narrative: A Study in Eighteenth and Nineteenth Century Hermeneutics*. New Haven: Yale University Press, 1974.

Fuller, Andrew. *The Complete Works of the Rev. Andrew Fuller*. Edited by Joseph Belcher. 3 vols. 1845. Repr., Harrisonburg, VA: Sprinkle, 1988.

Gallaty, Robby, and Steven W. Smith. *Preaching for the Rest of Us: Essentials for Text-Driven Preaching*. Nashville: B&H Academic, 2017.

Gane, Erwin R. "The Exegetical Methods of Some Sixteenth-Century Puritan Preachers: Hooper, Cartwright, and Perkins." *Andrews University Seminary Studies* 19 (1981) 21–36.

Garrett, James Leo, Jr. *Baptist Theology: A Four-Century Study*. Macon: Mercer University Press, 2009.

———. *Systematic Theology: Biblical, Historical, and Evangelical*. Vol. 1. 4th ed. Eugene, OR: Wipf & Stock, 2014.

George, Timothy. Foreword to *Baptists and the Christian Tradition: Toward an Evangelical Baptist Catholicity*, edited by Matthew Y. Emerson et al., ix–xii. Nashville: B&H Academic, 2020.

———. "The Future of Baptist Theology." In *Theologians of the Baptist Tradition*, edited by Timothy George and David S. Dockery, 5–10. Nashville: Broadman & Holman, 2001.

———. "John Gill." In *Baptist Theologians*, edited by Timothy George and David S. Dockery, 77–101. Nashville: Broadman, 1990.

———. "Retrieval for the Sake of Renewal." *Reformed Faith & Practice* 2 (2017) 72–73.

Gerrish, B. A. *Grace and Gratitude: The Eucharistic Theology of John Calvin*. Eugene, OR: Wipf and Stock, 2002.

———. "The Lord's Supper in the Reformed Confessions." *Theology Today* 23 (1966) 224–43.

Gill, John. *The Cause of God and Truth*. New ed. London: Tegg, 1838.

———. *A Complete Body of Doctrinal and Practical Divinity: or, A System of Evangelical Truths, Deduced from the Sacred Scriptures*. Vol. 2. New ed. London: Tegg, 1839.

Gillette, A. D., ed. *Minutes of the Philadelphia Baptist Association, from A.D. 1707, to A.D. 1807: Being the First One Hundred Years of Its Existence*. Philadelphia: American Baptist Publication Society, 1851.

Glowasky, Michael. *Rhetoric and Scripture in Augustine's Homiletic Strategy: Tracing the Narrative of Christian Maturation*. Boston: Brill, 2020.

Goodwin, Thomas. *The Works of Thomas Goodwin*. Vol. 11. Edinburgh: Nichol, 1865.

Gordan, Bruce. Introduction to *Architect of Reformation: An Introduction to Heinrich Bullinger, 1504–1575*, edited by Bruce Gordon and Emidio Campi, 1–18. Grand Rapids: Baker Academic, 2004.

———. "Late Medieval Christianity." In *The Oxford History of the Reformation*, edited by Peter Marshall, 17–38. Oxford: Oxford University Press, 2022.

Grace, W. Madison, II. "Early English Baptists' View of the Lord's Supper." *Southwestern Journal of Theology* 57 (2015) 159–79.

Grant, Keith S. *Andrew Fuller and the Evangelical Renewal of Pastoral Theology*. Studies in Baptist History and Thought 36. Carlisle, UK: Paternoster, 2013.

Grantham, Thomas. *Christianismus Primitivus, or, The Ancient Christian Religion*. London: Smith, 1678.

Grasso, Domenico. *Proclaiming God's Message: A Study in the Theology of Preaching*. Notre Dame, IN: Notre Dame Press, 1965.

Greenhaw, David W. "Theology of Preaching." In *Concise Encyclopedia of Preaching*, edited by William H. Willimon and Richard Lischer, 477–82. Louisville: Westminster John Knox, 1995.

Gregory, Joel. "Expository." In *The New Interpreter's Handbook of Preaching*, edited by Paul Scott Wilson et al., 176–79. Nashville: Abingdon, 2008.

Gribben, Crawford. *John Owen and English Puritanism: Experiences of Defeat*. Oxford Studies in Historical Theology. Oxford: Oxford University Press, 2016.

Hall, David D. *The Puritans: A Transatlantic History*. Princeton: Princeton University Press, 2019.

Halstead, Aaron S. "*Verbum Dei*: Toward a Baptist Acceptance of a Bullingerian Helvetic Theology of Proclamation." PhD diss., Southwestern Baptist Theological Seminary, 2024.

Hanna, Christopher R. *Retrieval for the Sake of Renewal: Timothy George as a Historical Theologian*. Eugene, OR: Wipf and Stock, 2022.

Hawkins, O. S., and Matt Queen. *The Gospel Invitation: Why Publicly Inviting People to Receive Christ Still Matters*. Nashville: Thomas Nelson, 2023.

Haykin, Michael A. G. *Amidst Us Our Beloved Stands: Recovering Sacrament in the Baptist Tradition*. Bellingham, WA: Lexham, 2022.

———, ed. *The Armies of the Lamb: The Spirituality of Andrew Fuller*. Dundas, Can.: Joshua, 2001.

———. "Great Admirers of the Transatlantic Divinity: Some Chapters in the Story of Baptist Edwardsianism." In *After Jonathan Edwards: The Courses of the New England Theology*, edited by Oliver D. Crisp and Douglas A. Sweeney, 197–208. Oxford: Oxford University Press, 2012.

———. *Kiffen, Knollys, and Keach: Rediscovering our English Baptist Heritage*. Peterborough, Can.: H&E, 2020.

———. *The Life and Thought of John Gill: (1697–1771) A Tercentennial Appreciation*. New York: Brill, 2017.

———. "'The Lord Is Doing Great Things, and Answering Prayer Everywhere': The Revival of the Calvinistic Baptists in the Long Eighteenth Century." In *Pentecostal Outpourings: Revival and the Reformed Tradition*, edited by Robert Davis Smart et al., 113–34. Grand Rapids: Reformation Heritage, 2016.

———. "Separatists and Baptists." In *The Post-Reformation Era, 1559–1689*, edited by John Coffey, 113–38. Vol. 1 of *The Oxford History of Protestant Dissenting Traditions*. Oxford: Oxford University Press, 2020.

———. "'Those Who Plead for Thee': English Particular Baptist Preaching in the Long Eighteenth Century." *Evangelical Quarterly* 94 (2023) 299–311.

Haymes, Brian. "Towards a Sacramental Understanding of Preaching." In *Baptist Sacramentalism*, edited by Anthony R. Cross and Philip E. Thompson, 263–70. Studies in Baptist History and Thought 5. Eugene, OR: Wipf & Stock, 2006.

Heal, Felicity. "The English, Scottish, and Irish Reformations." In *The Oxford Handbook of The Protestant Reformations*, edited by Ulinka Rublack, 233–52. Oxford: Oxford University Press, 2017.

Healey, Jonathan. *The Blazing World: A New History of Revolutionary England, 1603–1689*. New York: Knopf, 2023.

Heisler, Greg. *Spirit-Led Preaching: The Holy Spirit's Role in Sermon Preparation and Delivery*. Nashville: B&H Academic, 2007.

Helwys, Thomas. *A Declaration of Faith of the English People Remaining in Amsterdam in Holland*. Amsterdam: 1611.

Henderson, Robert W. *The Teaching Office in the Reformed Tradition: A History of the Doctoral Ministry*. Philadelphia: Westminster, 1962.

Herr, Alan Fager. *The Elizabethan Sermon: A Survey and a Bibliography*. New York: Octagon, 1969.

Hicks, Thomas Eugene, Jr. "An Analysis of the Doctrine of Justification in the Theologies of Richard Baxter and Benjamin Keach." PhD diss., Southern Baptist Theological Seminary, 2009.

Hoare, Elizabeth. "Bernard of Clairvaux: Preaching to Foster a Love and Devotion to God." In *A Legacy of Preaching: Apostles to the Revivalists*, edited by Benjamin K. Forrest et al., 1:177–90. Grand Rapids: Zondervan, 2018.

Hobbs, Herschel H. "People of the Book: The Baptist Doctrine of the Holy Scripture." In *Baptist Why and Why Not Revisited*, edited by Timothy George and Richard D. Land, 11–22. Nashville: Broadman & Holman, 1997.

Hofer, Andrew. *The Power of Patristic Preaching: The Word in Our Flesh*. Washington, DC: Catholic University of America Press, 2023.

Holifield, E. Brooks. *The Covenant Sealed: The Development of Puritan Sacramental Theology in Old and New England, 1570–1720*. Eugene, OR: Wipf & Stock, 2002.

Holmes, James Christopher. "The Role of Metaphor in the Sermons of Benjamin Keach, 1640–1704." PhD diss., Southern Baptist Theological Seminary, 2009.

Holmes, Stephen R. "Nonconformist Preaching and Liturgy." In *T&T Clark Companion to Nonconformity*, edited by Robert Pope, 247–56. London: Bloomsbury T&T Clark, 2013.

Hooker, Thomas. *The Soul's Preparation for Christ*. London: 1638.

Houser, William G. "Puritan Homiletic: A Caveat." *Concordia Theological Quarterly* 53 (1989) 257.

Howson, Barry H. *Christ Exalted: Pastoral Writings of Hanserd Knollys with an Essay on His Eschatological Thought*. Eugene, OR: Pickwick, 2019.

Hunt, Arnold. *The Art of Hearing: English Preachers and Their Audiences, 1590–1640*. Cambridge Studies in Early Modern British History. Cambridge: Cambridge University Press, 2011.

Hyperius, Andreas. *De formandis concionibus sacris: seu de interpretation scripturarum populari*. Marburg: 1553.

Ivimey, Joseph. *A History of the English Baptists*. 4 vols. London: 1811–1830.

Jue, Jeffrey K. "Andrew Fuller: Heir of the Reformation." *Eusebeia* 8 (2008) 27–52.

Kater, Maarten J. "Puritan Preaching and Pathos: Some Uses from 'Puritan Rhetoric.'" *Studies in Puritanism and Piety* 1 (2019) 43–56.

Kay, James F. *Preaching and Theology*. St. Louis: Chalice, 2007.

———. "Theology of Proclamation." In *The New Interpreter's Handbook of Preaching*, edited by Paul Scott Wilson, 493–96. Nashville: Abingdon, 2008.

Keach, Benjamin. *The ax laid to the root, or, One blow more at the foundation of infant baptism and church-membership containing an exposition of that metaphorical text of Holy Scripture, Mat. 3, 10*. London: 1693.

———. *The Baptist Catechism, Commonly Called Keach's Catechism: or, A Brief Instruction in the Principles of the Christian Religion*. Philadelphia: American Baptist Publication Society, 1851.

———. *Beams of divine light: or, Some brief hints of the being and attributes of God and of the three persons in the God-Head. Also proving the deity of Christ, and of the Holy-Ghost. Written at the request of a most pious, and honourable citizen of London. And published by him for the sake of the poorer sort of Christians, in these perilous times*. London: Allwood, 1700.

———. *The breach repaired in God's worship, or, Singing of psalms, hymns, and spiritual songs, proved to be an holy ordinance of Jesus Christ with an answer to all objections: As also, an examination of Mr. Isaac Marlow's two papers, one called, A discourse against singing, &c., the other, An appendix: Wherein his arguments and cavils are detected and refuted*. London: 1691.

———. *Christ Alone the Way to Heaven; or, Jacob's Ladder Improved*. London: Harris, 1698.

———. *A counter-antidote, to purge out the malignant effects of a late counterfeit [. .] An answer to Mr. Shute's reply to Mr. Collins's half-sheet*. London: Bernard, 1694.

———. *The Display of Glorious Grace, or, The Covenant of Peace, Opened: In Fourteen Sermons*. London: Bridge, 1698.

———. *Distressed Sion relieved, or, The garment of praise for the spirit of heaviness wherein are discovered the grand causes of the churches trouble and misery under* the late dismal dispensation: With a compleat history of, and lamentation for those renowned worthies that fell in England by popish rage and cruelty, from the year 1680 to 1688. London: Crouch, 1689.

———. *The Everlasting Covenant: A Sweet Cordial for a Drooping Soul: or, The Excellent Nature of the Covenant of Grace Opened*. London: Barnard, 1693.

———. *An Exposition of the Parables and Express Similitudes of Our Lord and Saviour Jesus Christ*. London: Aylott, 1858.

———. *The glory of a true church, and its discipline display'd wherein a true gospel church is described: Together with the power of the keys, and who are to be let in, and who to be shut out*. London: 1697.

———. *God acknowledged, or, The true interest of the nation and all that fear God opened in a sermon preached December the 11th, 1695: Being the day appointed by the king for publick prayer and humiliation*. London: Marshall, 1696.

———. *A Golden Mine Opened: or, The Glory of God's Rich Grace Displayed in the Mediator to Believers: And His Direful Wrath against Impenitent Sinners: Containing the Substance of near Forty Sermons upon Several Subjects*. London: 1694.

———. *Gold Refin'd, or, Baptism in Its Primitive Purity*. London: 1689.

———. *The gospel minister's maintenance vindicated. Wherein, a regular ministry in the churches, is first asserted, and the objections against a Gospel maintenance for ministers, answered. Also, the dignity, necessity, difficulty, use and excellency of the ministry of Christ is opened. Likewise, the nature and vveghtiness of that sacred vvorkand office clearly evinc'd. Recommended to the baptized congregations, by several elders in and about the City of London*. London: Harris, 1689.

———. *The grand impostor discovered: or, The Quakers doctrine weighed in the ballance, and found wanting. A poem, by way of dialogue: wherein their chief, and most concerning principles are laid down, and by the authority of Gods holy word clearly refuted*. London: Harris, 1675.

———. *Instructions for Children: Or, The Child's and Youth's Delight; Teaching an Easy Way to Spell and Read True English*. 4th ed. London: Mead and Harris, 1699.

———. *The Jewish Sabbath abrogated, or, The Saturday Sabbatarians confuted in two parts: first, proving the abrogation of the old seventh-day Sabbath: secondly, that the Lord's Day is of divine appointment: containing several sermons newly preach'd upon a special occasion, wherein are many new arguments not found in former authors*. London: Marshall, 1700.

———. *The Marrow of True Justification, or, Justification without Works*. London: Newman, 1692.

———. *A Medium Betwixt Two Extremes: Wherein It Is Proved, That the Whole First Adam Was Condemned, and the Whole Second Adam Justified. Being a Sermon Lately Preached in London, and Now Offered to Publick View*. London: Bell, 1698.

———. *A short confession of faith containing the substance of all the fundamental articles in the larger confession put forth by the elders of the Baptist churches, owning persona; election and final perseverance*. London: 1697.

———. *Spiritual Songs: Being the Marrow of the Scripture, in Songs of Praise to Almighty God; From the Old and New Testament*. 2nd ed. London: Marshal, 1700.

———. *A summons to the grave, or, The necessity of a timely preparation for death demonstrated in a sermon preached at the funeral of that most eminent and faithful servant of Jesus Christ Mr. John Norcott who departed this life March 24, 1675/6*. London: Harris, 1676.

———. "To All the Baptized Churches and Faithful Brethren in England and Wales; Christian Salutations." In *Faith and Life for Baptists: The Documents of the London Particular Baptist General Assemblies, 1689-1694*, edited by James M. Renihan, 105-12. Palmdale, CA: RBAP, 2016.

———. *The travels of true godliness, from the beginning of the world to this present day in an apt and pleasant allegory*. London: Dunton, 1684.

———. *Tropologia: A Key to Open Scripture Metaphors*. London: Collingridge, 1856.

Keeble, Neil H. *The Literary Culture of Nonconformity in Later Seventeenth-Century England*. Leicester: Leicester University Press, 1987.

Kennedy, George A. *Classical Rhetoric & Its Christian and Secular Tradition from Ancient to Modern Times*. 2nd ed. Chapel Hill: University of North Carolina Press, 1999.

Kidd, Thomas S. *God of Liberty: A Religious History of the American Revolution*. New York: Basic, 2010.

Kidd, Thomas S., and Barry Hankins. *Baptists in America: A History*. Oxford: Oxford University Press, 2015.

King, Kevin L. "Ulrich Zwingli: Pastor, Patriot, Prophet, and Protestant." In *Apostles to the Revivalists*, edited by Benjamin K. Forrest et al., 294-312. Vol. 1. of *A Legacy of Preaching*. Grand Rapids: Zondervan, 2018.

Kirby, Torrance, and Paul Stanwood, eds. *Paul's Cross and the Culture of Persuasion in England, 1520-1640*. Studies in the History of Christian Traditions. Boston: Brill, 2014.

Kneidel, Greg. "*Ars Praedicandi*: Theories and Practice." In *The Oxford Handbook of The Early Modern Sermon*, edited by Peter McCullough et al., 3-20. Oxford: Oxford University Press, 2011.

Knollys, Hanserd. *Christ Exalted: In a Sermon*. London: 1645.

———. *An Exposition of the First Chapter of the Song of Solomon. Wherein the Texta is Analysed, the Allegories are Explained, and the Hidden Mysteries are Unveiled, According to the Proportion of Faith, With Spiritual Meditations upon Every Verse*. London: Godbid, 1656.

———. *Pamphlets on Religion*. Edited by Rady Roldán-Figueroa and William Lee Pitts. Early English Baptist Texts. Macon: Mercer University Press, 2017.

Kreitzer, L. Joseph. *William Kiffen and His World*. Centre for Baptist History and Heritage Studies: Re-Sourcing Baptist History; Seventeenth Century Series 1-6. Oxford: Regent's Park College, 2018.

Kuivenhoven, Maarten. "Condemning Coldness and Sleepy Dullness: The Concept of Urgency in the Preaching Models of Richard Baxter and William Perkins." *Puritan Reformed Journal* 4 (2012) 180-200.

Kuruvilla, Abraham. *Privilege the Text: A Theological Hermeneutic for Preaching*. Chicago: Moody, 2013.

Latimer, Hugh. "Sermon of the Plough." In *Sermons by Hugh Latimer*, edited by George Elwes Corrie, 1:59-78. The Parker Society. Cambridge: Cambridge University Press, 1844.

———. "Sermon the Second on the Lord's Prayer." In *Sermons by Hugh Latimer*, edited by George Elwes Corrie, 1:335-60. The Parker Society. Cambridge: Cambridge University Press, 1844.

Lea, Thomas D. "The Hermeneutics of the Puritans." *Journal of the Evangelical Theological Society* 39 (1996) 271-84.

Leith, John H. "Calvin's Doctrine of the Proclamation of the Word and Its Significance for Today in the Light of Recent Research." *Review and Expositor* 86 (1989) 29–44.

Lewis, Peter. *The Genius of Puritanism*. 1977. Repr., Grand Rapids: Soli Deo Gloria, 1997.

Lischer, Richard. *A Theology of Preaching: The Dynamics of the Gospel*. Eugene, OR: Wipf and Stock, 2001.

Lloyd-Jones, Martyn. *Preaching and Preachers*. Grand Rapids: Zondervan, 1972.

Lumpkin, William L. *Baptist Confessions of Faith*. Edited by Bill J. Leonard. 2nd rev. ed. Valley Forge, PA: Judson, 2011.

Maag, Karin. *Worshiping with the Reformers*. Reformation Commentary on Scripture. Downers Grove, IL: IVP Academic, 2021.

MacDonald, Murdina D. *London Calvinistic Baptists, 1689–1727: Tensions with a Dissenting Community Under Toleration*. Centre for Baptist Studies in Oxford Publications 23. Oxford: Regent's Park College, 2022.

MacLeod, Donald. *Compel Them to Come: Calvinism and the Free Offer of the Gospel*. Ross Shire, UK: Christian Focus, 2020.

Maclure, Millar. *The Paul's Cross Sermons, 1534–1642*. Toronto: Toronto University Press, 1957.

Madigan, Kevin. *Medieval Christianity: A New History*. New Haven: Yale University Press, 2015.

Maier, Christoph T. *Preaching the Crusades: Mendicant Friars and the Cross in the Thirteenth Century*. Cambridge: Cambridge University Press, 1994.

Manetsch, Scott M. *Calvin's Company of Pastors: Pastoral Care and the Emerging Reformed Church, 1536–1609*. Oxford Studies in Historical Theology Series. Oxford: Oxford University Press, 2013.

Marlow, Isaac. *The Purity of Gospel Communion*. London: 1694.

———. *Some Short Observations made on a Book Newly Published by Mr. Benjamin Keach Intituled, the Breach Repaired in God's Worship, &c. Wherein is Contained a Pretended Answer to Isaac Marlow's Brief Discourse Concerning Singing in the Publick Worship of God; as also to an Appendix, Lately Published, and Thereunto Added*. London: 1691.

Marshall, Peter. *Heretics and Believers: A History of the English Reformation*. New Haven: Yale University Press, 2017.

———. *The Oxford History of the Reformation*. Oxford: Oxford University Press, 2022.

Mathews, Ned L. "The Disciplines of a Text-Driven Preacher." In *Text-Driven Preaching: God's Word at the Heart of Every Sermon*, edited by Daniel L. Akin et al., 75–98. Nashville: B&H Academic, 2010.

Maxwell, Jaclyn L. *Christianization and Communication in Late Antiquity: John Chrysostom and His Congregation in Antioch*. Cambridge: Cambridge University Press, 2006.

Mayor, J. E. B. *Autobiography of Matthew Robinson*. Cambridge: Cambridge University Press, 1856.

McBeth, Leon. *The Baptist Heritage*. Nashville: Broadman, 1987.

McClure, John S. *Preaching Words: 144 Key Terms in Homiletics*. Louisville: Westminster John Knox, 2007.

McDill, Wayne. *The 12 Essential Skills for Great Preaching*. Nashville: Broadman & Holman, 1994.

McGrath, Alister E. *Reformation Thought: An Introduction.* Hoboken, NJ: Wiley Blackwell, 2021.

McKibbens, Thomas R., Jr. "Disseminating Biblical Doctrine Through Preaching." *Baptist History and Heritage* 19 (1984) 42–57.

———. *The Forgotten Heritage: A Lineage of Great Baptist Preaching.* Macon: Mercer University Press, 1986.

———. "John A. Broadus: Shaper of Baptist Preaching." *Baptist History and Heritage* 40 (2005) 18–24.

McKim, Donald K. "The Functions of Ramism in William Perkins' Theology." *The Sixteenth Century Journal* 16 (1985) 503–17.

———. *The Westminster Dictionary of Theological Terms.* 2nd ed. Rev. ed. Louisville: Westminster John Knox, 2014.

McMullen, Michael D., and Timothy D. Whelan, eds. *The Diary of Andrew Fuller, 1780–1801.* Vol. 1 of *The Complete Works of Andrew Fuller.* Boston: De Gruyter, 2016.

Merida, Tony. *The Christ-Centered Expositor: A Field Guide for Word-Driven Disciple Makers.* Nashville: B&H Academic, 2016.

Milioni, Dwayne. "William Perkins: Prince of Puritan Preaching." In *Apostles to the Revivalists*, edited by Benjamin K. Forrest et al., 363–77. Vol. 1. of *A Legacy of Preaching.* Grand Rapids: Zondervan, 2018.

Miller, Donald. *Fire in Thy Mouth.* New York: Abingdon, 1954.

Miller, Perry. *The New England Mind: The Seventeenth Century.* Cambridge: Harvard University Press, 1939.

Mitchell, W. Fraser. *English Pulpit Oratory from Andrews to Tillotson: A Study of Its Literary Aspects.* London: Macmillan, 1939.

Mohler, R. Albert, Jr. *He Is Not Silent: Preaching in a Postmodern World.* Chicago: Moody, 2008.

———. "A Theology of Preaching." In *Handbook of Contemporary Preaching*, edited by Michael Duduit, 12–20. Nashville: Broadman, 1992.

Moore, Susan Hardman. "Reformed Theology and Puritanism." In *The Cambridge Companion to Reformed Theology*, edited by Paul T. Nimmo and David A. S. Fergusson, 199–214. Cambridge Companions to Religion. Cambridge: Cambridge University Press, 2016.

Morden, Peter J. "Andrew Fuller and *The Gospel Worthy of All Acceptation*." In *Pulpit and People: Studies in Eighteenth-Century Baptist Life and Thought*, edited by John H. Y. Briggs, 128–51. Eugene, OR: Paternoster, 2009.

———. *The Life and Thought of Andrew Fuller, 1754–1815.* Studies in Evangelical History and Thought. Milton Keynes, UK: Paternoster, 2015.

———. *Offering Christ to the World: Andrew Fuller (1754–1815) and the Revival of Eighteenth-Century Particular Baptist Life.* Studies in Baptist History and Thought 8. Carlisle, UK: Paternoster, 2003.

Morgan, Edward. *The Incarnation of the Word: The Theology of Language of Augustine of Hippo.* New York: T&T Clark, 2010.

Morgan, Irvonwy. *Puritan Spirituality.* London: Epworth, 1973.

Morrill, John. "The Puritan Revolution." In *The Cambridge Companion to Puritanism*, edited by John Coffey and Paul C. H. Lim, 67–88. Cambridge: Cambridge University Press, 2008.

Morrissey, Mary. "Scripture, Style, and Persuasion in Seventeenth-Century England Theories of Preaching." *Journal of Ecclesiastical History* 53 (2002) 686–706.

Mounce, Robert H. *The Essential Nature of New Testament Preaching*. Eugene, OR: Wipf & Stock, 2005.

Muller, Richard A. *Calvin and the Reformed Tradition: On the Work of Christ and the Order of Salvation*. Grand Rapids: Baker Academic, 2012.

———. *Holy Scripture: The Cognitive Foundation of Theology*. Vol. 2 of *Post-Reformation Reformed Dogmatics*. Grand Rapids: Baker Academics, 1993.

Mullett, Michael. "Radical Sects and Dissenting Churches, 1600–1750." In *A History of Religion in Britain: Practice and Belief from Pre-Roman Times to the Present*, edited by Sheridan Gilley and W. J. Sheils, 194–216. Cambridge: Blackwell, 1994.

Neale, J. M. *Medieval Preachers and Medieval Preaching: A Series of Extracts, Translated from the Sermons of the Middle Ages, Chronologically Arranged: With Notes and an Introduction*. London: Mozley, 1856.

Nettles, Thomas J. "Baptist Revivals in America in the Eighteenth and Nineteenth Centuries." In *Pentecostal Outpourings: Revival and the Reformed Tradition*, edited by Robert Davis Smart et al., 194–229. Grand Rapids: Reformation Heritage, 2016.

———. *Beginnings in Britain*. Vol. 1 of *The Baptists: Key People Involved in Forming a Baptist Identity*. Ross-shire, UK: Mentor Imprint, 2005.

———. *By His Grace and for His Glory*. Rev. 20th anniv. ed. Cape Coral, FL: Founders, 2006.

———. "The Enduring Impact and Relevance of *A Treatise on the Preparation and Delivery of Sermons*." In *John A. Broadus: A Living Legacy*, edited by David S. Dockery and Roger D. Duke, 176–211. Studies in Baptist Life and Thought. Nashville: B&H Academic, 2008.

Nimmo, Paul T. "The Theology of Preaching: A Reformed Perspective." *Theology in Scotland* 25 (2018) 12–19.

Nimmo, Paul T., and David A. S. Fergusson. Introduction to *The Cambridge Companion to Reformed Theology*, edited by Paul T. Nimmo and David A. S. Fergusson, 1–10. Cambridge Companions to Religion. Cambridge: Cambridge University Press, 2016.

Noll, Mark A. *America's God: From Jonathan Edwards to Abraham Lincoln*. Oxford: Oxford University Press, 2002.

———. *A History of Christianity in the United States and Canada*. Grand Rapids: Eerdmans, 1992.

———. *The Rise of Evangelicalism: The Age of Edwards, Whitefield, and the Wesleys*. Downers Grove, IL: IVP Academic, 2003.

O'Kelly, Steve. "The Influence of Separate Baptists on Revivalistic Evangelism and Worship." PhD diss., Southwestern Baptist Theological Seminary, Fort Worth, 1978.

Old, Hughes Oliphant. *The Age of the Reformation*. Vol. 4 of *The Reading and Preaching of the Scriptures in the Worship of the Christian Church*. Grand Rapids: Eerdmans, 2002.

———. *The Medieval Church*. Vol. 3 of *The Reading and Preaching of the Scriptures in the Worship of the Christian Church*. Grand Rapids: Eerdmans, 1999.

———. *The Modern Age*. Vol. 6 of *The Reading and Preaching of the Scriptures in the Worship of the Christian Church*. Grand Rapids: Eerdmans, 2007.

———. *The Patristic Age*. Vol. 2 of *The Reading and Preaching of the Scriptures in the Worship of the Christian Church*. Grand Rapids: Eerdmans, 1998.

Olford, Stephen F. "Restoring the Scriptures to Baptist Worship." *Review & Expositor* 85 (1988) 19–30.

Orme, Nicholas. *Going to Church in Medieval England*. New Haven: Yale University Press, 2021.

An Orthodox Creed: or, A Protestant Confession of Faith Being An Essay to Unite, and Confirm all true Protestants in the Fundamental Articles of the Christian Religion, against the Errors and Heresies of the Church of Rome. London: 1679.

Ortlund, Gavin. *Theological Retrieval for Evangelicals: Why We Need Our Past to Have a Future*. Wheaton, IL: Crossway, 2019.

Owen, John. *The Works of John Owen*. 16 vols. Carlisle, PA: Banner of Truth, 1966.

Ozment, Steven. *The Age of Reform, 1250–1550: An Intellectual and Religious History of Late Medieval and Reformation Europe*. New Haven: Yale University Press, 2020.

Pace, R. Scott. *Preaching by the Book: Developing and Delivering Text-Driven Sermons*. Edited by Heath A. Thomas. Hobbs College Library. Nashville: B&H Academic, 2018.

Packer, J. I. *The Quest for Godliness: The Puritan Vision of the Christian Life*. Wheaton, IL: Crossway, 1990.

Parker, T. H. L. *Calvin's Preaching*. Louisville: Westminster John Knox, 1992.

———. *John Calvin: A Biography*. Louisville: Westminster John Knox, 2007.

Pasquarello, Mike, III. *Christian Preaching: A Trinitarian Theology of Proclamation*. Eugene, OR: Wipf and Stock, 2006.

Patterson, Paige. "Ancient Rhetoric: A Model for Text-Driven Preachers." In *Text-Driven Preaching: God's Word at the Heart of Every Sermon*, edited by Daniel L. Akin et al., 163–80. Nashville: B&H Academic, 2010.

Pederson, Randall J. *Unity in Diversity: English Puritans and the Puritan Reformation, 1603–1689*. Leiden: Brill, 2014.

Pelikan, Jaroslav. *The Growth of Medieval Theology (600–1300)*. Vol. 3 of *The Christian Tradition: A History of the Development of Doctrine*. Chicago: University of Chicago Press, 1978.

Perkins, William. *The Art of Prophesying; or, A Treatise Concerning the Sacred and Only True Manner and Method of Preaching*. In *The Works of William Perkins*, edited by Joseph A. Pipa and J. Stephen Yuille, 10:281–356. Grand Rapids: Reformation Heritage, 2020.

Pipa, Joseph A. "William Perkins and the Development of Puritan Preaching." PhD diss., Westminster Theological Seminary, 1985.

Piper, John. *Expository Exultation: Christian Preaching as Worship*. Wheaton, IL: Crossway, 2018.

———. *The Supremacy of God in Preaching*. Rev. ed. Wheaton, IL: Crossway, 2015.

Plumlee, Spencer Franklin. "Baptist Primitivist: Internal and External Religion in the Theology of Thomas Grantham, 1633–1692." PhD diss., Southwestern Baptist Theological Seminary, 2013.

Poole, Matthew. *Annotations upon the Holy Bible: Wherein the Sacred Text Is Inserted, and Various Readings Annex'd, Together with the Parallel Scriptures*. Vol. 3. London: Roberts, 1685.

Ray, Jefferson Davis. *Expository Preaching*. Grand Rapids: Zondervan, 1940.

Renihan, James M. *Edification and Beauty: The Practical Ecclesiology of the English Particular Baptists, 1675–1705*. Studies in Baptist History and Thought 17. Eugene, OR: Wipf & Stock, 2008.

———. *For the Vindication of the Truth: A Brief Exposition of the First London Confession of Faith*. Baptist Symbolics 1. Cape Coral, FL: Founders, 2022.

———. *To the Judicious and Impartial Reader: An Exposition of the 1689 London Baptist Confession of Faith*. Baptist Symbolics 2. Cape Coral, FL: Founders, 2022.

———. *True Confessions: Baptist Documents in the Reformed Family*. Owensboro, KY: Reformed Baptist Academic, 2004.

Renihan, Samuel D. *From Shadow to Substance: The Federal Theology of the English Particular Baptists (1642–1704)*. Center for Baptist History and Heritage Studies 16. Oxford: Regent's Park College, 2018.

Richardson, Caroline Francis. *English Preachers and Preaching, 1640–1670*. New York: Macmillan, 1928.

Riker, David Bowman. *A Catholic Reformed Theologian: Federalism and Baptism in the Thought of Benjamin Keach, 1640–1704*. Eugene, OR: Wipf and Stock, 2009.

———. "A Catholic Reformed Theologian: Federalism and Baptism in the Thought of Benjamin Keach, 1640–1704." PhD diss., University of Aberdeen, 2007.

Rindels, Ryan. *Andrew Fuller's Theology of Revival: Divine Sovereignty and Human Responsibility in Spiritual Renewal*. Eugene, OR: Pickwick, 2021.

Robinson, Haddon W. *Biblical Preaching: The Development and Delivery of Expository Messages*. 3rd ed. Grand Rapids: Baker Academic, 2014.

Ryken, Leland. *Worldly Saints: The Puritans as They Really Were*. Grand Rapids: Zondervan, 1986.

Ryland, John, Jr. *The Work of Faith, the Labour of Love, and the Patience of Hope, Illustrated in the Life and Death of Rev. Andrew Fuller*. 2nd ed. London: Button & Son, 1818.

Ryrie, Alec. *Being Protestant in Reformation Britain*. Oxford: Oxford University Press, 2015.

———. *The English Reformation: A Very Brief History*. Very Brief Histories. London: SPCK, 2019.

Schreiner, Thomas R., and Matthew R. Crawford. *The Lord's Supper: Remembering and Proclaiming Christ Until He Comes*. NAC Studies in Bible & Theology 10. Nashville: B&H Academic, 2011.

Schreiner, Thomas R., and Shawn D. Wright, eds. *Believer's Baptism: Sign of the New Covenant in Christ*. NAC Studies in Bible & Theology 2. Nashville: B&H Academic, 2006.

Schuringa, H. David. "The Vitality of Reformed Preaching." *Calvin Theological Journal* 30 (1995) 184–93.

Seaver, Paul S. *Puritan Lectureship: The Politics of Religious Dissent, 1560–1662*. Stanford: Stanford University Press, 1970.

Smith, Brandon D. "The Trinity Debate (2016–2017): A Selected Bibliography." Biblical Reasoning, April 25, 2018. https://secundumscripturas.com/2018/04/25/the-trinity-debate-2016-2017-a-selected-bibliography/.

Smith, Steven W. *Dying to Preach: Embracing the Cross in the Pulpit*. Grand Rapids: Kregel, 2009.

———. *Recapturing the Voice of God: Shaping Sermons Like Scripture*. Nashville: B&H Academic, 2015.

Smyth, Charles. *The Art of Preaching: A Practical Survey of Preaching in the Church of England, 747–1939*. London: Society for Promoting Christian Knowledge, 1940.

Spears, William Eugene. "The Baptist Movement in England and in the Late Seventeenth Century as Reflected in the Work and Thought of Benjamin Keach, 1640–1704." PhD diss., University of Edinburgh, 1953.
Spilsbury, John. *Gods Ordinance, the Saints Priviledge. Discovered and Proved in Two Treatises. The First, the Saints Interest by Christ in all the Priviledges of Grace: Wherein their Right to the use of Baptisme, and the Lords Supper, Even Now during the Reign of Antichrist, is Cleared; and the Objections of those that Oppose the Same, are Answered. The Second, the Peculiar Interest of the Elect in Christ, and His Saving Grace. Wherein it is Proved that Christ Hath Not Presented to His Father Justice a Satisfaction for the Sinnes of all Men; but Onely for the Sinnes of Those that Doe, Or Shall Believe in Him; which are His Elect Onely: And the Objections of those that Maintaine the Contrary, are also Answered.* London: 1646.
Spradlin, Michael R. "Adrian Rogers and Reformed Theology." Michael R. Spradlin, March 9, 2023. https://michaelrspradlin.blog/2023/03/09/adrian-rogers-and-reformed-theology/.
Spurgeon, Charles Haddon. *1834–1854*. Vol. 1 of *C. H. Spurgeon's Autobiography: Compiled from His Diary, Letters, and Records*. London: Passmore and Alabaster, 1899.
———. *Lectures to My Students*. London: Passmore and Alabaster, 1875.
———. *The Metropolitan Tabernacle Pulpit Sermons*. 63 vols. London: Passmore & Alabaster, 1855–1917.
Stansbury, Ronald. *A Companion to Pastoral Care in the Late Middle Ages (1200–1500)*. Brill's Companions to the Christian Tradition. Leiden: Brill, 2010.
Stanton, Matthew. *Liturgy and Identity: London Baptists and the Hymn-Singing Controversy*. Centre for Baptist Studies in Oxford Publications 21. Oxford: Regent's Park College, 2022.
Stout, Harry S. *The New England Soul: Preaching and Religious Culture in Colonial New England*. New York: Oxford, 1986.
Streett, R. Alan. *The Effective Invitation: A Practical Guide for the Pastor*. Grand Rapids: Kregel, 1984.
———. "The Public Invitation and Calvinism." In *Whosoever Will: A Biblical Theological Critique of Five-Point Calvinism*, edited by David L. Allen and Steve W. Lemke, 225–50. Nashville: B&H Academic, 2010.
Sutton, Jerry. *The Baptist Reformation: The Conservative Resurgence in the Southern Baptist Convention*. Nashville: Broadman & Holman, 2000.
Thomas, Hugh M. *The Secular Clergy in England, 1066–1216*. Oxford: Oxford University Press, 2014.
Thompson, Mark D. "The Declarative God: Toward a Theological Description of Preaching." In *Theology Is for Preaching: Biblical Foundations, Method, and Practice*, edited by Chase R. Kuhn and Paul Grimmond, 18–33. Bellingham, WA: Lexham, 2021.
———. "Sola Scriptura." In *Reformation Theology: A Systematic Summary*, edited by Matthew Barrett, 145–87. Wheaton, IL: Crossway, 2017.
Tillotson, John. *Sermons, and Discourses some of which Never before Printed, the Third Volume*. London: Aylmer and Rogers, 1687.
Tolbert, Mark. "The Public Invitation and Altar Call." In *Calvinism: A Biblical and Theological Critique*, edited by David L. Allen and Steve W. Lemke, 457–80. Nashville: B&H Academic, 2022.

Todd, Obbie Tyler. *A Baptist at the Crossroads: The Atonement in the Writings of Richard Furman (1755–1825)*. Eugene, OR: Pickwick, 2021.

———. *Let Men Be Free: Baptist Politics in the Early United States (1776–1835)*. Eugene, OR: Pickwick, 2022.

———. *Southern Edwardseans: The Southern Baptist Legacy of Jonathan Edwards*. New Directions in Jonathan Edwards Studies 8. Göttingen, Ger.: Vandenhoeck & Ruprecht, 2022.

Toon, Peter. *The Emergence of Hyper-Calvinism in England Nonconformity, 1689–1765*. Eugene, OR: Wipf & Stock, 2011.

Trueman, Carl R. "Scripture and Exegesis in Early Modern Reformed Theology." In *The Oxford Handbook of Early Modern Theology, 1600–1800*. Edited by Ulrich L. Lehner et al., 1–18. Oxford: Oxford University Press, 2016.

Turley, Thomas P. "The Theology of Preaching in St. Augustine." *Dunwoodie Review* 8 (1968) 12.

Tyacke, Nicholas. *Anti-Calvinists: The Rise of English Arminianism, c. 1590–1640*. Oxford: Clarendon, 1986.

———. *Aspects of English Protestantism, 1530–1700*. Manchester: Manchester University Press, 2001.

Underwood, Ted LeRoy. *Primitivism, Radicalism, and the Lamb's War: The Baptist Quaker Conflict in Seventeenth-Century England*. Oxford Studies in Historical Theology. New York: Oxford University Press, 1997.

Van Dixhoorn, Chad. *God's Ambassadors: The Westminster Assembly and The Reformation of the English Pulpit, 1643–1653*. Grand Rapids: Reformation Heritage, 2017.

Van Hof, Charles. "The Theory of Sermon Rhetoric in Puritan New England: Its Origins and Expressions." PhD diss., Graduate School of Loyola University of Chicago, 1979.

Vaughn, James Barry. "Benjamin Keach." In *Baptist Theologians*, edited by Timothy George and David S. Dockery, 49–76. Nashville: Baptist Sunday School Board, 1990.

———. "Public Worship and Practical Theology in the Work of Benjamin Keach (1640–1704)." PhD diss., University of St. Andrews, 1989.

Vines, Jerry. *A Guide to Effective Sermon Delivery*. Chicago: Moody, 1986.

———. *A Practical Guide to Sermon Preparation*. Chicago: Moody, 1985.

Vines, Jerry, and Jim Shaddix. *Power in the Pulpit: How to Prepare and Deliver Expository Sermons*. Rev. ed. Chicago: Moody, 2017.

Wabuda, Susan. *Preaching During the English Reformation*. Cambridge: Cambridge University Press, 2002.

Walker, Austin. "Benjamin Keach (1640–1704) Tailor Turned Preacher." In *Pulpit and People: Studies in Eighteenth-Century Baptist Life and Thought*, edited by John H. Y. Briggs, 25–42. Studies in Baptist History and Thought 28. Eugene, OR: Wipf and Stock, 2009.

———. *The Excellent Benjamin Keach*. Ontario, Can.: Joshua, 2015.

———. "The Life of Benjamin Keach." In *The Works of Benjamin Keach*, edited by Matthew Stanton and Ian Campbell, 1:1–66. Knightstown, IN: Particular Baptist Heritage, 2023.

Walker, Kyle. *Let the Text Talk: Preaching That Treats the Text on Its Own Terms*. Fort Worth: Seminary Hill, 2018.

Wallace, Ronald S. *Calvin's Doctrine of the Word and Sacrament*. Eugene, OR: Wipf and Stock, 1997.

Walzer, Michael. *The Revolution of the Saints: A Study in the Origins of Radical Politics*. Cambridge: Harvard University Press, 1965.

Wandel, Lee Palmer. "Switzerland." In *Preachers and People in the Reformations and Early Modern Period*, edited by Larissa Taylor, 221–47. A New History of the Sermon 2. Leiden: Brill, 2001.

Ward, Matthew. *Pure Worship: The Early English Baptist Distinctive*. Eugene, OR: Pickwick, 2014.

Ward, Timothy. "Preaching and Revelation: Is the Sermon the Word of God?" In *Theology Is for Preaching: Biblical Foundations, Method, and Practice*, edited by Chase R. Kuhn and Paul Grimmond, 53–66. Studies in Historical and Systematic Theology. Bellingham, WA: Lexham, 2021.

Watson, Thomas. *A Body of Practical Divinity In a Series of Sermons on the Shorter Catechism Composed by the Reverend Assembly of Divines at Westminster: To which are Appended, Select Sermons on Various Subjects; Including the Art of Divine Contentment; and Christ's Various Fulness*. Philadelphia: Wardle, 1833.

Wax, Trevin. "Epilogue: Calvinists and Non-Calvinists Together for the Gospel." In *Calvinism: A Biblical and Theological Critique*, edited by David L. Allen and Steve W. Lemke, 481–503. Nashville: B&H Academic, 2022.

Wayland, Francis. *Letters on the Ministry of the Gospel*. Boston: Gould and Lincoln, 1864.

Wenkel, David H. "Only and Alone the Naked Soul: The Anti-Preparation Doctrine of The London Baptist Confessions of 1644/1646." *Baptist Quarterly* 50 (2019) 19–29.

Wenzel, Siegfried. *Medieval "Artes Praedicandi": A Synthesis of Scholastic Sermon Structure*. Toronto: University of Toronto Press, 2001.

Westminster Assembly. "The Directory for Public Worship." In *The Westminster Confession of Faith, Larger and Shorter Catechisms, and Subordinate Standards*, 475–501. Edinburgh ed. Philadelphia: Young, 1851.

———. "The Larger Catechism." In *The Westminster Confession of Faith, Larger and Shorter Catechisms, and Subordinate Standards*, 163–384. Edinburgh ed. Philadelphia: Young, 1851.

White, B. R. *The English Baptists of the 17th Century*. London: Baptist Historical Society, 1983.

———. *The English Separatist Tradition: From the Marian Martyrs to the Pilgrim Fathers*. Oxford: Oxford University Press, 1971.

Whitley, William Thomas. *A History of British Baptists*. London: Griffin, 1923.

Whitt, Donald Brad. "Come to Jesus: An Examination of the Public Invitation in the Preaching of Adrian Rogers." PhD diss., Southwestern Baptist Theological Seminary, 2022.

Willimon, William. *Conversations with Barth on Preaching*. Nashville: Abingdon, 2006.

———. *Proclamation and Theology*. Nashville: Abingdon, 2005.

Wingren, Gustaf. *The Living Word: A Theological Study of Preaching and the Church*. Eugene, OR: Wipf and Stock, 2002.

Winship, Michael P. *Hot Protestants: A History of Puritanism in England and America*. London: Yale University Press, 2018.

———. "Weak Christians, Backsliders, and Carnal Gospelers: Assurance of Salvation and the Pastoral Origins of Puritan Practical Divinity in the 1580s." *Church History* 70 (2001) 462–81.

Wollrich, Humphry. *A declaration to the Baptists: Concerning the name of the Lord, and what it is to be baptized thereinto, and the nature of the Lord, and what it is to be made partaker thereof: And sheweth that none can be saved, but such as are baptized into the name of the Father, Son, and Holy Ghost, into which name and nature, the apostles were sent to baptize, and not into water: Shewing also, that the apostles were made the administrators of the Spirits baptism: Also a discovery of the Baptists foundation*. London: Simmons, 1659.

Worcester, Thomas. "Catholic Sermons." In *Preachers and People in the Reformations and Early Modern Period*, edited by Larissa Taylor, 3–33. A New History of the Sermon 2. Boston: Brill, 2001.

Worden, Blair. *God's Instruments: Political Conduct in the England of Oliver Cromwell*. Oxford: Oxford University Press, 2012.

Wright, Abraham. *Five sermons, in five several styles; or Waies of preaching*. London: Archer, 1656.

Wright, Steele B. "The Preacher and His Sermon: Andrew Fuller's Reading of Jean Claude." *Journal of Andrew Fuller Studies* (2021) 35–47.

Wymer, Andrew. "The Word of God 'Enfleshed Anew': The Implications of a Latent Baptist Sacramental Sensibility for the Lord's Supper." *Worship* 89 (2015) 425–47.

Yeung, Celine S. *Received by Christ: A Biblical Reworking of the Reformed Theology of the Lord's Supper*. Re-Envisioning Reformed Dogmatics. Eugene, OR: Cascade, 2023.

York, Herschael W., and Bert Decker. *Preaching With Bold Assurance: A Solid and Enduring Approach to Engaging Exposition*. Nashville: Broadman & Holman, 2003.

Yuille, J. Stephen. "A Simple Method: William Perkins and the Shaping of the Protestant Pulpit." *Puritan Reformed Journal* 9 (2017) 215–30.

Zuidema, Jason. "'Lords and Labourers': Hugh Latimer's Homiletical Hermeneutics." In *Paul's Cross and the Culture of Persuasion in England, 1520–1640*, edited by Torrance Kirby and Paul Stanwood, 175–86. Studies in the History of Christian Traditions. Boston: Brill, 2014.

Zwingli, Ulrich. "Of the Clarity and Certainty of the Word of God." In *Zwingli and Bullinger*, edited by G. W. Bromiley, 49–95. Library of Christian Classics 24. Philadelphia: Westminster, 1953.

www.ingramcontent.com/pod-product-compliance
Lightning Source LLC
Chambersburg PA
CBHW070318230426
43663CB00011B/2177